# FRENCH

D0735754

# FRENCH

**PHRASEBOOK • DICTIONARY**

by
Alex Silverman
M.A.T. Program Director
School for International Training
Brattleboro, Vermont

Crown Publishers, Inc., New York

*To Jori*
*My traveling companion through life*

*My sincerest appreciation to all those who helped with*
*the preparation of this book: Jori Ross, Gabriel Silver-*
*man, Al and Bea Fantini, Joy Wallens, and Joanne*
*Thibault*

Copyright © 1989 by Crown Publishers, Inc.

Published by Crown Publishers, Inc., 201 East 50th Street, New York,
New York 10022

CROWN, LIVING LANGUAGE, LIVING LANGUAGE TRAVELTALK,
and colophon are trademarks of Crown Publishers, Inc.

Manufactured in the United States of America

Library of Congress Cataloging-in-Publication Data
Silverman, Alex.
    Living language traveltalk French.

    Includes index.
    1. French language—Textbooks for foreign speakers—English.
2. French language—Conversation and phrase books—English. I. Title.
PC2129.E5S545     1989          448.3′421          88-34093
ISBN 0-517-56993-0

10 9 8 7 6 5 4

First Edition

# CONTENTS

# PREFACE

Are you planning a trip to France, Belgium, Switzerland, or any other French-speaking country? If so, this book will help you to make the most of your trip. The *Traveltalk*™ phrasebook/dictionary features over 2,200 French expressions to use in the various situations you may encounter as a tourist. Each word has a phonetic transcription to help you with pronunciation.

No prior knowledge of French is necessary. All you have to do to make yourself understood is read the phonetics as you would any English sentence. We also recommend using the *Traveltalk*™ French cassette so you can hear French spoken by native speakers and practice pronunciation. However, this book is useful on its own, as it offers the following features.

**Pronunciation Guide**   The transcription system for this volume is presented in this section through the use of simple English examples and explanations. Reading through it first will enable you to use the phrases in subsequent chapters with full confidence that your pronunciation is comprehensible.

**Essential Phrases**   Many common phrases are used over and over in a variety of contexts. For your convenience, these phrases have been grouped together in Chapter 1.

**Chapters 2–13** reflect the full range of the visitor's experience. From arrival at the airport to saying farewell to new friends, *Traveltalk* provides a comprehensive resource for every important context of your visit.

**Sample Dialogues** give you a sense of how the language sounds in conversation.

**Travel Tips and Cultural Highlights**   Interspersed throughout the chapters are brief narratives highlighting cultural attractions and offering insider's tips for getting the most out of your visit.

**General Information** is given throughout. Essential facts are presented to ease your transition into a new setting:

• legal holidays
• metric conversion tables
• important signs
• common abbreviations
• clothing/shoe size conversion charts

**Grammar Guide** A concise and easy-to-follow grammar summary is included for those who would like to understand the structure of the language.

**Two-way 1,600-Word Dictionary** All of the key words presented in this volume are listed in the French-English/English-French dictionary. They also provide a phonetic transcription of every French word and phrase.

This book will be useful in any French-speaking country, but the primary focus of the book is on France, its geographic, cultural, culinary, and human treasures. Enjoy the book—and your trip!

# BEFORE YOU LEAVE
## VISAS

The French government has issued the following information regarding the new visa regulations for U.S. citizens.

As of this writing, visas are required for all U.S. citizens visiting France. As a special convenience, the French Consulates now routinely issue a three-year multiple-entry visa to American citizens. A three-month multiple-entry visa and a seventy-two-hour transit visa can also be obtained. Application forms are available from the French Consulates as well as the French Government Tourist Offices in the United States. The completed form should be brought or mailed to the French Consulate with jurisdiction over your state (see list below for addresses). The form must be accompanied by:

- Your valid passport
- Visa fee as per schedule below, in cash at the Consulate, or by certified check or money order if by mail (no personal checks accepted):
    - $15.00 for a three-year multiple-entry visa
    - $9.00 for a three-month multiple-entry visa
    - $3.00 for a seventy-two-hour transit visa
- A stamped self-addressed envelope for applications made by mail

The visa is valid for tourism and business travel only. Each stay cannot exceed ninety days. For those wishing to work or study in France, please contact the French Consulate for information on the necessary procedure.

### French Consulates in the United States.

BOSTON
535 Boylston Street, MA 02116
Tel. (617) 266-3141 Telex 940985
(ME, MA, NH, RI, VT)

CHICAGO
444 North Michigan Avenue, Suite 3140, IL 60611
Tel. (312) 787-5359/60/61, 787-5385 Telex 190229
(ND, SD, IL, IN, IA, KS, KY, MN, MO, NE, WI)

DETROIT
100 Renaissance Center, Suite 1550, MI 48243
Tel. (313) 568-0993 Telex 164102
(MI, OH, WV)

HOUSTON
2727 Allen Parkway, Suite 975, TX 77019
Tel. Visa (713) 528-2173, (713) 528-2181 Telex 825078
(OK, TX)

LOS ANGELES
8350 Wilshire Boulevard, Suite 310, Beverly Hills, CA 90211
Tel. (213) 653-3120 Telex 691183
(AZ, NM, CO, CA counties: Mono, Inyo, Kings, San Luis
  Obispo, Kern, Santa Barbara, Ventura, Los Angeles, San
  Bernardino, Orange, Riverside, Imperial, San Diego; NV
  counties: Clark, Lincoln, Nye, Esmeralda, Mineral)

MIAMI
1 Biscayne Tower, 17th Floor, 2 South Biscayne Boulevard, FL
  33131
Tel. (305) 372-9798/99
(FL)

NEW YORK
*To apply in person* (U.S. citizens only):
75 Vanderbilt Avenue (at the corner of 46th Street, street
  level)
Tel. (212) 983-5660

*To apply by mail* (also non-U.S. citizens):
934 Fifth Avenue, NY 10021
Tel. (212) 606-3600 Telex 640060
(CT, NY, NJ, PA, Bermuda)

NEW ORLEANS
3305 Saint Charles Avenue, LA 70115
Tel. (504) 897-6381/82 Telex 587399
(AL, AR, GA, LA, MS, TN)

SAN FRANCISCO
530 Bush Street, CA 94108
Tel. (415) 397-4893 Telex 34225
(AK, CA, NV [except counties under Los Angeles jurisdiction]
   OR, UT, WA, WY, Hawaii, Pacific Islands under U.S. jurisdic-
   tion)

WASHINGTON, D.C.
4101 Reservoir Road, NW 20007
Tel. (202) 944-6000
(NC, SC, DE, DC, VA, MD)


## WHERE TO GET INFORMATION ON FRANCE IN THE UNITED STATES

The French government maintains Tourist Offices in the United
States at the addresses listed below. You may call, write, or visit
any of these offices for information on particular regions or cities
in France.

NEW YORK
610 Fifth Avenue, NY 10020
Tel. (212) 757-1125

CHICAGO
645 North Michigan Avenue, IL 60611
Tel. (312) 337 6301

DALLAS
P.O. Box 58610, TX 75258
Tel. (214) 742-7011

LOS ANGELES
9401 Wilshire Boulevard, Beverly Hills, CA 90212
Tel. (213) 272-2661

SAN FRANCISCO
1 Hallidie Plaza, Suite 250, CA 94102
Tel. (415) 986-4161

# FRANCE

# PRONUNCIATION GUIDE

Every French word or phrase in this book is presented along with its English equivalent and an easy-to-follow transcription (sound key) that provides the correct pronunciation. Simply read the transcription as you would read regular English and you will be speaking comprehensible French. Of course, there are differences between many English and French sounds. You can learn to imitate the French pronunciation more accurately by using the *Traveltalk French* cassette and by listening to the French speakers around you in your travels.

## FRENCH-ENGLISH PRONUNCIATION CHART

The pronunciation chart presented below is your guide to the transcriptions used in the book. You will find it useful to spend some time learning what sounds are represented by the various French spellings. Then you will be able to follow the transcriptions without having to consult the chart. Pay special attention to the vowels; they determine the overall sound of the word and are crucial to comprehension.

### Consonants

| French Spelling | Approximate Sound | Symbol | Example |
|---|---|---|---|
| **b, d, k, l, m, n, p, s, t, v, z** | same as in English (see Note) | | |
| **c** (before e, i, y) | s | [s] | **cinéma** seenaymah |
| **c** (before a, o, u) | k | [k] | **cave** kahv |
| **ç** (appears only before a, o, u) | s | [s] | **français** frah (n)seh (see Note) |

| French Spelling | Approximate Sound | Symbol | Example |
|---|---|---|---|
| **ch** | *sh* | [sh] | **chaud** shoh |
| **g** (before e, i, y) | *s* (as in measure) | [zh] | **âge** ahzh |
| **g** (before a, o, u) | *g* in game | [g] | **gâteau** gahtoh |
| **gn** | *ny* in onion | [ny] | **agneau** ahnyoh |
| **h** | always silent | | **homme** ohm |
| **j** | *s* in measure | [zh] | **Jacques** zhahk |
| **qu**, final **q** | *k* | [k] | **qui** kee |
| **r** | pronounced in back of mouth, rolled like light gargling sound | [r] | **Paris** pahree |
| **ss** | *s* | [s] | **tasse** tahs |
| **s** (beginning of word or before consonant) | *s* | [s] | **salle** sahl **disque** deesk |
| **s** (between vowels) | *z* in Zelda | [z] | **maison** mayzoh(n) |
| **th** | *t* | [t] | **thé** tay |
| **x** | *x* in exact | [gz] | **exact** ehgzahkt |
| **x** | *x* in excellent | [ks] | **excellent** ehksehlah(n) |
| **ll** | *y* in yes | [y] | **volaille** vohlahy |
| **ll** | as in ill | [l] | **elle** ehl |

Note: Final consonants are most often silent in French, e.g., *Paris* [pahree]. There are four letters, however, that are usually pronounced when final. These are *c, r, f,* and *l*. Please be *careful* about this rule!

7

## Vowels

| French Spelling | Approximate Sound | Symbol | Example |
| --- | --- | --- | --- |
| **a, à, â** | *a* in father | [ah] | **la** lah |
| **é, er, ez** (end of word) | *ay* in lay | [ay] | **thé** tay<br>**parler** pahrlay<br>**allez** ahlay |
| **e** plus final pronounced consonant | *e* in met | [eh] | **belle** behl (l is the final pronounced consonant) |
| **è, ai, aî** | *e* in met | [eh] | **père** pehr<br>**chaîne** shehn |
| **e, eu** | *u* in put | [uh] | **le** luh |
| **i** | *ee* in beet | [ee] | **ici** eesee |
| **i** plus vowel | *y* in yesterday | [y] | **lion** lyoh(n) |
| **o, au, eau, ô** | *o* in both | [oh] | **mot** moh<br>**chaud** shoh<br>**beau** boh<br>**hôte** oht |
| **ou** | *oo* in toot | [oo] | **vous** voo |
| **oi, oy** | *wa* in watt | [wah] | **moi** mwah |
| **u** | no equivalent in English—say *ee*, then round your lips | [ew] or [oo] | **tu** tew<br>**fumeurs** foomuhr |
| **u** plus **i** | *wee* as in week | [wee] | **lui** lwee |
| **euille** | no equivalent in English—say *uh* and follow it with *y* | [uhy] | **feuille** fuhy |
| **eille** | *ay* as in hay | [ehy] | **merveilleux** mehrvehyuh |

## Nasal Vowels

Nasal vowels are sounds produced when air is expelled from both the mouth and the nose. In French, a consonant that follows a nasal vowel is not fully pronounced. For example, the French word *on*: We pronounce the nasal vowel *o* through the mouth and nose, but we do not sound the following consonant *n* or *m*. That is, we do not touch the roof of our mouth with the tip of the tongue. In our transcription of French nasal vowels, we will therefore include an (n) or (m) in parentheses.

| French Spelling | Approximate Sound | Symbol | Example |
|---|---|---|---|
| **an, en** | vowel in balm | [ah(n)] | **France** frah(n)s |
| **em** | vowel in balm | [ah(m)] | **emmener** ah(m)uhnay |
| **in, ain, ein** | vowel in man | [a(n)] | **fin** fa(n) |
| **im, aim** | vowel in man | [a(m)] | **faim** fa(m) |
| **ien** | *y* + vowel in men | [yeh(n)] | **bien** byeh(n) |
| **ion** | *y* + vowel in song | [yoh(n)] | **station** stahsyohn(n) |
| **oin** | *w* + vowel in man | [wa(n)] | **loin** lwa(n) |
| **on** | vowel in song | [oh(n)] | **bon** boh(n) |
| **om** | vowel in song | [oh(m)] | **tomber** toh(m)bay |
| **un** | vowel in lung | [uh(n)] | **un** uh(n) |

## STRESS

English, we stress certain syllables in a word (ri*dic*ulous) and certain words in a sentence (I *want* to go *home*). Stressed syllables are pronounced with greater force and loudness and are made longer than other syllables. In French, all syllables in a word and words in a sentence receive equal stress. Your French will be more comprehensible if you give every syllable a full, clear pronunciation.

## LIAISON

Liaison means linking. French speakers pronounce *some* final consonants when the next word begins with a vowel. In this way, the two words are linked and the result is a more flowing, harmonious sound. For example:

*Nous parlons français.* [Noo pahrloh(n) frah(n)seh.]

Here the *s* in *nous* is not pronounced since the next word begins with a consonant. There is no liaison.

*Nous allons chez Philippe.* [Noo zahloh(n) shay Feeleep.]

Here the *s* in *nous* is pronounced since the next word begins with a vowel. This is a case of liaison. Note that *s* in liaison is pronounced *z*. In this volume, liaison consonants will be shown as the first sound in the second word.

## ELISION

Another way that French preserves the ear-pleasing alternation of vowels and consonants is to drop the vowel in certain words when the next sound is a vowel. The most important of such elisions is with the definite articles *le* and *la* (masculine and feminine equivalents for *the* in English).

| masculine singular | **le film** | luh feelm |
| *but* | **l'ami** | lahmee |

| feminine singular | **la dame** | lah dahm |
| *but* | **l'orange** | lohrah(n)zh |

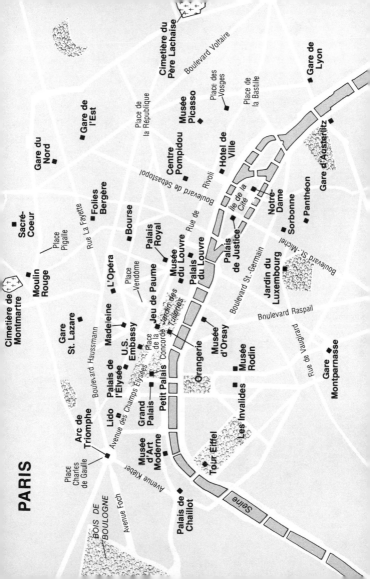

# 1/USEFUL EXPRESSIONS

## COURTESY

| | | |
|---|---|---|
| Please. | **S'il vous plaît.** | Seel voo pleh. |
| Thank you. | **Merci.** | Mehrsee. |
| You're welcome. | **De rien.** | Duh ryeh(n). |
| Excuse me. | **Pardon.** | Pahrdoh(n). |
| It doesn't matter. | **Ça ne fait rien.** | Sah nuh fay ryeh(n). |

## GREETINGS

| | | |
|---|---|---|
| Good morning.<br>Good afternoon.<br>Hello. (formal)* | **Bonjour.** | Boh(n)zhoor. |
| Good evening. | **Bonsoir.** | Boh(n)swahr. |
| Good night.<br>(bedtime) | **Bonne nuit.** | Bohn nwee. |
| Hello. (telephone) | **Allô.** | Ahloh. |
| Goodbye. | **Au revoir.** | Oh rvwahr. |
| See you soon. | **À bientôt.** | Ah byeh(n)toh. |
| See you later. | **À tout à l'heure.** | Ah toot ah luhr. |
| See you tomorrow. | **À demain.** | Ah duhma(n). |
| Let's go! | **Allons-y!** | Ahloh(n)-zee! |

*You may hear people greeting each other with "Salut" [sahlew]. This is a very informal slang expression used among friends. Until you get to know someone very well, it's best to stick to the more formal *bonjour* [boh(n)zhoor].

## APPROACHING SOMEONE FOR HELP

| | | |
|---|---|---|
| Excuse me, | **Pardon,** | Pahrdoh(n), |
| • Sir. | • **Monsieur.** | • Muhsyuh. |
| • Ma'am/Mrs./Ms. | • **Madame.** | • Mahdahm. |
| • Miss. | • **Mademoiselle.** | • Mahdmwahzehl. |

13

| | | |
|---|---|---|
| Do you speak English? | **Parlez-vous anglais?** | Pahr-lay voo ah(n)gleh? |
| Do you understand English? | **Comprenez-vous anglais?** | Koh(m)prehnay-voo ah(n)gleh? |
| Yes./No. | **Oui./Non.** | Wee. Noh(n). |
| I'm sorry. | **Je suis désolé(e).** * | Zhuh swee dayzohlay. |
| I don't speak French. | **Je ne parle pas français.** | Zhuh nuh pahrl pah frah(n)seh. |
| I don't understand. | **Je ne comprends pas.** | Zhuh nuh koh(m)prah(n) pah. |
| I understand a little. | **Je comprends un peu.** | Zhuh koh(m)prah(n) uh(n) puh. |
| I'm a tourist. | **Je suis un(e) touriste.**† | Zhuh swee zuh(n) [zewn] tooreest. |
| I speak very little French. | **Je parle un petit peu de français.** | Zhuh pahrl uh(n) ptee puh duh frah(n)seh. |
| Please speak more slowly. | **Parlez plus lentement, s'il vous plaît.** | Pahrlay plew lah(n)-tmah(n), seel voo pleh. |

*In French, adjectives agree in number and gender with the nouns they modify. *Désolé* is the masculine form and *désolée* is the feminine. Herein, the feminine endings will appear in parentheses. See also Chapter 15, Grammar in Brief (page 197), regarding the gender of adjectives.

† Note: In French, you generally add *e* to masculine nouns and adjectives to make them feminine, unless they already end in *e* (*touriste*, for example). To make masculine and feminine nouns and adjectives plural, just add *s*. So, if you're an American man, you'd say, "Je suis américai*n*." If you're an American woman, you'd say, "Je suis américai*ne*." A group of American women would say, "Nous sommes américai*nes*," while a mixed group of men and women would use the plural form, "Nous sommes américai*ns*."

14

| Please repeat. | **Répétez, s'il vous plaît.** | Raypaytay, seel voo pleh. |
| May I ask a question? | **Une question, s'il vous plaît?** | Ewn kehstyoh(n), seel voo pleh? |
| Could you please help me? | **Pourriez-vous m'aider, s'il vous plaît?** | Pooryay-voo mehday, seel voo pleh? |
| Okay. | **D'accord.** | Dahkohr. |
| Of course. | **Bien sûr.** | Byeh(n) sewr. |
| Where is . . . ? | **Où est . . . ?** | Oo eh . . . ? |
| Thank you very much. | **Merci beaucoup.** | Mehrsee bohkoo. |

## QUESTION WORDS

| Who? | **Qui?** | Kee? |
| What? | **Quoi?** | Kwah? |
| Why? | **Pourquoi?** | Poorkwah? |
| When? | **Quand?** | Kah(n)? |
| Where? | **Où?** | Oo? |
| Where from? | **D'où?** | Doo? |
| Where are you going? | **Où allez-vous?** | Oo ahlay voo? |
| How? | **Comment?** | Kohmah(n)? |
| How much is it? | **C'est combien?** | Seh koh(m)byeh(n)? |

15

## NUMBERS

Take the time to learn how to count in French. You'll find that knowing the numbers will make everything easier during your trip.

| 0  | **zéro**        | zayroh         |
|----|-----------------|----------------|
| 1  | **un**          | uh(n)          |
| 2  | **deux**        | duh            |
| 3  | **trois**       | trwah          |
| 4  | **quatre**      | kahtr          |
| 5  | **cinq**        | sa(n)k*        |
| 6  | **six**         | sees*          |
| 7  | **sept**        | seht           |
| 8  | **huit**        | weet*          |
| 9  | **neuf**        | nuhf           |
| 10 | **dix**         | dees*          |
| 11 | **onze**        | oh(n)z         |
| 12 | **douze**       | dooz           |
| 13 | **treize**      | trehz          |
| 14 | **quatorze**    | kahtohrz       |
| 15 | **quinze**      | ka(n)z         |
| 16 | **seize**       | sehz           |
| 17 | **dix-sept**    | dee-seht       |
| 18 | **dix-huit**    | dee-zweet      |
| 19 | **dix-neuf**    | deez-nuhf      |
| 20 | **vingt**       | va(n)          |
| 21 | **vingt et un** | va(n) tay uh(n)|
| 22 | **vingt-deux**  | va(n)-duh      |
| 23 | **vingt-trois** | va(n)-trwah    |
| 24 | **vingt-quatre**| va(n)-kahtr    |
| 25 | **vingt-cinq**  | va(n)-sa(n)k   |
| 26 | **vingt-six**   | va(n)-sees     |
| 27 | **vingt-sept**  | va(n)-seht     |
| 28 | **vingt-huit**  | va(n)-tweet    |
| 29 | **vingt-neuf**  | va(n)-nuhf     |

*Note: The final consonants are not pronounced when the next word begins with a consonant. For example, huit fois (wee fwah) vs. huit ans (weet ah[n]).

| 30 | **trente** | trah(n)t |
| 31 | **trente et un** | trah(n)t ay uh(n) |
| 32 | **trente-deux** | trah(n)t-duh |
| 40 | **quarante** | kahrah(n)t |
| 50 | **cinquante** | sa(n)kah(n)t |
| 60 | **soixante** | swahsah(n)t |
| 61 | **soixante et un** | swahsah(n)t ay uh(n) |
| 62 | **soixante-deux** | swahsah(n)t-duh |
| 70* | **soixante-dix** | swahsah(n)t-dees |
| 71 | **soixante et onze** | swahsah(n)t ay oh(n)z |
| 72 | **soixante-douze** | swahsah(n)t-dooz |
| 73 | **soixante-treize** | swahsah(n)t-trehz |
| 74 | **soixante-quatorze** | swahsah(n)t-kahtohrz |
| 75 | **soixante-quinze** | swahsah(n)t-ka(n)z |
| 76 | **soixante-seize** | swahsah(n)t-sehz |
| 77 | **soixante-dix-sept** | swahsah(n)t-dee-seht |
| 78 | **soixante-dix-huit** | swahsah(n)t-dee-zweet |
| 79 | **soixante-dix-neuf** | swahsah(n)t-deez-nuhf |
| 80* | **quatre-vingts** | kahtruh-va(n) |
| 81 | **quatre-vingt-un** | kahtruh-va(n)-uh(n) |
| 82 | **quatre-vingt-deux** | kahtruh-va(n)-duh |
| 83 | **quatre-vingt-trois** | kahtruh-va(n)-trwah |
| 90* | **quatre-vingt-dix** | kahtruh-va(n)-dees |
| 91 | **quatre-vingt-onze** | kahtruh-va(n)-oh(n)z |
| 92 | **quatre-vingt-douze** | kahtruh-va(n)-dooz |
| 100 | **cent** | sah(n) |
| 101 | **cent un** | sah(n) uh(n) |
| 102 | **cent deux** | sah(n) duh |
| 110 | **cent dix** | sah(n) dees |
| 120 | **cent vingt** | sah(n) va(n) |

*Note: In French, the number 70 *(soixante-dix)* is literally translated as "60-10." You must add *onze* (11) through *dix-neuf* (19) to *soixante* (60) to get the numbers 71 through 79. The number 80 *(quatre-vingts)* is literally translated as four twenties. The numbers 90 through 99 are formed the same way as the 70s, by adding the numbers *onze* (11) through *dix-neuf* (19) to the number *quatre-vingts* (80).

Practice counting aloud from 60 to 100 so you become comfortable with these numbers.

| 200 | **deux cents** | duh sah(n) |
| 210 | **deux cent dix** | duh sah(n) dees |
| 300 | **trois cents** | trwah sah(n) |
| 400 | **quatre cents** | kahtruh sah(n) |
| 500 | **cinq cents** | sa(n) sah(n) |
| 600 | **six cents** | see sah(n) |
| 700 | **sept cents** | seht sah(n) |
| 800 | **huit cents** | wee sah(n) |
| 900 | **neuf cents** | nuhf sah(n) |
| 1,000 | **mille** | meel |
| 1,100 | **mille cent** | meel sah(n) |
| 1,200 | **mille deux cents** | meel duh sah(n) |
| 2,000 | **deux mille** | duh meel |
| 10,000 | **dix mille** | dee meel |
| 50,000 | **cinquante mille** | sa(n)kah(n)t meel |
| 100,000 | **cent mille** | sah(n) meel |
| 1,000,000 | **un million** | uh(n) meelyoh(n) |
| 1,000,000,000 | **un milliard** | uh(n) meelyahr |

## Ordinal Numbers

| first (m) | **premier (1er)** | pruhmyay |
| first (f) | **première (1ère)** | pruhmyehr |
| second | **deuxième (2e)** | duhzyehm |
| third | **troisième (3e)** | trwahzyehm |
| fourth | **quatrième** | kahtreeyehm |
| fifth | **cinquième** | sa(n)kyehm |
| sixth | **sixième** | seezyehm |
| seventh | **septième** | sehtyehm |
| eighth | **huitième** | weetyehm |
| ninth | **neuvième** | nuhvyehm |
| tenth | **dixième** | deezyehm |
| twentieth | **vingtième** | va(n)tyehm |
| hundredth | **centième** | sah(n)tyehm |

Note: In French, decimal points are indicated by commas. For example, 6.5 would be written 6,5 (six virgule cinq) and pronounced sees veergewl sa(n)k.

## QUANTITIES

| | | |
|---|---|---|
| a half | **une moitié** | ewn mwahtyay |
| half of | **un demi de** | uh(n) duhmee duh |
| a half hour | **une demie heure** | ewn duhmee uhr |
| a third | **un tiers** | uh(n) tyehr |
| a quarter | **un quart** | uh(n) kahr |
| two-thirds | **deux tiers** | duh tyehr |
| 3 percent | **trois pour cent** | trwah poor sah(n) |
| a lot of, many | **beaucoup de** | bohkoo duh |
| a little of | **un peu de** | uh(n) puh duh |
| a dozen (of) | **une douzaine de** | ewn doozehn duh |
| half a kilo of | **un demi-kilo de** | uh(n) duhmee keeloh duh |
| | | |
| a few | **quelques** | kehlkuh |
| enough | **assez de** | ahsay duh |
| too little | **trop peu de** | troh puh duh |
| too much | **trop de** | troh duh |
| a kilo of | **un kilo de** | uh(n) keeloh duh |
| a glass of | **un verre de** | uh(n) vehr duh |
| a cup of | **une tasse de** | ewn tahs duh |
| once | **une fois** | ewn fwah |
| twice | **deux fois** | duh fwah |
| last | **dernier (dernière)** | dehrnyehr |

## ABOUT THE CURRENCY

In each of the French-speaking European countries—France, Belgium, and Switzerland—the monetary unit is the *franc* [frah(n)], divided into 100 *centimes* [sah(n)tcem]. Of course, the value of the franc relative to the dollar is in constant flux (exchange rates are posted daily in the banks) and differs from country to country. The chart below shows the variety of coins and banknotes you will find in these nations.

| | Coins | Banknotes |
|---|---|---|
| France | 5, 10, 20, 50 centimes 1, 2, 5, 10 francs | 10, 20, 50, 100, 200, 500 francs |

| Switzerland | 5, 10, 20, 50 centimes | 10, 20, 50, 100, 500, |
|---|---|---|
|  | 1, 2, 5 francs | 1000 francs |
| Belgium | 50 centimes | 50, 100, 500, 1000, |
|  | 1, 5, 10, 20 francs | 5000 francs |

In Canada, the monetary system is similar to that of the United States (dollars and cents). In recent years the Canadian dollar has been worth somewhat less than the U.S. dollar.

## DIALOGUE: À LA BANQUE (AT THE BANK)

| Le client: | **Pouvez-vous me changer cent dollars?** | Pooveh-voo muh shah(n)zhay sah(n) dohlahr? |
|---|---|---|
| La caissière: | **Certainement, monsieur. Le cours est à six francs aujourd'hui. Ça vous fait donc six cent francs.** | Sehrteh(n)mah(n), muhsyuh. Luh koor eh tah see frah(n) ohzhoordwee. Sah voo feh doh(n)k see sah(n) frah(n). |
| Le client: | **Bien. Voici mes chèques de voyage.** | Byeh(n). Vwahsee may shek duh vwahyahzh. |
| La caissière: | **Voulez-vous bien les signer, monsieur.** | Vooleh-voo byeh(n) lay seenyay, muhsyuh. |
| Le client: | **Bien sûr. Eh bien, voilà.** | Byeh(n) sewr. Ay byeh(n), vwahlah. |
| La caissière: | **Et votre passeport, s'il vous plaît.** | Ay vohtruh pahspohr, seel voo pleh. |
| Le client: | **Le voici.** | Luh vwahsee. |

• • • • • • • • • • • • • • • • • • • • • • • • • • • • • • • • • • • • • • • • • •

| Customer: | Could you change $100 for me? |
|---|---|
| Teller: | Certainly, sir. The rate is six francs to the dollar today. So that would be 600 francs. |
| Customer: | Fine. Here are my traveler's checks. |

20

| | |
|---|---|
| Teller: | Would you please sign them, sir? |
| Customer: | Of course. Here they are. |
| Teller: | And your passport, please. |
| Customer: | Here it is. |

## BANKS

Banks are generally open from 9:00 to 12:00 and 2:00 to 5:00, although many of the larger banks remain open during the lunch break. The *bureaux de change* [bewroh duh shah(n)zh] (currency exchange offices) are open beyond normal banking hours. Your best bet on money exchange is generally a bank. Airport and hotel exchange rates are usually less advantageous. You may also wish to compare bank rates if you're changing large sums. Usually three rates are posted:

**1. l'achat** [lahshah]—the rate for buying dollars. This is the relevant rate for you since the bank is buying your dollars.

**2. la vente** [lah vah(n)t]—the rate for selling dollars. The dollar is worth less at this rate. Generally you're better off waiting until you return to the United States to change back your dollars.

**3. chèques de voyage** [shehk duh vwahyahzh]—traveler's check rates, which differ slightly from cash rates.

Don't forget your passport whenever you're changing money or doing any other monetary transaction.

Your major credit card will be accepted at most hotels, restaurants and stores. Signs indicating which cards are acceptable are usually prominently displayed in the establishment.

| | | |
|---|---|---|
| Where is the nearest bank? | **Où est la banque la plus proche?** | Oo eh lah bah(n)k lah plew prohsh? |

21

| English | French | Pronunciation |
|---|---|---|
| Is there a currency exchange office nearby? | **Y a-t-il un bureau de change près d'ici?** | Yahteel uh(n) bewroh duh shah(n)zh preh deesee? |
| I want to telex my bank in Chicago. | **Je voudrais envoyer un télex à ma banque à Chicago.** | Zhuh voodreh ah(n)vwahyay uh(n) taylehks ah mah bah(n)k ah Sheekahgoh. |
| Has my money arrived from my bank in New York? | **Est-ce que mon argent est arrivé de ma banque à New York?** | Ehskuh moh(n) nahrzhah(n) eh tahreevay duh mah bah(n)k ah Noo Yohrk? |
| I'd like to change some dollars. | **Je voudrais changer des dollars.** | Zhuh voodreh shah(n)zhay day dohlahr. |
| How much is the dollar worth? | **Combien vaut le dollar?** | Koh(m)byeh(n) voh luh dohlahr? |
| I'd like to buy... | **Je voudrais acheter...** | Zhuh voodreh zahshtay... |
| • French francs | • **des francs français** | • day frah(n) frah(n)seh |
| • Belgian francs | • **des francs belges** | • day frah(n) behlzh |
| • Swiss francs | • **des francs suisses** | • day frah(n) swees |
| Can I change traveler's checks? | **Est-ce que je peux changer des chèques de voyage?** | Ehskuh zhuh puh shah(n)zhay day shehk duh vwahyahzh? |
| Can I cash this check? | **Est-ce que je peux toucher ce chèque?** | Ehskuh zhuh puh tooshay suh shehk? |
| Where do I sign? | **Où est-ce que je dois signer?** | Oo ehskuh zhuh dwah seenyay? |

| Can you give me . . . | **Pouvez-vous me donner. . .** | Pooveh-voo muh dohnay. . . |
|---|---|---|
| • large bills | • **l'argent en grosses coupures** | • lahrzhah(n) ah(n) grohs koopewr |
| • small bills | • **l'argent en petites coupures** | • lahrzhah(n) ah(n) puhteet koopewr |
| • five 20-franc notes | • **cinq billets de vingt francs** | • sa(n) beeyay duh va(n) frah(n) |
| • some change | • **de la monnaie** | • duh lah mohneh |

## TIPPING

Tipping should be the least of one's problems in France. There's a fifteen percent service charge built into all restaurant and hotel bills and charges at barbers and beauty parlors.

The cabdriver gets between ten and fifteen percent above the basic meter charge, before the extras are added on, such as so many francs for transporting your luggage, a surcharge involved in airport and railway station pickups, and night differentials.

Airport and railway porters charge a posted fee. Two or three francs more is enough. The bellman delivering your bags to your room gets more or less the franc equivalent of what you would tip in dollars in a similar class hotel in the United States. If you would tip two dollars at New York's Plaza, you would tip the corresponding amount (ten to twelve francs) at the Crillon. Tip the concierge if he has performed any special services, such as procuring hard-to-get theater or concert tickets. Tip doormen getting cabs five francs. Room service warrants a tip, even though there is already a room service charge. Since over fifteen percent of your hotel bill is for service, it seems redundant to leave extra tips for the chambermaids.

Bus tour guides and museum guides leave no doubt that they expect tips. Two or three francs is plenty. Tip movie ushers about two francs per person, theater ushers a little more.

At bars and in cafés and restaurants the service charge is always included in the bill. The register slip handed to you for whatever you order at a sidewalk café is *service compris* [sehr-vees koh(m)pree], meaning "tip included."

In the case of restaurants, the service charge may or may not be incorporated into the price of the posted menu or the menu you get at the table. If not, then at a bottom corner of the menu it will say "15% *service en sus*" [sehrvees ah(n) sews], which means it will be added. *The service charge is always included in the bill you get.* There are no exceptions. Set your mind at ease. Whatever you leave above and beyond is up to you. The French leave no more than the small change breakage, maybe a few francs on an average dinner bill.

An exception to all this may occur in a truly great restaurant with outstanding service, where the captain, waiter, and sommelier (wine steward) go out of their way to turn your meal into a really memorable experience. In that case, any extras will be appreciated. But distribute individually, with *merci*s and handshakes, in the French style. Do not just leave money on the table and walk out.

## PAYING THE BILL

| | | |
|---|---|---|
| The bill, please. | **L'addition, s'il vous plaît.** | Lahdeesyoh(n), seel voo pleh. |
| How much is it? | **C'est combien?** | Seh koh(m)byeh(n)? |
| Is service included? | **Le service est compris?** | Luh sehrvees eh koh(m)pree? |
| This is for you. | **C'est pour vous.** | Seh poor voo. |

## TELLING TIME

| | | |
|---|---|---|
| What time is it? | **Quelle heure est-il?** | Kehl uhr ehteel? |
| It's . . . | **Il est . . .** | Eel eh . . . |
| • three o'clock | • **trois heures** | • trwah zuhr |
| • three-fifteen | • **trois heures et quart** | • trwah zuhr ay kahr |

24

| | | |
|---|---|---|
| • three-thirty | • **trois heures et demie** | • trwah zuhr ay duh-mee |
| • two forty-five | • **trois heures moins le quart** | • trwah zuhr mwah(n) luh kahr* |
| • three-ten | • **trois heures dix** | • trwah zuhr dees |
| • two-fifty | • **trois heures moins dix** | • trwah zuhr mwah(n) dees |
| It's . . . | **Il est . . .** | Eel eh . . . |
| • midnight | • **minuit** | • meenwee |
| • noon | • **midi** | • meedee |
| • three A.M. | • **trois heures du matin** | • trwah zuhr dew mahta(n) |
| • three P.M. | • **trois heures de l'après-midi** | • trwah zuhr duh lahpreh meedee |
| • six P.M. | • **six heures du soir** | • see zuhr dew swahr |
| five minutes ago | **il y a cinq minutes** | eel yah sa(n) meenewt |
| in a half hour | **dans une demi-heure** | dah(n) zewn duhmee-uhr |
| since seven P.M. | **depuis sept heures du soir** | duhpwee seht uhr dew swahr |
| after eight P.M. | **après huit heures du soir** | ahpreh weet uhr dew swahr |
| before nine A.M. | **avant neuf heures du matin** | ahvah(n) nuh vuhr dew mahta(n) |
| When does it begin? | **A quelle heure est-ce que ça commence?** | Ah kehl uhr ehskuh sah kohmah(n)s? |
| He came . . . | **Il est venu . . .** | Eel ay vnew . . . |
| • on time | • **à l'heure** | • ah luhr |
| • early | • **tôt** | • toh |
| • late | • **en retard** | • ah(n) ruhtahr |

*Note: After the half hour on the clock, minutes are subtracted from the next hour. The literal translation of the French for 2:45 is "it's three minus a quarter (of an hour)."

25

## The 24-Hour Clock

In European countries, after 12 o'clock P.M. (noon) time is often stated as 13 hours, 14 hours, etc., similar to military time in the United States. This system—from 1 hour (1 A.M.) to 24 hours (12 A.M. midnight)—is generally used for transportation schedules and theater times. Simply add 12 to all times beyond 12 P.M. (noon), hence 3 P.M. is 3 plus 12, or 15 hours. The following chart will help you for quick reference.

### Official Time Chart

| | | | |
|---|---|---|---|
| 1 A.M. | 1h00 | **Une heure** | Ewn uhr |
| 2 A.M. | 2h00 | **Deux heures** | Duh zuhr |
| 3 A.M. | 3h00 | **Trois heures** | Trwah zuhr |
| 4 A.M. | 4h00 | **Quatre heures** | Kahtr uhr |
| 5 A.M. | 5h00 | **Cinq heures** | Sah(n)k uhr |
| 6 A.M. | 6h00 | **Six heures** | See zuhr |
| 7 A.M. | 7h00 | **Sept heures** | Seht uhr |
| 8 A.M. | 8h00 | **Huit heures** | Weet uhr |
| 9 A.M. | 9h00 | **Neuf heures** | Nuh vuhr |
| 10 A.M. | 10h00 | **Dix heures** | Dee zuhr |
| 11 A.M. | 11h00 | **Onze heures** | Oh(n)z uhr |
| 12 P.M. | 12h00 | **Douze heures (midi)** | Dooz uhr (meedee) |
| 1 P.M. | 13h00 | **Treize heures** | Trehz uhr |
| 2 P.M. | 14h00 | **Quatorze heures** | Kahtohrz uhr |
| 3 P.M. | 15h00 | **Quinze heures** | Ka(n)z uhr |
| 4 P.M. | 16h00 | **Seize heures** | Sehz uhr |
| 5 P.M. | 17h00 | **Dix-sept heures** | Dees-seht uhr |
| 6 P.M. | 18h00 | **Dix-huit heures** | Deez-weet uhr |
| 7 P.M. | 19h00 | **Dix-neuf heures** | Deez-nuh vuhr |
| 8 P.M. | 20h00 | **Vingt heures** | Vah(n) tuhr |
| 9 P.M. | 21h00 | **Vingt-et-une heures** | Vah(n) tay ewn uhr |
| 10 P.M. | 22h00 | **Vingt-deux heures** | Vah(n)-duh zuhr |
| 11 P.M. | 23h00 | **Vingt-trois heures** | Vah(n)-trwah zuhr |
| 12 A.M. | 24h00 | **Vingt-quatre heures** | Vah(n)-kahtr uhr |

The show you're planning to see might start at 7:30 P.M. or 19h30 *(dix-neuf heures et demie)*.

# 2/AT THE AIRPORT

Bienvenue en France! Welcome to France! As an American traveling in Europe, you should proceed through Customs *(Douanes)* smoothly and as rapidly as the volume of arriving visitors will allow. Generally, objects for personal use, such as clothing, tobacco products, alcohol, and perfume, enter the country duty-free. You may bring in up to 2 liters of wine, 1 liter of hard liquor, 400 cigarettes, and 50 grams of perfume or ¼ liter of eau de toilette without charge.

Customs officials at major airports generally have a working knowledge of English. However, you may find the following phrases useful at the airport. First we present a typical exchange at passport control.

## DIALOGUE: CONTRÔLE DES PASSEPORTS (CUSTOMS AND IMMIGRATION)

| | | |
|---|---|---|
| Douanière: | **Bonjour, monsieur. Votre passeport, s'il vous plaît.** | Boh(n)zhoor, muhsyuh. Vohtr pahspohr, seel voo pleh. |
| Touriste: | **Voici mon passeport.** | Vwahsee moh(n) pahspohr. |
| Douanière: | **Vous êtes américain?** | Voo zeht ahmehreeka(n)? |
| Touriste: | **Oui, je suis américain.** | Wee, zhuh swee zahmehreeka(n). |
| Douanière: | **Combien de temps allez-vous rester en France?** | Koh(m)byeh(n) duh tah(m) ahlay-voo rehstay ah(n) frah(n)s? |
| Touriste: | **Je vais rester une semaine.** | Zhuh veh rehstay ewn suhmehn. |
| · · · · · · · · · · · · · · · · · · · · · · · · · · · · · · · · · · · · · · · · · · | | |
| Customs Official: | Hello, sir. Your passport, please. | |

| Tourist: | Here's my passport. |
| Customs Official: | Are you American? |
| Tourist: | Yes, I'm American. |
| Customs Official: | How long will you be in France? |
| Tourist: | I'll be here for a week. |

## AIRPORT ARRIVAL

| What is your nationality? | **Quelle est votre nationalité?** | Kehl eh vohtr nah-syohnahleetay? |
| I am . . . | **Je suis . . .** | Zhuh swee . . . |
| • American (m) | • **américain** | • ahmayreeka(n) |
| • American (f) | • **américaine** | • ahmayreekehn |
| What's your name? | **Comment vous appelez-vous?** | Kohmah(n) voo zahplay-voo? |
| My name is . . . | **Je m'appelle . . .** | Zhuh mahpehl . . . |
| Where are you staying? | **Où est-ce que vous logez?** | Oo ehskuh voo lohzhay? |
| I'm staying at the ___ Hotel. | **Je loge à l'hôtel ___ .** | Zhuh lohzh ah lohtehl ___ . |
| Are you here on vacation? | **Vous êtes en vacances?** | Voo zeht ah(n) vahkah(n)s? |
| Yes, I'm on vacation. | **Oui, je suis en vacances.** | Wee, zhuh swee zah(n) vahkah(n)s. |
| I'm just passing through. | **Je suis de passage.** | Zhuh swee duh pahsahzh. |
| I'm here on a business trip. | **Je suis en voyage d'affaires.** | Zhuh swee zah(n) vwahyahzh dahfehr. |
| I'll be here . . . | **Je vais rester . . .** | Zhuh vay rehstay . . . |
| • a week. | • **une semaine.** | • ewn smehn. |
| • several weeks. | • **plusieurs semaines.** | • plewzyuhr smehn. |

28

| • a few days. | • **quelques jours.** | • kehlkuh zhoor. |
| • until ___. | • **jusqu'à ___.** | • zhewskah ___. |
| Nothing to declare | **Rien à déclarer** | Ryeh(n) nah day-klahray |
| Goods to declare | **Articles à déclarer** | Ahrteekl ah day-klahray |
| Do you have anything to declare? | **Avez-vous quelque chose à déclarer?** | Ahvay-voo kehlkuh shohz ah dayklahray? |
| I have nothing to declare. | **Je n'ai rien à déclarer.** | Zhuh neh reeya(n) nah dayklahray. |
| Can you open the bag? | **Pouvez-vous ouvrir cette valise?** | Pooveh-voo zoo' ,eer seht vahleez? |
| You have to pay duty on these items. | **Il faut payer des droits de douane sur ces articles.** | Eel foh payay day drwah duh dwahn sewr say zahrteekl. |
| It's for my own personal use. | **C'est pour mon usage personnel.** | Seh poor moh(n) new-zahzh pehrsohnehl. |
| These are gifts. | **Ce sont des cadeaux.** | Suh soh(n) day kahdoh. |
| Have a nice stay! | **Bon séjour!** | Boh(n) sayzhoor! |

## LUGGAGE AND PORTERS

Porters are usually available at the principal airports and train stations. You may prefer to use the baggage cart to get your luggage to your ground transportation.

| I need . . . | **Il me faut . . .** | Eel muh foh . . . |
| • a porter. | • **un porteur.** | • uh(n) pohrtuhr. |
| • a baggage cart. | • **un chariot.** | • uh(n) sharyoh. |
| Here's my luggage. | **Voici mes bagages.** | Vwahsee may bahgahzh. |
| This is mine. | **C'est à moi.** | Seh tah mwah. |

29

| Take my bags... | **Portez mes bagages...** | Pohrtay may bahgahzh... |
|---|---|---|
| • to the taxi. | • **au taxi.** | • oh takhsee. |
| • to the bus stop. | • **à l'arrêt d'autobus.** | • ah lahreh dohtohbews. |
| • to the automatic lockers. | • **à la consigne automatique.** | • ah lah koh(n)-seenyuh ohtohma-teek. |
| Be careful, please! | **Faites attention, s'il vous plaît!** | Feht zahtah(n)syoh(n), seel voo pleh! |
| How much is that? | **C'est combien?** | Seh koh(m)byeh(n)? |

## AIRPORT TRANSPORTATION AND SERVICES

| Where is/are... | **Où est/sont...** | Oo eh/soh(n)... |
|---|---|---|
| • the car rental agencies? | • **les agences de location de voiture?** | • lay zahzhah(n)s duh lohkahsyoh(n) duh vwahtewr? |
| • the taxis? | • **les taxis?** | • lay tahksee? |
| • the duty-free shop? | • **le magasin hors-taxe?** | • luh mahgahza(n) ohr-tahks? |
| • the bus stop? | • **l'arrêt d'autobus?** | • lahray dohtohbews? |
| • the bus to the city? | • **le bus qui va en ville?** | • luh bews kee vah ah(n) veel? |
| • an information booth? | • **le bureau de renseignements?** | • luh bewroh duh rah(n)sehnyuhma(n)? |
| • the ticket counter? | • **le guichet?** | • luh gheeshay? |
| • the luggage check-in? | • **la consigne?** | • lah koh(n)seenyuh? |
| • the lost baggage office? | • **le bureau d'objets trouvés?** | • luh bewroh dohbzhay troovay? |
| • the currency exchange? | • **le bureau de change?** | • luh bewroh duh shah(n)zh? |
| • the bathroom? | • **les toilettes?** | • lay twahleht? |
| • the exit? | • **la sortie?** | • lah sohrtee? |
| • the phone? | • **le téléphone?** | • luh taylayfohn? |

30

## FLIGHT ARRANGEMENTS

| English | French | Pronunciation |
|---|---|---|
| Is there a direct flight to Brussels? | Y a-t-il un vol direct pour Bruxelles? | Yahteel uh(n) vohl deerehkt poor Brewsehl? |
| What time does it leave? | A quelle heure part l'avion? | Ah kehl uhr pahr lahvyoh(n)? |
| I'd like . . . | Je voudrais . . . | Zhuh voodreh . . . |
| • a one-way ticket. | • un aller. | • uh(n) nahlay. |
| • a round-trip. | • un aller-retour. | • uh(n) nahlay ruhtoor. |
| • a seat in first class. | • une place en première classe. | • ewn plahs ah(n) pruhmyehr klahs. |
| • a seat in tourist (coach) class. | • une place en deuxième classe. | • ewn plahs ah(n) duhzyehm klahs. |
| • a seat in the no-smoking section. | • une place dans la section non-fumeurs. | • ewn plahs dah(n) lah sehksyo(h)n noh(n)-fumuhr. |
| • a window seat. | • une place à côté de la fenêtre. | • ewn plahs ah kohtay duh lah fuhnehtr. |
| • an aisle seat. | • une place côté couloir. | • ewn plahs kohtay koolwahr. |
| What is the arrival time? (lit., At what time does one arrive?) | A quelle heure est-ce qu'on arrive? | Ah kehl uhr ehs koh(n) nahreev? |
| Do I need to change planes? | Faut-il changer d'avions? | Fohteel shuh(n)zhay dahvyoh(n)? |
| There's a connection in Geneva. | Il y a une correspondance à Genève. | Eel yah ewn kohrehspoh(n)dah(n)s ah Zhuhnehv. |
| When is check-in? | A quelle heure est l'enregistrement? | Ah kehl uhr eh lah(n)-rehzheestruhmah(n)? |
| What is the flight number? | Quel est le numéro du vol? | Kehl eh luh newmayroh dew vohl? |
| From what gate does this flight leave? | De quelle porte part ce vol? | Duh kehl pohrt pahr suh vohl? |

31

| | | |
|---|---|---|
| I'd like to ___ my reservation for flight number 43. | **Je voudrais ___ ma réservation pour le vol numéro quarante-trois.** | Zhuh voodreh ___ mah rayzehrvah-syoh(n) poor luh vohl newmayroh kahrah(n)t-trwah. |
| • confirm | • **confirmer** | • koh(n)feermay |
| • cancel | • **annuler** | • ahnewlay |
| • change | • **changer** | • shah(n)zhay |
| I'd like to check these bags. | **Je voudrais enregistrer ces bagages.** | Zhuh voodreh ah(n)rehzheestray say bahgahzh. |
| I only have these carry-ons. | **J'ai seulement ceci que je garde avec moi.** | Zheh suhlmah(n) suh-see kuh zhuh gahrd ahvehk mwah. |
| How late is take-off going to be? | **L'avion va partir avec combien de minutes de retard?** | Lahvyoh(n) vah pahr-teer ahvehk koh(m)-byeh(n) duh meenewt duh ruhtahr? |
| Can I have my boarding pass? | **Puis-je avoir ma carte d'accès à bord?** | Pweezh ahvwahr mah kahrt dahkseh ah bohr? |
| Will they be serving a meal? | **Va-t-on servir un repas?** | Vahtoh(n) sehrveer uh(n) ruhpah? |
| I missed my plane. | **J'ai manqué mon avion.** | Zhay mah(n)kay moh(n) nahvyoh(n). |
| Will my ticket be good for the next flight? | **Est-ce que mon billet sera valide pour le prochain vol?** | Ehskuh moh(n) beeyay srah vahleed poor luh prohsha(n) vohl? |

## HELPFUL SIGNS

Below is a list of the various signs you are likely to encounter as you move about in a French-speaking country. Road signs, as well as the international picture road signs, are included in Chapter 9, On the Road (page 119).

32

| **A louer** | Ah looay | For Rent |
| **Ascenseur** | Ahsah(n)suhr | Elevator |
| **Attention** | Ahtah(n)syoh(n) | Caution |
| **A vendre** | Ah vah(n)dr | For Sale |
| **Caisse** | Kehs | Cashier |
| **Chaud** | Shoh | Hot |
| **Chemin privé** | Shuhma(n) preevay | Private Road |
| **Chien méchant** | Shyeh(n) mayshah(n) | Beware of the Dog |
| **Chiens interdits** | Shyeh(n) a(n)tehrdee | No Dogs |
| **Dames** | Dahm | Women |
| **Danger** | Dah(n)zhay | Danger |
| **Danger de mort** | Dah(n)zhay duh mohr | Danger of Death |
| **Défense de . . .** | Dayfah(n)s duh . . . | Do Not . . . |
| **Défense d'entrer** | Dayfah(n)s dah(n)tray | Keep Out |
| **Défense de cracher** | Dayfah(n)s duh krahshuy | No Spitting |
| **Défense de fumer** | Dayfah(n)s duh foomay | No Smoking |
| **Eau non potable** | Oh noh(n) pohtahbl | Do Not Drink the Water |
| **Eau potable** | Oh pohtahbl | Drinking Water |
| **Ecole** | Aykohl | School |
| **Entrée** | Ah(n)tray | Entrance |
| **Entrez sans frapper** | Ah(n)tray sah(n) frahpay | Enter without Knocking |
| **___ est en dérangement** | ___ eh tah(n) dayrah(n)zhmah(n) | ___ is out of order |
| **Fermé** | Fehrmay | Closed |
| **Froid** | Frwah | Cold |
| **Fumeurs** | Foomuhr | Smoking |
| **Guichet** | Gheeshay | Ticket Window |
| **Haute tension** | Oht tah(n)syoh(n) | High Voltage |
| **Heures d'ouverture** | Uhr doovehrtewr | Business Hours |
| **Hommes** | Ohm | Men |
| **Hôpital** | Ohpeetahl | Hospital |
| **Horaire** | Ohrehr | Schedule |
| **Hors service** | Ohr sehrvees | Out of Order |
| **Il est défendu de . . .** | Eel eh dayfah(n)dew duh . . . | It is Forbidden to . . . |
| **Jours fériés** | Zhoor fayryay | Holidays |

33

| Libre | Leebr | Free, Unoccupied |
|---|---|---|
| Messieurs | Maysyuh | Men |
| Ne pas déranger | Nuh pah day-rah(n)zhay | Do Not Disturb |
| Ne pas toucher | Nuh pah tooshay | Do Not Touch |
| Non fumeurs | Noh(n) foomuhr | No Smoking |
| Occupé | Ohkewpay | Occupied |
| Ouvert de . . . à . . . | Oovehr duh . . . ah . . . | Open from . . . to . . . |
| Passage souter-rain | Pahsahzh sootehra(n) | Underground Passage |
| Peinture fraiche | Pa(n)tewr frehsh | Wet Paint |
| Poussez | Poosay | Push |
| Prière de ne pas déranger | Preeyehr duh nuh pah dayrah(n)zhay | Do Not Disturb |
| Privé | Preevay | Private |
| Quai | Keh | Track |
| Renseignements | Rah(n)sehnyuhmah(n) | Information |
| Réouverture le . . . | Rayoovehrtewr luh . . . | We Will Reopen on . . . |
| Réservé | Rayzehrvay | Reserved |
| Salle d'attente | Sahl dahtah(n)t | Waiting Room |
| Soldes | Sohld | Sales, Discounts |
| Sonnez | Sohnay | Ring |
| Sortie | Sohrtee | Exit |
| Sortie de secours | Sohrtee duh suhkoor | Emergency Exit |
| Sur rendez-vous | sewr rah(n)day-voo | By Appointment |
| Stationnement in-terdit | Stahsyohnmah(n) a(n)tehrdee | No Parking |
| Tirez | Teeray | Pull |
| Toilettes | Twahleht | Restrooms |
| Voie | Vwah | Platform |
| WC | Vay Say | Restrooms |

34

# 3/FINDING YOUR WAY
## DIALOGUE: DANS LA RUE (ON THE STREET)

| | | |
|---|---|---|
| Touriste: | **Pardon, monsieur, pour aller au Musée de la Gare d'Orsay?** | Pahrdoh(n), muhsyuh, poor ahlay oh Mewzay duh lah Gahr dohrsay? |
| Parisien: | **Oui, ce n'est pas loin d'ici. Continuez tout droit et le musée sera à gauche.** | Wee, suh nay pah lwa(n) deesee. Koh(n)teeneway too drwah ay luh mewzay suhrah ah gohsh. |
| Touriste: | **Merci. Alors, je peux y aller à pied?** | Mehrsee. Ahlohr, zhuh puh ee ahlay ah pyay? |
| Parisien: | **Ah oui! Bien sûr! Mais le musée est fermé aujourd'hui. Il est fermé le lundi.** | Ah wee! Byeh(n) sewr! May luh mewzay ay fehrmay ohzhoordwee. Eel ay fehrmay luh luh(n)dee. |
| Touriste: | **Tant pis. J'irai demain.** | Tah(n) pee. Zheeray duhma(n). |
| Parisien: | **Alors, bon séjour à Paris!** | Ahlohr, boh(n) sayzhoor ah Pahree! |

· · · · · · · · · · · · · · · · · · · · · · · · · · · · · · · · · ·

| | |
|---|---|
| Tourist: | Excuse me, sir, how can I get to the Gare d'Orsay Museum? |
| Parisian: | Yes, it's not far from here. Continue straight ahead and the museum will be on the left. |
| Tourist: | Thanks. So I can walk there? |
| Parisian: | Yes, of course! But the museum is closed today. It's closed on Mondays. |
| Tourist: | Too bad. I'll go tomorrow. |
| Parisian: | Well, have a good stay in Paris! |

## FINDING YOUR WAY IN PARIS

If you are staying in Paris for any length of time or if you plan to go anywhere that is not a major tourist attraction, well-known hotel, or restaurant, you might do well to purchase any of the handy little map-guides to the city. Paris is divided into 20 *arrondissements,* or districts, and Parisian addresses will include the number of the arrondissement. The map-guides include a complete index of street names plus individual arrondissement maps and a map of the entire city. The city maps will also indicate the nearest *métro* station for any location. Some of these guides also feature lists of churches, embassies, hospitals, theaters, parks, cinemas, police stations, gardens, department stores, etc., along with their addresses. Two of the common publishers of such guides are *Taride* and *Le Conte.* These materials can be found at bookstores and street kiosks.

## WALKING AROUND

It is hard to dispute the old adage that the best way to get to know a new city is to explore it on foot. Fortunately, many of the better guide books encourage this by providing self-guided walking tours of the prominent landmarks and neighborhoods in major cities. The following section is designed to help you orient yourself and get directions from natives as you move about the city.

You may notice that in providing street directions, the French rarely talk about numbers of *blocks* (*rue* [rew], or *pâtés de maisons* [pahtay duh mehzoh(n)]). They are much more likely to refer to the distance in meters (*mètres* [mehtr]) or point out landmarks such as traffic lights (*feux de circulation* [fuh duh seerkewlahsyoh(n)]). This is understandable when you consider how irregular and unpredictable street patterns are in many European cities!

| | | |
|---|---|---|
| Excuse me, sir/madam/miss. | **Pardon, monsieur/ madame/ mademoiselle.** | Pahrdoh(n), muhsyuh/ mahdahm/ mahduhmwahzehl. |

| English | French | Pronunciation |
|---|---|---|
| Where is the Pantheon? | **Où est le Panthéon?** | Oo eh luh pah(n)tay-oh(n)? |
| Do you have a map of the city? | **Avez-vous un plan de la ville?** | Ahvay-voo uh(n) plah(n) duh lah veel? |
| Could you show me on my map, please? | **Montrez-moi sur mon plan, s'il vous plaît?** | Moh(n)tray-mwah sewr moh(n) plah(n), seel voo pleh? |
| Can I get there on foot? | **Puis-je y aller à pied?** | Pweezh ee ahlay ah pyay? |
| How far is it? | **C'est à quelle distance?** | Seh tah kehl dees-tah(n)s? |
| I think I'm lost. | **Je crois que je suis perdu(e).** | Zhuh krwah kuh zhuh swee pehrdew. |
| Where can I find this address? | **Où puis-je trouver cette adresse?** | Oo pweezh troovay seht ahdrehs? |
| How long does it take on foot? | **Combien de temps est-ce que cela prend à pied?** | Koh(m)byeh(n) duh tah(m) ehskuh slah prah(n) ah pyay? |

Here are a few possible responses you may get to your questions:

| French | Pronunciation | English |
|---|---|---|
| **C'est tout droit.** | Seh too drwah. | It's straight ahead. |
| **Tournez à gauche (à droite).** | Toornay ah gohsh (ah drwaht). | Turn left (right). |
| **C'est là-bas.** | Seh lah-bah. | It's down there. |
| **C'est . . .** | Seh . . . | It's . . . |
| • **derrière** ___ | • dehryehr ___ | • behind ___ |
| • **devant** ___ | • duhvah(n) ___ | • in front of ___ |
| • **à côté de** ___ | • ah kohtay duh ___ | • next to ___ |
| • **près de** ___ | • preh duh ___ | • near ___ |
| • **au-delà de** ___ | • oh-dlah duh ___ | • after ___ |
| **Tournez à gauche après le carrefour.** | Toornay ah gohsh ahpreh luh kahrfoor. | Turn left after the intersection. |
| **On ne peut pas y aller à pied.** | Oh(n) nuh puh pah zee ahlay ah pyay. | You can't get there on foot. |

37

| **Vous êtes sur le** | Voo zeht sewr luh | You're on the wrong |
| **mauvais chemin.** | mohveh shma(n). | road. |
| **C'est après les** | Seh tahpreh lay fuh. | It's beyond the traf- |
| **feux.** | | fic light. |

## PUBLIC TRANSPORTATION

Paris is endowed with the greatest public transportation system of any of Europe's major cities. If you haven't been to Paris in five or six years, you cannot help but see the changes. New express suburban lines are tied into the in-city system, with new cars, revamped stations, and bigger and better "super" buses. It's all the result of a highly subsidized program that keeps everything moving in Paris, and at prices that everyone can afford.

The fare system sounds more complicated than it is. These are the choices: you can buy tickets one at a time, either at a Metro station or on the bus, or in blocks of ten (Metro stations only) by asking for *un carnet* [uh(n) kahrnay]. On a ten-ride basis, the price is cut almost in half!

On the Metro, one ticket will get you one ride anywhere on the system, regardless of the number of transfers. By bus, one ticket gets you a ride according to distance—so many sections, or zones. If you go farther, it means two tickets, which gets you to the end of the line.

But for a visitor there are far better schemes. There's the so-called *Formule 1,* which means unlimited rides for one day on all public transportation within city limits at great savings. Then there are tourist tickets *(Paris sésame)* for two, four, and seven days at reasonable rates.

If you are staying in Paris longer, the biggest money-saver of all is the *Carte orange.* This is actually the commutation ticket geared to natives on a monthly basis, but it is also issued by the week—Monday to Sunday—and can be bought by visitors. What you get is unlimited transportation for seven days.

For the *Carte orange,* you need a passport-type photo, although most railway station Metro sections have photo machines for do-it-yourself picture-taking.

With all of these you get a pass, with a slot containing what looks like a regular Metro ticket, except that the magnetic tape is computer-set for constant reuse in Metro turnstiles. *Note: You must put your name and signature on the pass. And you must write the pass number on the ticket.* On buses, simply flash the pass (with ticket in it) at the driver as you get on.

To make it easier to use the bus and Metro, the entire system is documented in easy-to-understand maps and diagrams.

## USING THE SUBWAY

| | | |
|---|---|---|
| Where's the nearest subway station? | **Où est la station de métro la plus proche?** | Oo eh lah stahsyoh(n) duh maytroh lah plew prohsh? |
| What line goes to ___? | **Quelle ligne va à ___?** | Kehl leenyuh vah ah ___? |
| Is this the train for ___? | **Est-ce bien le train qui va à ___?** | Ehs byeh(n) luh tra(n) kee vah ah ___? |
| Where do I change to go to ___? | **Où faut-il changer pour aller à ___?** | Oo fohteel shah(n)zhay poor ah-lay ah ___? |
| Do I get off here to go to ___? | **Est-ce que je descends ici pour aller à ___?** | Ehskuh zhuh dehsah(n) zeesee poor ahlay ah ___? |

### Subway Signs

| | |
|---|---|
| **Guichet** | Ticket Window |
| **Tête de station** | Head of Station (the train stops here) |
| **Défense de cracher** | No Spitting |

## ON THE BUS

| | | |
|---|---|---|
| What bus do I take to go to ___? | **Quel bus dois-je prendre pour aller à ___?** | Kehl bews dwahzh prah(n)dr poor ahlay ah ___? |

39

| | | |
|---|---|---|
| Where is the nearest bus stop? | **Où est l'arrêt de bus le plus proche?** | Oo eh lahreh duh bews luh plew prohsh? |
| Does this bus go to ___? | **Est-ce que ce bus va à ___?** | Ehskuh suh bews vah ah ___? |
| When is the next bus to ___? | **Quand part le prochain bus pour ___?** | Kah(n) pahr luh proh-sha(n) bews poor ___? |
| What is the fare to ___? | **Quel est le prix du trajet pour ___?** | Kehl eh luh pree dew trahzhay poor ___? |
| Do you need exact change? | **Faut-il avoir la monnaie exacte?** | Fohteel ahvwahr lah mohnay ehgzahkt? |
| I want to get off at ___. | **Je veux descendre à ___.** | Zhuh vuh dehsah(n)dr ah ___. |
| Please tell me when to get off? | **Pourriez-vous me dire quand je dois descendre?** | Pooryay-voo muh deer kah(n) zhuh dwah dehsah(n)dr? |
| Do I need to change buses? | **Faut-il changer de bus?** | Fohteel shah(n)zhay duh bews? |

## Bus Signs

| | |
|---|---|
| **Défense de parler au conducteur** | Do Not Talk to the Driver |
| **Arrêt fixe** | Regular Stop |
| **Arrêt sur demande** | Stop on Demand |

## TAKING A TAXI

Taxi travel in French-speaking Europe follows the same basic patterns as in the United States. Meters are in use except for certain out-of-city trips. In Paris, make sure you have a metered cab by checking for the lighted sign on the roof of the vehicle. Parisian taxis use a system of differential rates. Rate A, the lowest, is used for trips within Paris on weekdays. Rate B, somewhat higher, applies for in-Paris trips from eight P.M. to 6:30 A.M. on weeknights, all day weekends and holidays, and for nearby suburbs (including airports) on weekdays. The C rate is the highest and is used evenings in the suburbs. Rates are clearly posted and will also indicate supplemental charges for luggage and a fourth adult passenger.

| Where is the nearest taxi stand? | **Où est la station de taxis la plus proche?** | Oo eh lah stahsyoh(n) duh tahksee lah plew prohsh? |
| Are there any taxis around here? | **Y a-t-il des taxis par ici?** | Yahteel day tahksee pahr eesee? |
| Taxi! | **Taxi!** | Tahksee! |
| Are you free? | **Etes-vous libre?** | Eht-voo leebr? |
| Please take me . . . | **S'il vous plaît, conduisez-moi . . .** | Seel voo pleh, koh(n)dweezay-mwah . . . |
| • to the airport. | • **à l'aéroport.** | • ah lah-ehrohpohr. |
| • to the train station. | • **à la gare.** | • ah lah gahr. |
| • to the bus station. | • **au terminus.** | • oh tehrmeenews. |
| • downtown. | • **au centre-ville.** | • oh sah(n)truh-veel. |
| • to the Hotel ___. | • **à l'hôtel ___.** | • ah lohtehl ___. |
| • to this address. | • **à cette adresse.** | • ah seht ahdrehs. |
| • to this restaurant. | • **à ce restaurant.** | • ah suh rehstohrah(n). |
| • to this store. | • **à ce magasin.** | • ah suh mahgahza(n). |
| How much is it to ___? | **C'est combien pour aller à ___?** | Seh koh(m)byeh(n) poor ahlay ah ___? |
| I'm in a hurry! | **Je suis pressé(e)!** | Zhuh swee prehsay! |
| Stop here, please. | **Arrêtez-vous ici, s'il vous plaît.** | Ahrehtay-voo zeesee seel voo pleh. |
| Wait here for me; I'll be right back. | **Attendez-moi ici; je reviens dans un moment.** | Ahtah(n)day mwah eesee; zhuh ruhvyeh(n) dah(n) zuh(n) mohmah(n). |

41

| Could you please drive more slowly! | **Conduisez plus lentement, s'il vous plaît!** | Koh(n)dweezay plew lah(n)tuhmah(n), seel voo pleh! |
| How much do I owe you? | **Combien est-ce que je vous dois?** | Koh(m)byeh(n) ehskuh zhuh voo dwah? |
| Keep the change. | **Gardez la monnaie.** | Gahrday lah mohneh. |
| Taxi stand | **Stationnement de taxis** | Stahsyoh(n)mah(n) duh tahksee |

## GOING BY TRAIN

As is the case in most European countries, there is a single state-run system in France, which is known as the SNCF (Société Nationale des Chemins de Fer Français). The train system in France is a source of pride for the entire country. It is rapid, economical and reliable. It is also extremely comprehensive, serving small towns and large cities alike.

### Types of Trains

**TGV (le Train à grande vitesse):** High-speed trains that cut traveling time between major French cities to a minimum.

**Rapide:** Trains that stop only at major cities.

**Express:** Long-distance trains stopping at large and middle-sized cities.

### Sleeping Arrangements

There are two principal types of sleeping accommodations. Be sure to reserve in advance.

*Couchette:* Bunk-style sleeping found in second class. Sleeps six per couchette.

*Wagon-lit:* First class private accommodations for one or two people.

42

## Eating Arrangements

The *wagon-restaurant* serves quality full-course meals. Prices are high. In addition, sandwiches, snacks, and soft drinks are available from vendors who pass by your window when your train has stopped briefly at a station.

Where is/are . . .
- the train station?
- the ticket window?
- the first-class compartments?

- the (second-class) sleeping cars?
- the first-class sleeping cars?
- the non-smoking section?

- the smoking section?
- the reservations office?
- the baggage check?
- the baggage lockers?
- the lost and found?
- the platform?

I'd like a ticket to Lyons . . .

- first class.
- second class.

- one way.
- round-trip.
- on the next train.

**Où est/sont . . .**
- **la gare?**
- **le guichet?**
- **les compartiments de première classe?**
- **les couchettes?**

- **les wagon-lits?**

- **le compartiment non-fumeurs?**

- **le compartiment fumeurs?**
- **le bureau de réservations?**
- **la consigne?**

- **la consigne automatique?**
- **le bureau des objets trouvés?**
- **les quais?**

**Je voudrais un billet pour Lyon . . .**
- **première classe.**
- **deuxième classe.**

- **aller simple.**
- **aller-retour.**
- **dans le prochain train.**

Oo eh/soh(n) . . .
- lah gahr?
- luh gheeshay?
- lay koh(m)pahr-teemah(n) duh pruh-myehr klahs?
- lay koosheht?

- lay vahgoh(n)-lee?

- luh koh(m)pahr-teemah(n) noh(n)-foomuhr?

- luh koh(m)pahr-teemah(n) foomuhr?
- luh bewroh duh ray-zehrvahsyoh(n)?
- lah koh(n)seenyuh?

- lah koh(n)seenyuh ohtohmahteek?
- luh bewroh day zohbzhay troovay?
- lay keh?

Zhuh voodreh zuh(n) beeyay poor Leeoh(n) . . .
- pruhmyehr klahs.
- duhzyehm klahs.

- ahlay sa(m)pl.
- ahlay-ruhtoor.
- dah(n) luh proh-sha(n) tra(n).

43

| | | |
|---|---|---|
| I'd like to reserve . . . | **Je voudrais réserver. . .** | Zhuh voodreh rayzehr-vay. . . |
| • a bunk on top. | • **une couchette supérieure.** | • ewn koosheht sew-payryuhr. |
| • a bunk in the middle. | • **une couchette au milieu.** | • ewn koosheht oh meelyuh. |
| • a bunk on the bottom. | • **une couchette en bas.** | • ewn koosheht ah(n) bah. |
| • a bed in the sleeping car. | • **une place en wagon-lit.** | • ewn plahs ah(n) vahgoh(n)-lee. |
| I'd like to check my bags. | **Je voudrais enregistrer mes bagages.** | Zhuh voodreh zah(n)rehzheestray may bahgahzh. |
| Does this train stop in ___? | **Ce train s'arrête à ___?** | Suh tra(n) sahreht ah ___? |
| From which platform does it leave? | **De quel quai part-il?** | Duh kehl keh pahr-teel? |
| Is the train on time? | **Le train est-il à l'heure?** | Luh tra(n) ehteel ah luhr? |
| Is there a change of trains in ___? | **Est-ce qu'il y a une correspon-dence à ___?** | Ehskeel yah ewn kohrehspoh(n)dah(n)s ah ___? |
| I'm going to Dijon; do I need to change trains? | **Je vais à Dijon; dois-je changer de train?** | Zhuh veh zah Dee-zhoh(n); dwahzh shah(n)zhay duh tra(n)? |
| Is this seat free? | **Cette place, est-elle libre?** | Seht plahs, eh tehl leebr? |
| This seat is occupied. | **Cette place est occupée.** | Seht plahs eh tohkew-pay. |
| Could you tell me when we get to Nancy? | **Pourriez-vous me dire quand nous arriverons à Nancy?** | Pooryay-voo muh deer kah(n) noo zahreevroh(n) ah Nah(n)see? |

44

## Train Signs

| | |
|---|---|
| **Entrée** | Entrance |
| **Sortie** | Exit |
| **Renseignements** | Information |
| **i** | Information |
| **Salle d'attente** | Waiting Room |
| **Bureau de réservations** | Reservations Office |
| **Accès aux quais** | To the Platform |
| **Fumeurs** | Smoking |
| **Non-fumeurs** | Non-smoking |
| **Enregistrement des bagages** | Baggage Check |

## TRAVELING BY BOAT

| | | |
|---|---|---|
| When is the next boat for ___? | **Quand part le prochain bateau pour ___?** | Kah(n) pahr luh proh-sha(n) bahtoh poor ___? |
| Where does the boat leave from? | **D'où part le bateau?** | Doo pahr luh bahtoh? |
| How long is the crossing? | **Combien de temps prend la traversée?** | Koh(m)byeh(n) duh tah(m) prah(n) lah trahvehrsay? |
| Where does the boat stop? | **Où est-ce qu'on fait escale?** | Oo ehs koh(n) feh tehskahl? |
| How much is a seat in . . . | **Combien coûte un billet . . .** | Koh(m)byeh(n) koot uh(n) beeyay. . . |
| • first class? | • **de première classe?** | • duh pruhmyehr klahs? |
| • second class? | • **de deuxième classe?** | • duh duhzyehm klahs? |
| • cabin class? | • **de cabine?** | • duh kahbeen? |
| I missed the boat. | **J'ai manqué le bateau.** | Zhay mah(n)kay luh bahtoh. |
| What should I do? | **Qu'est-ce que je dois faire?** | Kehskuh zhuh dwah fehr? |

# 4/ACCOMMODATIONS

One of the joys of traveling in French-speaking Europe is the abundance of clean, comfortable, well-run hotels in a variety of price ranges. There are also lots of choices for accommodations other than the traditional hotel, as we shall describe below.

In France, hotels are officially classified in five categories: from one to four stars, plus L for luxury accommodations. The hotel's category is listed at its entrance, and room rates will reflect this classification.

If you do arrive in a city without reservations, your best bet is to check in with the official tourist office (*Le Syndicat d'initiative* [luh Sa(n)deekah deeneesyahteev]), often located downtown near the train station. They will help you find a hotel in the price range and location you desire.

In addition to the standard hotel, many other varieties of accommodations are available to the traveler, especially outside of Paris. Start with the rural top-of-the-line *Relais et châteaux* [Ruhlay zay shahtoh] chain—not really a chain, but some 150 independently owned and operated castle hotels and manor houses in various parts of France, banded together in name only for purposes of advertising, promotion, and working through a central reservation system. (U.S. representative: David B. Mitchell & Co., 200 Madison Avenue, New York, NY 10016; tel. 1 (800) 372-1323.)

A similar group of castle and manor-house properties (somewhat less luxuriously outfitted and much less expensive) is the collection of 146 *châteaux* and manor houses that goes by the name *Châteaux hôtels indépendants et hôtelleries d'atmosphère* [Shahtoh ohtehl a(n)daypah(n)dah(n) ay ohstehlree dahtmohsfehr]. Another group calls itself *Châteaux et demeures de tradition* [Shahtoh zay duhmuhr duh trahdeesyoh(n)].

*Relais du silence* [Ruhlay dew seelah(n)s], for country living with guaranteed peace and quiet, and the *Logis de France* [Lohzhee duh Frah(n)s] are some 3,700 minor country inns that must meet certain standards to belong to the organization and invariably offer good country cooking at low prices. They are definitely worth checking out while driving about France.

*Auberges rurales* [Ohbehrzh ruhrahl] offer no-frills country accommodations. *Gîtes ruraux* [Zheet rewroh] are apartments or small country homes in rural areas, which can be rented by the week or month. Information on all of these can be had from the French Government Tourist Office.

Other low-cost alternatives abound throughout the country. *Chambres d'hôte* [shah(m)bruh doht] are bed-and-breakfast type accommodations offering comfortable rooms at attractive prices and a chance to meet local families and sample their way of life.

*Pensions* [pah(n)syoh(n)] are a traditional favorite for the budget-minded traveler in Europe, offering accommodations and some or all daily meals. And, finally, a good alternative for the long-distance automobile traveler, *motels* [mohtehl] have begun to spring up on main roads in suburban locations and near airports all over the country.

## DIALOGUE: À LA RÉCEPTION (AT THE FRONT DESK)

| | | |
|---|---|---|
| Cliente: | **Bonjour, monsieur. Avez-vous une chambre pour deux personnes pour une nuit?** | Boh(n)zhoor, muhsyuh. Ahvay-voo ewn shah(m)br poor duh pehrsohn poor ewn nwee? |
| Gérant: | **Un moment, madame. Je vais voir ... Oui, j'en ai une au troisième étage avec un lit à deux places.** | Uh(n) mohmah(n), mahdahm. Zhuh veh voir ... Wee, zhah(n) nay ewn oh trwahzyehm aytahzh ahvehk uh(n) lee ah duh plahs. |
| Cliente: | **C'est parfait. Y a-t-il une salle de bain?** | Say pahrfeh. Yahteel ewn suhl duh ba(n)? |
| Gérant: | **Non, mais il y a un cabinet de toilette et une douche.** | Noh(n), may eel yah uh(n) kahbeenay duh twahleht ay ewn doosh. |

47

| Cliente: | **Très bien. Est-ce que je pourrais la voir?** | Treh byeh(n). Ehskuh zhuh poorray lah vwahr? |
|---|---|---|
| Gérant: | **Oui, bien sûr. Suivez-moi, madame.** | Wee, byeh(n) sewr. Sweevay mwah, mahdahm. |

. . . . . . . . . . . . . . . . . . . . . . . . . . . . . . . . . . . . . . . . .

| Customer: | Hello. Do you have a room for two people for one night? |
|---|---|
| Manager: | One moment, madam. Let me see . . . Yes, I have one on the fourth floor* with a double bed. |
| Customer: | Perfect. Does it have a bathroom? |
| Manager: | No, but it does have a toilet and a shower. |
| Customer: | Fine. Could I see it? |
| Manager: | Yes, of course. Follow me, madam. |

*Our first floor is the *rez-de-chaussée* [rehduhshohsay] (ground floor) in France. Thus, their *premier étage* [pruhmyeh raytahzh] (first floor) is our second floor, etc.

## HOTEL ARRANGEMENTS AND SERVICES

| I have a reservation. | **J'ai une réservation.** | Zhay ewn raysehrvah-syoh(n). |
|---|---|---|
| I'd like a room . . . | **Je voudrais une chambre . . .** | Zhuh voodreh zewn shah(m)br . . . |
| • for tonight. | • **pour ce soir.** | • poor suh swahr. |
| • with one bed. | • **à un lit.** | • ah uh(n) lee. |
| • with two beds. | • **à deux lits.** | • ah duh lee. |
| • with a double bed. | • **avec un grand lit.** | • ahvehk uh(n) grah(n) lee. |
| • with twin beds. | • **avec des lits jumeaux.** | • ahvehk day lee zhewmoh. |

48

| English | French | Pronunciation |
|---|---|---|
| • with a bathroom. | • **avec salle de bain.** | • ahvehk sahl duh ba(n). |
| • with a shower. | • **avec douche.** | • ahvehk doosh. |
| • with air-conditioning. | • **climatisée.** | • kleemahteezay. |
| • with a view. | • **avec vue.** | • ahvehk vew. |
| Is there . . . | **Y a-t-il . . .** | Yahteel . . . |
| • hot water? | • **de l'eau chaude?** | • duh loh shohd? |
| • a private toilet? | • **des toilettes privées?** | • day twahleht pree-vay? |
| • a radio? | • **un poste de radio?** | • uh(n) pohst duh rah-dyoh? |
| We're going to stay. . . | **Nous allons rester. . .** | Noo zahloh(n) rehstay. . . |
| • one night. | • **une nuit.** | • ewn nwee. |
| • a few days. | • **quelques jours.** | • kehlkuh zhoor. |
| • a week. | • **une semaine.** | • ewn suhmehn. |
| I'd like to see the room. | **Je voudrais voir la chambre.** | Zhuh voodreh vwahr lah shah(m)br. |
| I'll take it. | **Je la prends.** | Zhuh lah prah(n). |
| I'm not going to take it. | **Je ne vais pas la prendre.** | Zhuh nuh vay pah lah prah(n)dr. |
| Do you have a room that's . . . | **Avez-vous une chambre . . .** | Ahvay-voo zewn shah(m)br. . . |
| • quieter? | • **plus tranquille?** | • plew trah(n)keel? |
| • bigger? | • **plus grande?** | • plew grah(n)d? |
| • less expensive? | • **moins chère?** | • mwa(n) shehr? |
| How much is it . . . | **Quel est le prix . . .** | Kehl eh luh pree . . . |
| • per night? | • **par nuit?** | • pahr nwee? |
| • per week? | • **par semaine?** | • pahr suhmehn? |
| • with all meals? | • **en pension complète?** | • ah(n) pah(n)syoh(n) koh(m)pleht? |
| • with breakfast? | • **avec petit déjeuner?** | • ahvehk puhtee day-zhuhnay? |
| • without meals? | • **sans repas?** | • sah(n) ruhpah? |

49

| Does the price include . . . | Est-ce que le prix comprend . . . | Ehskuh luh pree koh(m)prah(n) . . . |
| • taxes? | • les taxes? | • lay tahks? |
| • service? | • le service? | • luh sehrvees? |

| Where can I park? | Où puis-je me garer? | Oo pweezh muh gahray? |

| Please have my bags sent up to my room. | Faites monter mes bagages à ma chambre, s'il vous plaît. | Feht moh(n)tay may bahgahzh ah mah shah(m)br seel voo pleh. |

| This is for your safe. | Ceci est pour votre coffre-fort. | Suhsee eh poor vohtr kohfruh-fohr. |

| I'd like to speak with . . . | Je voudrais parler avec . . . | Zhuh voodreh pahrlay ahvehk . . . |
| • the manager. | • le gérant. | • luh zhayrah(n). |
| • the hall porter. | • le concierge. | • luh koh(n)syehrzh. |
| • the maid. | • la femme de chambre. | • lah fahm duh shah(m)br. |
| • the bellboy. | • le chasseur. | • luh shahsuhr. |

| May I have . . . | Puis-je avoir. . . | Pweezh ahvwahr. . . |
| • a blanket? | • une couverture? | • ewn koovehrtewr? |
| • hangers? | • des cintres? | • day sa(n)tr? |
| • some ice? | • des glaçons? | • day glahsoh(n)? |
| • a pillow? | • un oreiller? | • uh(n) nohrayay? |
| • some stationery? | • du papier à lettres? | • dew pahpyay ah lehtr? |
| • some soap? | • du savon? | • dew sahvoh(n)? |
| • a towel? | • une serviette? | • ewn sehrvyeht? |
| • toilet paper? | • du papier hygiénique? | • dew pahpyay eezheeyayneek? |

| Where is . . . | Où est . . . | Oo eh . . . |
| • the elevator? | • l'ascenseur? | • lahsah(n)suhr? |
| • the garage? | • le garage? | • luh gahrahzh? |
| • the dining room? | • la salle à manger? | • lah sahl ah mah(n)zhay? |
| • the laundry? | • la blanchisserie? | • lah blah(n)sheesree? |
| • the beauty salon? | • le salon de coiffure? | • luh sahloh(n) duh kwahfewr? |

50

| There's a problem with . . . | Il y a un problème avec . . . | Eel yah uh(n) prohblehm ahvehk . . . |
|---|---|---|
| • the key. | • la clé. | • lah klay. |
| • the heat. | • le chauffage. | • luh shohfahzh. |
| • room service. | • le service à l'étage. | • luh sehrvees ah laytahzh. |
| • the hot water. | • l'eau chaude. | • loh shohd. |
| • the air-conditioner. | • le climatiseur. | • luh kleemahteezuhr. |
| Could you make up the room now? | Pouvez-vous faire la chambre tout de suite? | Poovay-voo fehr lah shah(m)br tood sweet? |
| I'm in room ___. | Je suis dans la chambre ___. | Zhuh swee dah(n) lah shah(m)br ___. |
| Can you get me a babysitter? | Pouvez-vous me trouver une garde d'enfants? | Poovay-voo muh troovay ewn gahrd dah(n)fah(n)? |
| We're leaving tomorrow. | Nous partons demain. | Noo pahrtoh(n) duhma(n). |
| Please prepare the bill. | Voulez-vous préparer la note. | Voolay-voo praypahray lah noht. |
| We're leaving at 10 A.M. | Nous partons à dix heures. | Noo pahrtoh(n) ah dee zuhr. |
| Could you please call us a taxi? | Pourriez-vous nous appeler un taxi? | Pooryay-voo noo zahplay uh(n) tahksee? |
| Please have my luggage brought downstairs. | Pourriez-vous descendre mes bagages. | Pooreeyay-voo daysah(n)druh may bahgahzh? |

# 5/SOCIALIZING

Meeting people, making new friends and acquaintances, discovering a new culture, and sharing your own through personal relationships are some of the most memorable experiences to be enjoyed through travel. A word of caution: people in French-speaking Europe generally take more time than Americans in establishing personal relationships and friendships. Formality and social etiquette are valued in human contacts and may lead you to perceive people as somewhat reserved or distant. Conversely, Europeans often see Americans as overly familiar or superficial. With good will, patience, and a sense of humor on both sides, these cultural differences can be a source of stimulation and enrichment and heighten your enjoyment of international travel.

Here are the names and addresses of some organizations that may make it easier to meet French people.

- Meet the French, 182 Blvd. Pereire, 75017 Paris. Tel. 45.74.77.12.
- American Club of Paris, 49 Rue Pierre Charron, 75008 Paris. Tel. 43.59.24.33.
- Club France-Amérique, 9 Av. Franklin Roosevelt, 75008 Paris. Tel. 43.59.51.00.

## DIALOGUE: DES INTRODUCTIONS (INTRODUCTIONS)

| Julie Johnson: | **Bonjour, monsieur. Permettez-moi de me présenter. Je m'appelle Julie Johnson.** | Boh(n)zhoor, muhsyuh. Pehrmehtay-mwah duh muh prayzah(n)tay. Zhuh mahpehl Julie Johnson. |
|---|---|---|
| Pierre Jacquot: | **Enchanté, madame. Je suis Pierre Jacquot.** | Ah(n)shah(n)tay, mahdahm. Zhuh swee Pyehr Zhakoh. |
| Julie Johnson: | **Très heureuse.** | Treh zuhruhz. |

| Pierre Jacquot: | **Vous êtes en vacances ici à Nice?** | Voo zeht ah(n) vahkah(n)s eesee ah Nees? |
| Julie Johnson: | **Oui, je vais rester ici encore une semaine.** | Wee, zhuh veh rehstay eesee ah(n)kohr ewn suhmehn. |
| Pierre Jacquot: | **Alors, bonne fin de séjour. Au revoir, madame.** | Ahlohr, bohn fa(n) duh sayzhoor. Oh ruhvwahr, mahdahm. |
| Julie Johnson: | **Merci. Au revoir, monsieur.** | Mehrsee. Oh ruhvwahr, muhsyuh. |

· · · · · · · · · · · · · · · · · · · · · · · · · · · · · · · · · · · · · · · · · ·

| Julie Johnson: | Hello! Allow me to introduce myself. My name is Julie Johnson. |
| Pierre Jacquot: | Pleased to meet you. I'm Pierre Jacquot. |
| Julie Johnson: | Nice meeting you. |
| Pierre Jacquot: | Are you here in Nice on vacation? |
| Julie Johnson: | Yes. I'll be here another week. |
| Pierre Jacquot: | Have a good stay. Goodbye now. |
| Julie Johnson: | Thank you. Goodbye. |

Note: The French use the titles "monsieur" and "madame" in speaking to acquaintances who are not close friends. In English, we would probably use first names or no form of address at all.

## INTRODUCTIONS

| I'd like to introduce you to___. | **Je voudrais vous présenter à___.** | Zhuh voodreh voo prayzah(n)tay ah___. |
| Pleased to meet you. | **Enchanté(e).** | Ah(n)shah(n)tay. |

| Allow me to introduce myself. | **Permettez-moi de me présenter.** | Pehrmehtay-mwah duh muh prayzah(n)tay. |
| What's your name? | **Comment vous appelez-vous?** | Kohmah(n) voo zahplay-voo? |
| My name is . . . | **Je m'appelle . . .** | Zhuh mahpehl . . . |
| I am . . . | **Je suis . . .** | Zhuh swee . . . |
| This is . . . | **C'est . . .** | Seh . . . |
| • my husband. | • **mon mari.** | • moh(n) mahree. |
| • my wife. | • **ma femme.** | • mah fam. |
| • my colleague. | • **mon/ma collègue.** | • moh(n)/mah kohlehg. |
| • my friend. | • **mon ami(e).** | • moh(n) nahmee. |
| How are you? | **Comment allez-vous?** | Kohmah(n) talay-voo? |
| Fine, thanks, and you? | **Très bien, merci, et vous?** | Treh byeh(n), mehr-see, ay voo? |
| How's it going? | **Ça va bien?** | Sah vah byeh(n)? |
| It's going well, thank you. | **Ça va bien, merci.** | Sah vah byeh(n), mehrsee. |

## FIRST CONTACT

| Where do you live? | **Où est-ce que vous habitez?** | Oo ehskuh voo zah-beetay? |
| I live in New York. | **J'habite à New York.** | Zhahbeet ah Noo Yohrk. |
| How do you like France? | **Qu'est-ce que vous pensez de la France?** | Kehskuh voo pah(n)say duh lah Frah(n)s? |
| I like France very much. | **J'adore la France.** | Zhahdohr lah Frah(n)s. |
| I just arrived. | **Je viens d'arriver.** | Zhuh vyeh(n) dahreevay. |
| I'm not sure yet. | **Je ne sais pas encore.** | Zhuh nuh seh pah zah(n)kohr. |

| I like the people very much. | **J'aime beaucoup les gens.** | Zhehm bohkoo lay zhah(n). |
| I like the countryside. | **J'aime le paysage.** | Zhehm luh pay-eezahzh. |
| Everything is so . . . <br> • interesting. <br> • different. | **Tout est si . . .** <br> • **intéressant.** <br> • **différent.** | Too teh see . . . <br> • a(n)tayrehsah(n). <br> • deefayrah(n). |
| That's . . . <br> • strange. <br> • stupid. <br> • wonderful. <br> • sad. <br> • beautiful. | **C'est . . .** <br> • **bizarre.** <br> • **stupide.** <br> • **merveilleux.** <br> • **triste.** <br> • **beau.** | Seh . . . <br> • beezahr. <br> • stewpeed. <br> • mehrvehyuh. <br> • treest. <br> • boh. |
| What's your profession? | **Quelle est votre profession?** | Kehl eh vohtr prohfeh-syoh(n)? |
| I'm a . . . <br> • businessman. <br><br> • businesswoman. <br><br> • doctor. <br> • lawyer | **Je suis . . .** <br> • **homme d'affaires.** <br> • **femme d'affaires.** <br> • **médecin.** <br> • **avocat(e).** | Zhuh swee . . . <br> • zohm dahfehr. <br><br> • fahm dahfehr. <br><br> • maydsa(n). <br> • ahvohkah(t). |
| I'm retired. | **Je suis à la retraite.** | Zhuh swee zah lah ruhtreht. |

## MAKING FRIENDS

| May I offer you a drink? | **Puis-je vous offrir à boire?** | Pweezh voo zohfreer ah bwahr? |
| Would you like to drink? | **Voulez-vous prendre un verre?** | Voolay-voo prah(n)dr uh(n) vehr? |
| With pleasure. | **Avec plaisir.** | Ahvehk plehzeer. |
| No, thanks. | **Merci.** * | Mehrsee. |

*Note: The French often decline an offer by saying "merci," sometimes accompanied by a slight shake of the head.

| | | |
|---|---|---|
| Would you like to come with us to a café? | **Est-ce que vous aimeriez nous accompagner au café?** | Ehskuh voo zehmuhryay noo zahkoh(m)panyay oh kahfay? |
| Gladly. | **Volontiers.** | Vohloh(n)tyay. |
| May I bring a friend? | **Est-ce que je peux emmener un ami (une amie)?** | Ehskuh zhuh puh ah(m)mnay uh(n) nahmee (ewn ahmee)? |
| Do you mind if I smoke? | **Ça vous dérange si je fume?** | Sah voo dayrah(n)zh see zhuh foom? |
| Not at all. | **Pas du tout.** | Pah dew too. |
| Yes, a bit. | **Oui, un peu.** | Wee, uh(n) puh. |
| May I telephone you? | **Est-ce que je peux vous téléphoner?** | Ehskuh zhuh puh voo taylayfohnay? |
| What's your phone number? | **Quel est votre numéro de téléphone?** | Kehl eh vohtr newmay-roh duh taylayfohn? |
| What is your address? | **Quelle est votre adresse?** | Kehl eh vohtr ahdrehs? |
| Can I give you a ride? | **Est-ce que je peux vous déposer quelque part?** | Ehskuh zhuh puh voo daypohzay kehlkuh pahr? |
| Are you married? | **Etes-vous marié(e)?** | Eht-voo mahryay? |
| No, but I have a girlfriend/boyfriend. | **Non, mais j'ai une petite amie/un petit ami.** | Noh(n), may zhay ewn pteet ahmee/uh(n) ptee tahmee. |
| I'm single. | **Je suis célibataire.** | Zhuh swee say-leebahtehr. |
| I'm a widow(er). | **Je suis veuve (veuf).** | Zhuh swee vuhv (vuhf). |
| I'm divorced. | **Je suis divorcé(e).** | Zhuh swee deevohrsay. |

SOCIALIZING

| | | |
|---|---|---|
| I'm traveling with a friend. | **Je voyage avec un ami (une amie).** | Zhuh vwahyahzh ahvehk uh(n) nahmee (ewn ahmee). |
| I'm alone. | **Je suis seul.** | Zhuh swee suhl. |
| You should come visit us at our house. | **Vous devez nous rendre visite à la maison.** | Voo duhvay noo rah(n)dr veezeet ah lah mayzoh(n). |
| You're so kind! | **Vous êtes si gentil(s)!** | Voo zeht see zhah(n)teey! |
| Are you free . . . • this evening? • tomorrow? | **Etes-vous libre . . . • ce soir? • demain?** | Eht voo leebr. . . • suh swahr? • duhma(n)? |
| I'll wait for you here. | **Je vous attends ici.** | Zhuh voo zahtah(n) eesee. |
| I'll pick you up in the hotel lobby. | **Je viendrai vous chercher à l'hôtel.** | Zhuh vyeh(n)dray voo shehrshay ah lohtehl. |
| It's getting late. | **Il se fait tard.** | Eel suh fay tahr. |
| It's time to get back. | **Il est temps de rentrer.** | Eel eh tah(m) duh rah(n)tray. |
| We're leaving tomorrow. | **Nous partons demain.** | Noo pahrtoh(n) duhma(n). |
| Thanks for everything. | **Merci pour tout.** | Mehrsee poor too. |
| I had a very good time. | **Je me suis très bien amusé(e).** | Zhuh muh swee treh byeh(n) nahmewzay. |
| We're going to miss you. | **Vous allez nous manquer.** | Voo zahlay noo mah(n)kay. |
| It was nice to have met you. | **Je suis très heureux (heureuse) d'avoir fait votre connaissance.** | Zhuh swee treh zuhruh (zuhruhz) dahvwahr fay vohtruh kohnay-sah(n)s. |
| Give my best to . . . | **Mes amitiés à . . .** | May zahmeetyay ah . . . |

57

## TALKING ABOUT LANGUAGE

| Do you speak... | **Parlez-vous...** | Pahrlay voo... |
|---|---|---|
| • English? | • **anglais?** | • zah(n)gleh? |
| • Spanish? | • **espagnol?** | • zehspahnyohl? |
| • German? | • **allemand?** | • zahlmah(n)? |

(For a list of languages, see page 188.)

| I only speak English. | **Je parle seulement anglais.** | Zhuh pahrl suhlmah(n) ah(n)gleh. |
|---|---|---|
| I speak a little French. | **Je parle un peu de français.** | Zhuh pahrl uh(n) puh duh frah(n)seh. |
| My French is so bad! | **Mon français est si mauvais!** | Moh(n) frah(n)seh eh see mohveh! |
| That is not true. Your French is excellent. | **Ce n'est pas vrai. Votre français est excellent.** | Suh nay pah vray. Vohtruh frah(n)say ay tehksehlah(n). |
| I really want to learn French. | **Je tiens à apprendre le français.** | Zhuh tyeh(n) ah ahprah(n)dr luh frah(n)seh. |
| Speak slowly. | **Parlez lentement.** | Pahrlay lah(n)tuhmah(n). |
| Could you repeat that? | **Répétez, s'il vous plaît.** | Raypaytay, seel voo pleh. |
| I don't understand. | **Je ne comprends pas.** | Zhuh nuh koh(m)prah(n) pah. |
| How do you write that? | **Comment ça s'écrit?** | Kohmah(n) sah say-kree? |
| How do you say "spoon" in French? | **Comment dit-on "spoon" en français?** | Kohmah(n) dee-toh(n) "spoon" ah(n) frah(n)seh? |
| Is there anyone who speaks English here? | **Y a-t-il quelqu'un ici qui parle anglais?** | Yah teel kehlkuh(n) ee-see kee pahrl ah(n)gleh? |

| Could you translate this for me? | **Pouvez-vous me traduire ceci?** | Poovay-voo muh trahdweer suhsee? |
| Can you understand me? | **Pouvez-vous me comprendre?** | Poovay-voo muh koh(m)prah(n)dr? |

## THE FAMILY

| I'm traveling with my family. | **Je voyage avec ma famille.** | Zhuh vwahyahzh ahvehk mah fahmeey. |
| I have . . . | **J'ai . . .** | Zheh . . . |
| • a husband. | • **un mari.** | • uh(n) mahree. |
| • a wife. | • **une femme.** | • ewn fahm. |
| • a daughter. | • **une fille.** | • ewn feey. |
| • a son. | • **un fils.** | • uh(n) fees. |
| • two daughters. | • **deux filles.** | • duh feey. |
| • two sons. | • **deux fils.** | • duh fees. |
| • a father. | • **un père** | • uh(n) pehr. |
| • a mother. | • **une mère.** | • ewn mehr. |
| • a grandfather. | • **un grand-père.** | • uh(n) grah(n)-pehr. |
| • a grandmother. | • **une grand-mère.** | • ewn grah(n)-mehr. |
| • a grandson | • **un petit fils.** | • uh(n) ptee fees. |
| • a granddaughter. | • **une petite fille.** | • ewn pteet feey. |
| • a cousin (m). | • **un cousin.** | • uh(n) kooza(n). |
| • a cousin (f). | • **une cousine.** | • ewn koozeen. |
| • an aunt. | • **une tante.** | • ewn tah(n)t. |
| • an uncle. | • **un oncle.** | • uh(n) noh(n)kl. |
| • a sister. | • **une soeur.** | • ewn suhr. |
| • a brother. | • **un frère.** | • uh(n) frehr. |
| • in-laws. | • **des beaux-parents.** | • day boh-pahrah(n). |
| • a father-in-law. | • **un beau père.** | • uh(n) boh-pehr. |
| • a mother-in-law. | • **une belle-mère.** | • ewn behl-mehr. |
| • a sister-in-law. | • **une belle-soeur.** | • ewn behl-suhr. |
| • a brother-in-law. | • **un beau-frère.** | • uh(n) boh-frehr. |
| My eldest son . . . | **Mon fils aîné . . .** | Moh(n) fees ehnay . . . |
| My eldest daughter . . . | **Ma fille aînée . . .** | Mah feey ehnay . . . |

| My youngest son . . . | **Mon fils cadet . . .** | Moh(n) fees kah-day... |
| My youngest daughter... | **Ma fille cadette . . .** | Mah feey kahdeht ... |
| How old are your children? | **Quel âge ont vos enfants?** | Kehl ahzh oh(n) voh zah(n)fah(n)? |
| My children are very young. | **Mes enfants sont très jeunes.** | May zah(n)fah(n) soh(n) treh zhuhn. |
| Peter is three years older than Paul. | **Peter a trois ans de plus que Paul.** | Peter ah trwah zah(n) duh plews kuh Paul. |

## IN THE HOME

| Make yourself at home. | **Faites comme chez vous.** | Feht kohm shay voo. |
| You may sit here. | **Asseyez-vous ici.** | Ahsehyay-voo zeesee. |
| What a pretty house! | **Quelle jolie maison!** | Kehl zhohlee mehzoh(n)! |
| I really like this neighborhood. | **J'aime beaucoup ce quartier.** | Zhehm bohkoo suh kahrtyay. |
| At our house . . . | **Chez nous . . .** | Shay noo... |
| At your house . . . | **Chez vous . . .** | Shay voo... |
| At my house . . . | **Chez moi . . .** | Shay mwah ... |

Note: *Chez* is an innocent-looking little word that has a wide range of meanings. As shown above, when combined with a personal pronoun, it often refers to one's dwelling: *chez moi* means (at) my house. In a different context, *chez moi* might mean "in my town," "in my country," etc.

| At home (i.e., in the States) we like baseball. | **Chez nous, on aime le baseball.** | Shay noo, oh(n) nehm luh baysbohl. |
| At your place (i.e., in France) people like soccer. | **Chez vous, on aime le football.** | Shay voo, oh(n) nehm luh footbohl. |

| English | French | Pronunciation |
|---|---|---|
| Here is . . . | Voici . . . | Vwahsee . . . |
| • the kitchen. | • la cuisine. | • lah kweezeen. |
| • the living room. | • le salon. | • luh sahloh(n) |
| • the dining room. | • la salle à manger. | • lah sahl ah mah(n)zhay. |
| • the bedrooms. | • les chambres. | • lay shah(m)br. |
| • the attic. | • le grenier. | • luh gruhnyay. |
| • the cellar. | • la cave. | • lah kahv. |
| • the closets. | • les armoires. | • lay zahrmwahr. |
| • the couch. | • le canapé. | • luh kahnahpay. |
| • the rug. | • le tapis. | • luh tahpee. |
| • the carpeting. | • la moquette. | • lah mohkeht. |
| • the appliances. | • les appareils ménagers. | • lay zahpahrehy may-nahzhay. |
| • the armchair. | • le fauteuil. | • luh fohtuhy. |
| • the table. | • la table. | • lah tahbl. |
| • the chair. | • la chaise. | • lah shehz. |
| • the ceiling. | • le plafond. | • luh plahfoh(n). |
| • the floor. | • le plancher. | • luh plah(n)shay. |
| It's . . . | C'est . . . | Seh . . . |
| • a house. | • une maison. | • ewn mehzoh(n). |
| • an apartment. | • un appartement. | • uh(n) nahpahr-tuhmah(n). |
| • a villa. | • une villa. | • ewn veelah. |
| • a condominium. | • une copropriété. | • ewn kohprohpreey-aytay. |
| • a second home. | • une résidence secondaire. | • ewn rayzeedah(n)s suhkoh(n)dehr. |
| Can I get you a drink? | Puis-je vous offrir un verre? | Pweezh voo zohfreer uh(n) vehr? |
| Thanks for having invited us to your home. | Merci de nous avoir invités chez vous. | Mehrsee duh noo zahvwahr a(n)veetay shay voo. |
| You must come and visit us at our home. | Vous devez venir nous rendre visite chez nous. | Voo duhvay vuhneer noo rah(n)dr veezeet shay noo. |

# 6/DINING OUT

The visitor to French-speaking countries will be delighted with the range and variety of food and types of restaurants. One of the glories of France is, in fact, its regional cuisines, and many unpretentious but high quality establishments are surprisingly affordable. The following is a partial list of categories of eating establishments.

**auberges, hôtellerie, relais de campagne** [Ohbehrzh, ohtehlree, ruhlay duh koh(n)pahnyuh]
Variations on the theme of country inn, many of these establishments serve excellent traditional food.

**bar** [bahr]
Bars serve drinks, coffee, and light meals such as omelettes and sandwiches.

**bistrot** [beestroh]
An unpretentious neighborhood restaurant with simple fare and a limited menu.

**brasserie** [brahsree]
A large café offering meals and drinks.

**cabaret** [kahbahray]
A type of supper club featuring entertainment that may include singing, dancing and political satire.

**café** [kahfay]
The quintessential French social institution, the place to hang out, refresh oneself, read, write, or people-watch. Cafés serve coffee, teas, infusions, beer, liquor, and wine plus light meals or snacks and soft drinks.

**crêperie** [krehpree]
May be a stand-up or sit-down restaurant. In any case, the bill of fare is crêpes—thin and tasty pancakes with a variety of meat, vegetable or dessert fillings available at the fancier places.

**restaurant** [rehstohrah(n)]
The range of style, ambiance and price category is impressive! Make sure you check the menu in the window to get an

idea of what it will cost before you decide to go in.

**routier** [rootyay]   The closest French equivalent to the diner or truck-stop. Don't expect refined atmosphere (or high prices), but the food in many *routiers* is tasty and attractively prepared.

**salon de thé** [sahloh(n) duh tay]   The French tearoom serves pastries and other desserts along with tea and coffee. Light meals are offered in some *salons*.

**snack-bar** [snahk-bahr]   Also called *buffet-express* [bewfay ehks-prehs], the *snack-bar* is often found near bus and train stations and is just what you think it is!

## MEALS AND MEALTIMES

**Breakfast (le petit déjeuner** [luh ptee dayzhuhnay]) is a light meal in France and is commonly served until about 10:00 A.M. If breakfast is included in the price of your hotel room, it may very well be what is called *café complet* [kahfay koh(m)play]. This consists of a bread (croissants or French bread in slices) with butter and jam, plus a steaming cup of *café au lait* [kahfay oh lay]. *Café au lait* is quite light, with hot milk mixed in equal amounts with strong coffee. Tea and hot chocolate are often available as well.

If breakfast is *not* included with your hotel room, you will probably find that it is a good deal cheaper at the café around the corner than at the hotel restaurant.

**Lunch (le déjeuner** [luh dayzhuhnay]) is traditionally the big meal of the day in many regions. Shorter midday breaks have led, in recent years, to lighter, quicker lunches for many working people, though the big Sunday noontime meal *en famille* [ah(n) fahmeey] remains the rule. Lunch is served from noon until 2:00 or 3:00 P.M. Since most businesses and many public services still close between 12:00 and 2:00, you may find that many restaurants fill up rather rapidly at this time.

**Dinner (le dîner** [luh deenay]) begins later in France than in the United States. Most restaurants do not begin serving until 8:00 P.M. Evening dining is a leisurely affair, with people lingering over their food and drinks. The formal structure of the French dinner certainly encourages this relaxed pace. The meal may begin with an *apéritif* (ahpayreeteef) such as vermouth or sherry, or wine-based drinks such as Dubonnet or Saint-Raphaël. Cocktails are not as common as in the States as before-dinner drinks but are available at most bars of course.

The meal proper may consist of the following courses: hors d'oeuvres, soup, fish, meat or poultry and vegetables, salad, cheese, dessert. Most restaurants provide options for fewer courses. One can order *à la carte* [ah lah kahrt]. In addition, most restaurants have a fixed-price menu—*menu à prix fixe* [muhnew ah pree feeks]. Often there are several fixed-price menus varying in price and in the number of courses served. Choices are limited in fixed-price menus. When you feel adventurous, you may wish to try the *menu gastronomique* [muhnew gahstrohnohmeek]. This menu features gourmet specialties and rare dishes. *Bon appétit* [boh(n) nahpaytee]!

## DIALOGUE: AU RESTAURANT (AT THE RESTAURANT)

| | | |
|---|---|---|
| Garçon: | **Qu'est-ce que vous prendrez, Madame?** | Kehskuh voo prah(n)dray, mahdahm? |
| Cliente: | **Je ne sais pas. Quelle est la spécialité du chef?** | Zhuh nuh seh pah . . . Kehl ay lah spaysyahl-eetay dew shehf? |
| Garçon: | **Je vous recommande ceci.** | Zhuh voo ruhkohmah(n)d suhsee. |
| Cliente: | **Ça me va.** | Sah muh vah. |
| Garçon: | **Et qu'est-ce que vous désirez boire?** | Ay kehskuh voo day-zeeray bwahr? |
| Cliente: | **Apportez-moi une bouteille d'eau** | Ahpohrtay mwah ewn bootehy doh meenay- |

| | **minérale, s'il vous plaît.** | rahl, seel voo pleh. |
|---|---|---|

. . . . . . . . . . . . . . . . . . . . . . . . . . . . . . . . . . . . .

| | |
|---|---|
| Waiter: | May I take your order, Ma'am? |
| Customer: | I don't know... What is the chef's specialty? |
| Waiter: | I recommend this. |
| Customer: | Fine. |
| Waiter: | Something to drink? |
| Customer: | Please bring me a bottle of mineral water. |

## EATING OUT

| | | |
|---|---|---|
| Do you know any good restaurants nearby? | **Connaissez-vous un bon restaurant près d'ici?** | Kohnehsay voo uh(n) boh(n) rehstohrah(n) preh deesee? |
| There are several. | **Il y en a plusieurs.** | Eel yah(n) nah plew-zyuhr. |
| Is it expensive? | **C'est cher?** | Seh shehr? |
| No, it's inexpensive. | **Non, c'est bon marché.** | Noh(n), seh boh(n) mahrshay. |
| What's the name of the restaurant? | **Comment s'appelle le restaurant?** | Kohmah(n) sahpehl luh rehstohrah(n)? |
| It's called Chez Pierre. | **Il s'appelle Chez Pierre.** | Eel sahpehl Shay Pyehr. |
| Do you need to make reservations? | **Est-ce qu'il faut réserver?** | Ehskeel foh rayzehr-vay? |
| I'd like to reserve a table ... | **Je voudrais réserver une table ...** | Zhuh voodreh rayzehr-vay ewn tahbl ... |
| • for two people | • **pour deux personnes.** | • poor duh pehrsohn. |
| • for tomorrow evening | • **pour demain soir.** | • poor duhma(n) swahr. |

| | | |
|---|---|---|
| • for eight P.M. | • **pour huit heures.** | • poor weet uhr. |
| • on the terrace. | • **sur la terrasse.** | • sewr lah tehrahs. |
| • by the window. | • **près de la fenêtre.** | • preh duh lah fuhnehtr. |
| • in the no-smoking section.* | • **dans la salle pour non-fumeurs.** | • dah(n) lah sahl poor noh(n)-foohmuhr. |
| Waiter/Waitress! | **Garçon/ Mademoiselle!** | Gahrsoh(n)/ Mahduhmwahzehl! |
| The menu, please. | **La carte, s'il vous plaît.** | Lah kahrt, seel voo pleh. |
| Do you have any special local dishes? | **Quelle est la spécialité de la région?** | Kehl eh lah spaysyahl-eetay duh la rayzhy-oh(n)? |
| I'd like a light meal. | **Je voudrais un repas léger.** | Zhuh voodreh uh(n) ruhpah layzhay. |
| I'll take the 60-franc menu. | **Je prendrai le menu à soixante francs.** | Zhuh prah(n)dreh luh muhnew ah swahsah(n)t frah(n). |
| Do you have children's portions? | **Est-ce qu'il y a des demi-portions pour enfants?** | Ehskeelyah day duhmee-pohrsyoh(n) poor ah(n)fah(n)? |
| I'm ready to order. | **Je suis prêt(e) à commander.** | Zhuh swee preht ah kohmah(n)day. |
| To begin (for starters) . . . | **Pour commen-cer. . .** | Poor koh(m)mah(n)-say. . . |
| Next . . . | **Ensuite . . .** | Ah(n)sweet . . . |
| Finally. . . | **Pour terminer. . .** | Poor tehrmeenay. . . |
| That's all. | **C'est tout.** | Seh too. |
| Have you finished? | **Vous avez terminé?** | Voo zahvay tehr-meenay? |

*Note: In France, smoking is more acceptable than in the United States, so you are less likely to find restaurants that have no-smoking sections.

| Could we have . . . | **Est-ce que nous pourrions avoir...** | Ehskuh noo pooryoh(n) ahvwahr... |
|---|---|---|
| • tap water? | • **de l'eau du robinet?** | • duh loh dew rohbeenay? |
| • silverware? | • **un couvert?** | • uh(n) koovehr? |
| • a napkin? | • **une serviette?** | • ewn sehrvyeht? |
| • a cup? | • **une tasse?** | • ewn tahs? |
| • a glass? | • **un verre?** | • uh(n) vehr? |
| • a fork? | • **une fourchette?** | • ewn foorsheht? |
| • a spoon? | • **une cuillère?** | • ewn kweeyehr? |
| • a knife? | • **un couteau?** | • uh(n) kootoh? |
| • an ashtray? | • **un cendrier?** | • uh(n) sah(n)dreeyay? |
| • a plate? | • **une assiette?** | • ewn ahsyeht? |
| • a toothpick? | • **un cure-dent?** | • uh(n) kewr-dah(n)? |
| • a saucer? | • **une soucoupe?** | • ewn sookoop? |
| • some bread? | • **du pain?** | • dew pa(n)? |
| • some butter? | • **du beurre?** | • dew buhr? |
| • some salt? | • **du sel?** | • dew sehl? |
| • some pepper? | • **du poivre?** | • dew pwahvr? |
| • some mustard? | • **de la moutarde?** | • duh lah mootahrd? |
| • some lemon? | • **du citron?** | • dew seetroh(n)? |
| • some sugar? | • **du sucre?** | • dew sewkr? |
| • some ketchup? | • **du ketchup?** | • dew kehchuhp? |
| • some horseradish? | • **du raifort?** | • dew rahyfohr? |
| • some saccharine? | • **de la saccharine?** | • duh lah sahkahreen? |
| • some mayonnaise? | • **de la mayonnaise?** | • duh lah mahyohnehz? |
| • a little more . . . ? | • **encore un peu de . . . ?** | • ah(n)kohr uh(n) puh duh . . . ? |
| Where is the bathroom? | **Où sont les toilettes?** | Oo soh(n) lay twahleht? |

## APPETIZERS (HORS D'OEUVRES)

Appetizers are extremely varied and especially delicious and attractively prepared in French cuisine. They may be either hot or cold and may be prepared with meat, fish, eggs, or vegetables.

67

Often the key to a successful appetizer is the subtle and careful mix of ingredients and spices. Here is a sampler of some of the major types of hors d'oeuvres a traveler may find.

**andouille**
[ah(n)dooy]
grilled and seasoned tripe sausage

**artichauts à la vinaigrette** [ahr-teeshoh ah lah veeneh-greht]
artichokes in vinaigrette dressing

**bouchée à la reine**
[booshay ah lah rehn]
creamed sweetbreads and mushrooms in a pastry shell

**crudités** [krew-deetay]
raw mixed vegetables such as carrots, tomatoes, beets, and celery served with a vinaigrette

**escargots à la bourguignonne**
[ehskahrgoh ah lah boorgeenyohn]
classic preparation of cooked snails served in butter and seasoned with lots of garlic, shallots, and other spices

**pâte** [pahtay]
very tasty liver purée that is spread on slices of crusty bread. *Pâté de campagne* [pahtay duh kah(m)pahnyuh] mixes several kinds of meats, while *pâté de foie gras* [pahtay duh fwah grah] is a loaf of duck or goose liver. If it's served *en croûte* [ah(n) kroot], it is wrapped in a pastry shell.

**quenelles** [kuhnehl]
pike dumplings in a white sauce

**rillettes** [reeyeht]
pork mix cooked in its own fat and served as a spread to go on bread

**terrine** [tehreen]
a type of deep pot in which this kind of pâté is served, hence the pâté itself

## EGG DISHES (LES OEUFS)

Eggs are served in a variety of ways as appetizers or light meals. Traditionally, they are not a breakfast staple as they are in the

United States. Note: In the singular, we say *un oeuf* [uh(n) nuhf], for *an egg* or *one egg*, but in the plural the *f* is silent—*des oeufs* [day zuh] for *some eggs*.

| | |
|---|---|
| **oeufs en cocotte** [uh zah(n) kohkoht] | baked in cups with cream and eaten with a spoon |
| **oeufs en gelée** [uh zah(n) zhuhlay] | poached and served cold in a gelled consommé |
| **omelette** [ohmleht] | The French variety is oval with a creamy center. There are numerous versions:<br>• **nature** [nahtewr]  plain<br>• **aux fines herbes** [oh feen zehrb]  with chives, tarragon, and parsley<br>• **au jambon** [oh zhah(m)boh(n)]  with ham<br>• **au fromage** [oh frohmahzh]  with cheese |
| **piperade** [pee-prahd] | a delightful mixture of tomato, onion, and pepper filling |
| **quiche** [keesh] | an egg or flan tart with a rich filling of cheese, seafood, or poultry. The best-known variety is quiche lorraine [keesh lohrehn], which features bacon and gruyère cheese. |
| **soufflé** [sooflay] | This well-known French export must be light and fluffy and can be made with cheese, ham, vegetables, or other ingredients |

## SOUPS (SOUPES)

| | | |
|---|---|---|
| **bisque**<br>• **d'écrevisse**<br>• **de homard** | beesk<br>• daykruhvees<br>• duh hohmahr | chowder<br>• crayfish<br>• lobster |
| **bouillabaisse** | booyahbehs | Provençal fish stew |
| **consommé**<br>• **madrilène**<br>• **printanier** | koh(n)sohmay<br>• mahdreelehn<br>• pra(n)tahnyay | broth<br>• with tomatoes<br>• with vegetables |

| | | |
|---|---|---|
| **crème** | krehm | cream |
| • **d'asperges** | • dahspehrzh | • of asparagus |
| • **de volaille** | • duh vohlahy | • of chicken |
| **garbure** | gahrbewr | cabbage soup with meat |
| **petite marmite** | puhteet mahrmeet | meat and vegetable soup |
| **potage** | pohtahzh | soup |
| • **à l'ail** | • ah lahy | • garlic |
| • **parmentier** | • pahrmah(n)tyay | • potato |
| **soupe** | soop | soup |
| • **aux choux** | • oh shoo | • cabbage |
| • **du jour** | • dew zhoor | • of the day |
| • **à l'oignon** | • ah lohnyoh(n) | • onion |
| • **au pistou** | • oh peestoo | • Provençal vegetable |
| **velouté** | vuhlootay | cream |
| • **de tomates** | • duh tohmaht | • of tomato |
| • **de volaille** | • duh vohlahy | • of chicken |
| **vichyssoise** | veesheeswahz | potato-leek soup |

## FISH AND SEAFOOD (POISSON ET FRUITS DE MER)

Fish may be served as a main course or a second appetizer. Many fish are local and have no equivalents in the United States. Also, familiar favorites such as lobster will look and taste somewhat different. What is really distinctive about French fish is their preparation and the delicate sauces in which they are served.

| | | |
|---|---|---|
| **Qu'est-ce que vous avez comme . . .** | Kehskhuh voo zahvay kohm . . . | What do you have in the way of . . . |
| • **poisson?** | • pwahsoh(n)? | • fish? |
| • **fruits de mer?** | • frwee duh mehr? | • seafood? |
| **l'aiglefin.** | lehgluhfa(n). | haddock. |
| **l'anchois.** | lah(n)shwa. | anchovies. |
| **l'anguille.** | lah(n)geey. | eel. |
| **le bar.** | luh bahr. | bass. |

70

| la baudroie. | lah bohdrwah. | angler. |
|---|---|---|
| le brochet. | luh brohshay. | pike. |
| le cabillaud. | luh kahbeeyoh. | cod (fresh). |
| le calmar. | luh kahlmahr. | squid. |
| le crabe. | luh krahb. | crab. |
| les coquillages. | lay kohkeeyahzh. | shellfish. |
| les coquilles St. Jacques. | lay kohkeey sa(n) zhahk. | scallops. |
| les crevettes. | lay kruhveht. | shrimp. |
| les cuisses de grenouilles. | lay kwees duh gruhnooy. | frog's legs. |
| les écrevisses. | lay zaykruhvees. | crayfish. |
| le hareng. | luh ahrah(n). | herring. |
| le homard. | luh ohmahr. | lobster. |
| le homard à l'américaine. | luh ohmahr ah lahmayreekehn. | lobster in butter with tomatoes and brandy. |
| les huîtres. | lay zweetr. | oysters. |
| la langouste. | lah lah(n)goost. | spiny lobster. |
| les langoustines. | lay lah(n)goosteen. | prawns. |
| le loup. | luh loo. | sea bass. |
| le maquereau. | luh mahkroh. | mackerel. |
| la morue. | lah mohrew. | cod. |
| les moules. | lay mool. | mussels. |
| les palourdes. | lay pahloord. | clams. |
| la perche. | lah pehrsh. | perch. |
| les poulpes. | lay poolp. | octopus. |
| le rouget. | luh roozhay. | red mullet. |
| les sardines. | lay sahrdeen. | sardines. |
| le saumon. | luh sohmoh(n). | salmon. |
| le saumon fumé. | luh sohmoh(n) fumay. | smoked salmon. |
| le scampi. | luh skah(m)pee. | shrimp. |
| le sole. | luh sohl. | sole. |
| le thon. | luh toh(n). | tuna. |
| la truite. | lah trweet. | trout. |
| le turbot. | luh tewrboh. | turbot. |

## Preparation Methods for Fish

| au four | oh foor | baked |
|---|---|---|
| frit | free | fried |
| grillé | greeyay | grilled |

| | | |
|---|---|---|
| mariné | mahreenay | marinated |
| poché | pohshay | poached |
| cuit à la vapeur | kwee ah lah vahpuhr | steamed |

## MEAT (LES VIANDES)

| | | |
|---|---|---|
| l'agneau | lahnyoh | lamb |
| les andouillettes | lay zah(n)dweeyeht | tripe sausages |
| le bifteck | luh beeftehk | steak |
| la blanquette de veau | lah blah(n)keht duh voh | veal stew |
| le boeuf | luh buhf | beef |
| le boudin | luh booda(n) | blood sausage |
| le carré d'agneau | luh kahray dahnyoh | rack of lamb |
| le cassoulet | luh kahsoolay | stew with sausage, white beans, and tomatoes |
| la cervelle | lah sehrvehl | brains |
| la charcûterie | lah shahrkewtree | coldcuts and pâtés |
| le châteaubriand | luh shahtohbreeah(n) | porterhouse steak |
| le cochon de lait | luh kohshoh(n) duh leh | suckling pig |
| la côte de boeuf | lah koht duh buhf | ribs of beef |
| les côtelettes | lay kohtleht | cutlets |
| les côtes | lay koht | chops |
| les cuisses de grenouille | lay kwees duh gruhn-ooy | frogs' legs |
| l'entrecôte | lah(n)truhkoht | sirloin steak |
| l'escalope | lehskahlohp | cutlet |
| le filet de boeuf | luh feelay duh buhf | filet of beef |
| le filet mignon | luh feelay meenyoh(n) | filet mignon |
| le foie | luh fwah | liver |
| le gigot d'agneau | luh zheegoh dahnyoh | leg of lamb |
| le jambon | luh zhah(m)boh(n) | ham |
| la langue | lah lah(n)g | tongue |
| le lard | luh lahr | bacon |
| les médaillons de veau | lay maydahyoh(n) duh voh | veal tenderloin |
| le navarin de mouton | luh nahvahra(n) duh mootoh(n) | lamb stew |
| le pot-au-feu | luh poh-toh-fuh | boiled beef stew |
| le ris de veau | luh ree duh voh | sweetbreads (veal) |

| les rognons | lay rohnyoh(n) | kidneys |
| le rosbif | luh rohsbeef | roast beef |
| les saucisses | lay sohsees | small sausages |
| les saucissons | lay sohseesoh(n) | large slicing sausages |
| la selle d'agneau | lah sehl dahnyoh | saddle of lamb |
| le steak | luh stehk | steak |
| le tournedos | luh toornuhdoh | small beef filets |
| les tripes | lay treep | tripe |

## Methods of Meat Preparation

| à l'étouffée | ah laytoofay | stewed |
| bouilli | booyee | boiled |
| braisé | brehzay | braised |
| frit | free | fried |
| grillé | greeyay | broiled |
| rôti | rohtee | roasted |
| sauté | sohtay | sautéed |
| Je préfère mon steak . . . | Zhuh prayfehr moh(n) stehk . . . | I like my steak . . . |
| • bleu. | • bluh. | • very rare. |
| • saignant. | • sehnyah(n). | • rare. |
| • à point. | • ah pwa(n). | • medium. |
| • bien cuit. | • byeh(n) kwec. | • well done. |

Note: In general, the French prefer their meats less well done than Americans. Bear that in mind when selecting one of the above categories.

## GAME AND POULTRY (GIBIER ET VOLAILLE)

| la caille | lah kahy | quail |
| la venaison | lah vuhnehzoh(n) | venison |
| le canard | luh kahnahr | duck |
| le caneton | luh kahntoh(n) | duckling |
| le chapon | luh shahpoh(n) | capon |
| la civette | lah seeveht | hare stew |
| le coq au vin | luh kohk oh va(n) | chicken in red wine sauce |
| la dinde | lah da(n)d | turkey |
| le faisan | luh fuhzah(n) | pheasant |

73

| le lapin | luh lahpa(n) | rabbit |
| le lièvre | luh lyehvr | hare |
| le marcassin | luh mahrkahsa(n) | wild boar |
| l'oie | lwah | goose |
| le perdreau/la perdrix | luh pehrdroh/lah pehrdree | partridge |
| le pigeonneau | luh peezhohnoh | squab |
| la poularde | lah poolahrd | pullet |
| la poule au pot | lah pool oh poh | chicken stew |
| le poulet | luh poolay | chicken |
| le poussin | luh poosa(n) | spring chicken |
| le salmis | luh sahlmee | game stewed in wine |
| le suprême de volaille | luh sewprehm duh vohlahy | chicken breast |
| le vol-au-vent | luh vohl-oh-vah(n) | pastry filled with chicken in cream sauce |

## SAUCES AND TYPES OF PREPARATION

The key to the success of so many French dishes is the use of absolutely fresh ingredients and the subtle combinations of flavors in the sauces that accompany the meat, fish, poultry, and vegetables. Below you will find a list of the most common preparations.

**aïoli** [ahyohli]                  mayonnaise and garlic

**allemande** [ahlmah(n)d]           white sauce with veal stock

**à la bonne femme** [ah lah bohn fahm]    creamy white sauce with vegetables

**américaine** [ahmayreekehn]        sauce of white wine, brandy, tomatoes, and spices

**béarnaise** [bayahrnehz]           sauce of butter, eggs, shallots, tarragon, and wine

**béchamel** [bayshahmehl]           thick white sauce

**bercy** [behrsee]                  wine sauce with fish stock

**beurre blanc** [buhr blah(n)] — butter sauce with shallots and wine

**beurre noir** [buhr nwahr] — browned butter sauce

**bigarrade** [beegahrahd] — orange sauce for duck

**blanquette** [blah(n)keht] — egg and cream sauce

**bordelaise** [bohrduhlehz] — the adjective form of Bordeaux; sauce made with Bordeaux wine, mushrooms and shallots

**bourguignonne** [boorgeen-yohn] — sauce made with Burgundy wine

**bretonne** [bruhtohn] — fish sauce with beans and mushrooms

**caen** [kah(n)] — made with apple brandy

**chantilly** [shah(n)teeyee] — sweet, rich whipped cream

**chasseur** [shahsuhr] — white sauce with mushrooms and parsley

**daube** [dohb] — stew with beef, red wine, garlic, and onions

**diable** [dyahbl] — spicy pepper sauce

**estragon** [ehstrahgoh(n)] — made with tarragon

**farci** [fahrsee] — stuffed

**fenouil** [fuhnooy] — made with fennel

**financière** [feenah(n)syehr] — with Madeira wine, truffles, and mushrooms

**fines herbes** [feen zehrb] — assortment of chopped herbs

**florentine** [flohrah(n)teen] — with spinach

**forestière** [fohrehstyehr] — with wild mushrooms

**gratin** [grahta(n)] — baked in a dish with cheese

**hollandaise** [ohlah(n)dehz] — lemony egg and butter sauce

**indienne** [a(n)dyehn] — with curry spices

75

**jardinière** [zhahrdeenyehr] — with French vegetables, "from the garden"

**lyonnaise** [lyohnehz] — with onions

**madère** [mahdehr] — with Madeira wine

**maître d'hôtel** [mehtr dohtehl] — light butter sauce with lemon and parsley

**marchand de vin** [mahrshah(n) duh va(n)] — red wine sauce with meat stock and shallots

**meunière** [muhnyehr] — cooked in flour and topped with lemon-butter sauce

**mornay** [mohrnay] — white wine and cheese sauce

**mousseline** [moosleen] — creamy Hollandaise sauce

**nantua** [nah(n)twah] — white sauce with cream, shellfish, and tomatoes

**normande** [nohrmah(n)d] — with mushrooms and eggs

**parmentier** [pahrmah(n)tyay] — with potatoes

**périgourdine** [payreegoordeen] — with truffles (named for the region of Périgord, known for its truffles)

**piquante** [peekah(n)t] — spicy sauce

**poivrade** [pwahvrahd] — dark sauce with peppers and onions

**porto** [pohrtoh] — made with Porto wine

**provençale** [prohvah(n)sahl] — in the style of Provence, the Mediterranean area around Nice; made with garlic, tomatoes, olives, and anchovies

**rémoulade** [raymoolahd] — mayonnaise and mustard

**velouté** [vuhlootay] — thickened chicken stock

**véronique** [vayrohneek] — with grapes

**verte** [vehrt] — mayonnaise with parsley and watercress

**vinaigrette** [veenehgreht]   oil, vinegar, and mustard dressing for salads, crudités, and vegetables

## VEGETABLES (LES LÉGUMES)

| | | |
|---|---|---|
| l'artichaut | lahrteeshoh | artichoke |
| le fond d'artichaut | luh foh(n) dahrteeshoh | artichoke heart |
| les asperges | lay zahspehrzh | asparagus |
| l'aubergine | lohbehrzheen | eggplant |
| la betterave | lah behtrahv | beets |
| les carottes | lay kahroht | carrots |
| le céleri | luh saylree | celery |
| les cèpes | lay sehp | flap mushrooms |
| les champignons | lay shah(m)peenyoh(n) | mushrooms |
| la chicorée | lah sheekohray | chicory |
| le chou | luh shoo | cabbage |
| le chou de Bruxelles | luh shoo duh Brewsehl | Brussels sprouts |
| le chou-fleur | luh shoo-fluhr | cauliflower |
| les concombres | lay koh(n)koh(m)br | cucumbers |
| les cornichons | lay kohrneeshoh(n) | pickles |
| la courgette | lah koorzheht | zucchini |
| le cresson | luh krehsoh(n) | watercress |
| les endives | lay zah(n)deev | endives |
| les épinards | lay zaypeenahr | spinach |
| les fèves | lay fehv | white beans |
| les flageolets | lay flahzhohlay | green shell beans |
| les haricots verts | lay ahreekoh vehr | green beans |
| la laitue | lah laytew | lettuce |
| les lentilles | lay lah(n)teey | lentils |
| le mäis | luh mah-ees | corn |
| les navets | lay nahvay | turnips |
| les oignons | lay zohnyoh(n) | onions |
| les petits pois | lay ptee pwah | peas |
| le piment | luh peemah(n) | green pepper |
| le poireau | luh pwaroh | leek |
| les pommes de terre | lay pohm duh tehr | potatoes |
| la tomate | lah tohmaht | tomato |

## Some Classic Vegetable Dishes

**artichauts à la grecque**
[ahrteeshoh ah lah grehk]
artichokes in herbs and olive oil, served cold

**asperges au gratin** [ahs-pehrzh oh grahta(n)]
asparagus in cheese sauce and bread crumbs

**aubergine farcie**
[ohbehrzheen fahrsee]
stuffed and baked eggplant

**choucroute garnie** [shookroot gahrnee]
sauerkraut and sausage served hot

**choux farcis** [shoo fahrsee]
stuffed cabbage

**épinards à la crème** [ay-peenahr ah lah krehm]
creamed spinach

**légumes panachés** [laygewm pahnahshay]
mixed vegetables

**macédoine de légumes** [mahsaydwahn duh laygewm]
mixed, chopped vegetables

**ratatouille** [rahtahtooy]
chopped eggplant with tomato, zucchini, onion, and olive oil

## HERBS AND SPICES (FINES HERBES ET ÉPICES)

| | | |
|---|---|---|
| **ail** | ahy | garlic |
| **aneth** | ahneht | dill |
| **anis** | ahnees | anise |
| **basilic** | bahzeeleek | basil |
| **cannelle** | kahnehl | cinnamon |
| **câpres** | kahpruh | capers |
| **cerfeuil** | sehrfuhy | chervil |
| **ciboulette** | seebooleht | chives |
| **clous de girofle** | kloo duh zheerohfl | cloves |
| **cumin** | kewma(n) | caraway |
| **échalote** | ayshaloht | shallot |
| **estragon** | ehstrahgoh(n) | tarragon |
| **gingembre** | zha(n)zhah(m)br | ginger |
| **laurier** | lohryay | bay leaf |
| **marjolaine** | mahrzhohlehn | marjoram |

78

| menthe | mah(n)t | mint |
| noix de muscade | nwah duh mewskahd | nutmeg |
| origan | ohreegah(n) | oregano |
| persil | pehrsee | parsley |
| piment | peemah(n) | pimiento |
| poivre | pwahvr | pepper |
| romarin | rohmahra(n) | rosemary |
| safran | sahfrah(n) | saffron |
| sauge | sohzh | sage |
| thym | ta(m) | thyme |

## POTATOES, PASTA, AND RICE (POMMES DE TERRE, PÂTES, ET RIZ)

| Je voudrais des pommes de terre... | Zhuh voodreh day pohm duh tehr... | I'd like some potatoes... |
| • à l'anglaise. | • ah lah(n)glehz. | • peeled and boiled. |
| • chip. | • sheep. | • potato chips. |
| • dauphine. | • dohfeen. | • baked with butter and Swiss cheese. |
| • frites. | • freet. | • French fries. |
| • lyonnaise. | • leeyohnehz. | • sautéed with onions. |
| • maître d'hôtel. | • mehtɪ dohtehl. | • cooked with milk, served with parsley. |
| • mousseline. | • moosleen. | • mashed, with cream. |
| • en purée. | • ah(n) pewray. | • mashed. |
| • rissolées. | • reesohlay. | • roasted. |
| • en robe des champs. | • ah(n) rohb day shah(m). | • in their jackets. |
| • sautées. | • sohtay. | • sautéed. |
| • soufflées. | • sooflay. | • whipped light and fluffy. |
| • vapeur. | • vahpuhr | • boiled. |
| Je voudrais... | Zhuh voodreh... | I'd like... |
| • des pâtes. | • day paht. | • some pasta. |
| • des nouilles. | • day nooy. | • some noodles. |
| • des spaghetti. | • day spahgehtee. | • some spaghetti. |

79

**Apportez-moi . . .**
- **du riz.**
- **du risotto à la turque.**
- **du riz à la créole.**
- **du riz à la valencienne.**

Ahpohrtay-mwah . . .
- dew ree.
- dew reezohtoh ah lah tewrk.
- dew ree ah lah kray-ohl.
- dew ree ah lah vahlah(n)syehn.

Bring me . . .
- some rice.
- rice with saffron and tomatoes.
- rice with tomatoes and peppers.
- rice with tomatoes, onions, saffron, and shellfish.

## SALADS (LES SALADES)

**salade de betterave** [sahlahd duh behtrahv]  beet salad

**salade de chou** [sahlahd duh shoo]  cole slaw

**salade italienne** [sahlahd eetahlyehn]  antipasto

**salade niçoise** [sahlahd neeswahz]  string beans, tomatoes, potatoes, olives, and hard-boiled eggs in oil and vinegar

**salade de romaine à l'estragon** [sahlahd duh rohmehn ah lehstrahgoh(n)]  romaine lettuce and tarragon

**salade russe** [sahlahd rews]  diced vegetables

**salade de saison** [sahlahd duh sehzoh(n)]  salad of the season

**salade de tomates** [sahlahd duh tohmaht]  tomato salad

**salade verte** [sahlahd vehrt]  mixed green salad

## CHEESE (LES FROMAGES)

**bleu d'auvergne** [bluh dohvehrnyuh]  soft cheese with a sharp flavor

**boursin** [boorsa(n)]  soft, mild cheese with herbs

**brie** [bree]  this famous creamy white cheese can be mild or strong

**camembert** [kahmah(m)behr]  the well-known cheese from Normandy

**cantal** [kah(n)tahl]  flavor varies with degree of aging; the older it is, the harder its texture and the stronger its flavor

**chèvre** [shehvr]  goat's milk cheese in many varieties and flavors (try some early in your trip; they take getting used to)

**demi-sel** [duhmee-sehl]  type of cream cheese

**emmenthal** [ehmah(n)tahl]  what we usually refer to as Swiss cheese (gruyère *with* the holes)

**fromage blanc** [frohmahzh blah(n)]  similar to cottage cheese

**fromage à la crème** [frohmahzh ah lah krehm]  rich, creamy cheese often mixed with cream and sugar for breakfast

**fromage de chèvre** [frohmahzh duh shehvr]  same as *chèvre*, above

**fromage de Hollande** [frohmahzh duh Ohlah(n)d]  "Dutch cheese," usually gouda

**gruyère** [grewyehr]  our "Swiss" without the holes

**muenster** [muh(n)stehr]  soft, somewhat sharp Alsatian cheese

**neufchâtel** [nuh-shahtehl]  mild and creamy

**petit suisse** [puhtee swees]  sprinkle with sugar and eat it for dessert

**pont l'Evèque** [poh(n) layvehk]  smooth cheese from Normandy

81

**port-salut** [pohr-sahlew]  a type of *St. Paulin* (see below)

**reblochon** [ruhbloh-shoh(n)]  mild and soft

**roquefort** [rohkfohr]  sharp and aromatic, blue-veined, made from ewe's milk

**St. Paulin** [Sa(n) Pohla(n)]  a mild, smooth cheese

## FRUIT (LES FRUITS)

Served after the cheese at a French meal, fruit is often a dessert selection.

| Qu'est-ce que vous avez comme fruits? | Kehskuh voo zahvay kohm frwee? | What kinds of fruit do you have? |
|---|---|---|
| **Je prendrai . . .** | Zhuh prah(n)dreh . . . | I'll have . . . |
| • **un abricot.** | • uh(n) nahbreekoh. | • an apricot. |
| • **de l'ananas.** | • duh lahnahnas. | • some pineapple. |
| • **une banane.** | • ewn bahnahn. | • a banana. |
| • **un brugnon.** | • uh(n) brewnyoh(n). | • a nectarine. |
| • **des cassis.** | • day kahsees | • some black currants. |
| • **des cerises.** | • day sreez. | • some cherries. |
| • **un citron.** | • uh(n) seetroh(n). | • a lemon. |
| • **un citron vert.** | • uh(n) seetroh(n) vehr. | • a lime. |
| • **des dattes.** | • day daht. | • some dates. |
| • **des figues.** | • day feeg. | • some figs. |
| • **des fraises.** | • day frehz. | • some strawberries. |
| • **des framboises.** | • day frah(m)bwahz. | • some raspberries. |
| • **des fruits sec.** | • day frwee sehk. | • some dried fruit. |
| • **des groseilles.** | • day grohzehy. | • some red currants. |
| • **une mandarine.** | • ewn mah(n)dahreen. | • a tangerine. |
| • **du melon.** | • dew muhloh(n). | • some melon. |

82

| | | |
|---|---|---|
| • des mûres. | • day mewr. | • some mulberries. |
| • des myrtilles. | • day meerteey. | • some blueberries. |
| • une orange. | • ewn ohrah(n)zh. | • an orange. |
| • un pample-mousse. | • uh(n) pah(n)pluh-moos. | • a grapefruit. |
| • de la pastèque. | • duh lah pahstehk. | • some water-melon. |
| • une pêche. | • ewn pehsh. | • a peach. |
| • une poire. | • ewn pwahr. | • a pear. |
| • une pomme. | • ewn pohm. | • an apple. |
| • des pruneaux. | • day prewnoh. | • some prunes. |
| • des prunes. | • day prewn. | • some plums. |
| • des raisins blancs. | • day rayza(n) blah(n). | • white grapes. |
| • des raisins noirs. | • day rayza(n) nwahr. | • black grapes. |
| • des raisins secs. | • day rayza(n) sehk. | • raisins. |

## NUTS (NOIX [nwah])

| | | |
|---|---|---|
| des noix | day nwah | walnuts |
| des amandes | day zahmah(n)d | almonds |
| des pistaches | day peestash | pistachios |
| des marrons | day mahroh(n) | chestnuts |
| des noisettes | day nwahzeht | hazelnuts |
| des noix d'acajou | day nwah dahkahzhoo | cashews |
| des cacahuètes | day kahkahweht | peanuts |

## DESSERTS (LES DESSERTS)

**un baba au rhum** [uh(n) bahbah oh ruhm] — yeasted cake in rum

**une bombe** [ewn boh(m)b] — ice cream concoction with fruit and whipped cream

**une coupe glacée** [ewn koop glahsay] — ice cream and whipped cream

**une crème cara-mel** [ewn krehm kahrahmehl] — caramel pudding

83

**des crêpes suzette** [day krehp sewzeht]  crêpes served flaming in an orange-flavored brandy sauce

Note: *Crêpes* (thin pancakes) are dessert items when *sucrées*, or sweet. Other dessert crêpes are made with fruit or chocolate sauce.

**un flan** [uh(n) flah(n)]  custard with a caramel sauce

**un gâteau** [uh(n) gahtoh]  cake or cake-like desserts

**une glace** [ewn glahs]  ice cream
- **à la vanille** [ah lah vahneey]  vanilla
- **au chocolat** [oh shohkohlah]  chocolate
- **aux fraises** [oh frehz]  strawberry
- **napolitaine** [nahpohleetehn]  combined with ices
- **panachée** [pahnahshay]  mixed flavors

**une macédoine de fruits** [ewn mah-saydwahn duh frwee]  fruit cup served with liqueur

**une mousse** [ewn moos]  light custard-like dessert made with eggs and whipped cream

**une mousse au chocolat** [ewn moos oh shohkohlah]  chocolate mousse

**une omelette norvégienne** [ewn ohmleht nohrvayzhy-ehn]  baked alaska

**une pâtisserie** [ewn pahteesree]  general term for pastry (or pastry shop); popular pastries include:

- **un éclair** [uh(n) nayklehr]  filled with custard and topped with a swab of chocolate or vanilla frosting
- **un mille-feuille** [uh(n) meel-fuhy]  ''a thousand leaves'' or layers of crisp, light, buttery pastry dough

84

| | | |
|---|---|---|
| **une pêche melba** [ewn pehsh mehlbah] | | vanilla ice cream topped with peaches and raspberry syrup |
| **une poire belle-hélène** [ewn pwahr behl-aylehn] | | pears and vanilla ice cream with chocolate sauce |
| **une pomme bonne femme** [ewn pohm bohn fahm] | | baked apple |
| **un sorbet** [uh(n) sohrbay] | | sherbet |
| **un soufflé** [uh(n) sooflay] | | egg yolks, beaten egg whites and a fruity flavoring |
| **une tarte aux pommes** [ewn tahrt oh pohm] | | apple pie |

## NON-ALCOHOLIC BEVERAGES (BOISSONS SANS ALCOOL)

| | | |
|---|---|---|
| **Garçon, apportez-moi . . .** | Gahrsoh(n), ahpohrtay-mwah . . . | Waiter, bring me . . . |
| **un café** | uh(n) kahfay | a cup of coffee |
| • **au lait.** | • oh leh. | • with milk. |
| • **crème.** | • krehm. | • with cream. |
| • **décaféiné.** or **déca.** | • daykahfayeenay. daykah. | • decaffeinated. or decaf. |
| • **express.** | • ehksprehs. | • espresso. |
| • **noir.** | • nwahr. | • black. |
| • **soluble.** | • sohlewbl. | • instant. |
| **du cidre.** | dew seedr. | some cider. |
| **une citronnade.** | ewn seetrohnahd. | a lemonade. |
| **un citron pressé.** | uh(n) seetroh(n) prehsay. | a "do-it-yourself" lemonade. |
| **de l'eau** | duh loh | some ___ water. |
| • **fraîche.** | • frehsh. | • cold |
| • **avec glaçons.** | • ahvehk glahsoh(n). | • ice |

85

| | | |
|---|---|---|
| • **minérale ga-zeuse.** | • meenayrahl gahzuhz. | • carbonated mineral |
| • **minérale non-gazeuse.** | • meenayrahl noh(n)-gahzuhz. | • non-carbonated mineral |
| **un frappé.** | uh(n) frahpay. | a milkshake. |
| **une infusion** | ewn a(n)fewzyoh(n) | an infusion |
| • **camomille.** | • kahmohmeel. | • chamomile. |
| • **verveine.** | • vehrvehn. | • verbena. |
| **un jus** | uh(n) zhew | a ___ juice. |
| • **de fruits.** | • duh frwee. | • fruit. |
| • **d'orange.** | • dohrah(n)zh. | • orange. |
| • **de pample-mousse.** | • duh pah(m)pluh-moos. | • grapefruit. |
| • **de pomme.** | • duh pohm. | • apple. |
| • **de tomate.** | • duh tohmaht. | • tomato. |
| **un soda.** | uh(n) sohdah. | a soda. |
| **un thé** | uh(n) tay | a cup of tea |
| • **citron.** | • seetroh(n). | • with lemon. |
| • **glacé.** | • glahsay. | • iced. |
| • **au lait.** | • oh leh. | • with milk. |
| • **sucré.** | • sewkray. | • with sugar. |

## ALCOHOLIC BEVERAGES (BOISSONS ALCOOLIQUES)

### Apéritifs

The *apéritif* [ahpayreeteef] is taken leisurely before dinner as an appetite stimulant. The stronger cocktail, used as an aid to "unwind," is less common.

| | |
|---|---|
| **byrrh** [beer] | dry red wine with herbs |
| **Campari** [Kah(m)pahree] | dry white Italian wine |
| **Dubonnet** [Dewbohnay] | popular, slightly sweet wine, comes in *rouge* (roozh—red) or *blanc* (blah(n)—white) |
| **Pernod** [Pehrnoh] | green, anisette-flavored (licorice) liqueur |

**Ricard** [Reekahr] — another licorice-flavored drink

**Saint-Raphaël** [Sa(n) rahfah-ehl] — wine and brandy-based drink

**sherry** [shchree] — amber wine from Spain; comes in degrees of sweetness

**vermouth** [vehrmoot] — red or white wine with herbs and bitters

**vermouth-cassis** [vehrmoot-kahsees] — vermouth and sweet black currant liqueur

## Phrases for Ordering Drinks

| straight | **sec** | sehk |
| on the rocks | **avec des glaçons** | ahvehk day glahsoh(n) |
| with water | **à l'eau** | ah loh |

## Beer (La Bière)

| I'd like a ___ beer. | **Je voudrais une bière . . .** | Zhuh voodray zewn byehr. . . |
| • bottled | • **en bouteille.** | • ah(n) booteh. |
| • local | • **du pays.** | • dew payee. |
| • draft | • **pression.** | • prehsyoh(n). |
| • light | • **blonde.** | • bloh(n)d. |
| • dark | • **brune.** | • brewn. |
| Bring me a beer. | **Apportez-moi un demi.** (lit., a half-liter) | Ahpohrtay-mwah uh(n) duhmee. |

## Wine (Les Vins)

France is one of the great wine-producing countries of the world, with a 2,000-year-old tradition and hundreds of distinctive wines to its credit. Virtually every region of the country with favorable climate and soil conditions produces some wine, but the vineyards of greatest renown are found in Burgundy, the Bordeaux area, Champagne, the Loire Valley, and Alsace.

Quality control is an elaborate and rigorous procedure carried out by an agency of the State. Only fine wines receive the title *Appelation d'origine contrôlée* [ahpuhlasyoh(n) dohreezheen koh(n)trohlay], which you will see printed on the label.

## Ordering Wine

| | | |
|---|---|---|
| What wine do you recommend? | **Quel vin me recommandez-vous?** | Kehl va(n) muh ruhkohmah(n)day-voo? |
| Where does this wine come from? | **D'où vient ce vin?** | Doo vyeh(n) suh vah(n)? |
| I'd like . . . | **Je voudrais . . .** | Zhuh voodreh . . . |
| • a bottle of . . . | • **une bouteille de . . .** | • ewn bootehy duh . . . |
| • red wine. | • **vin rouge.** | • va(n) roozh. |
| • rosé wine. | • **vin rosé.** | • va(n) rohzay. |
| • white wine. | • **vin blanc.** | • va(n) blah(n). |
| • sparkling wine. | • **vin mousseux.** | • va(n) moosuh. |
| • robust wine. | • **vin corsé.** | • va(n) kohrsay. |
| • sweet wine. | • **vin doux.** | • va(n) doo. |
| • dry wine. | • **vin sec.** | • va(n) sehk. |
| • light wine. | • **vin léger.** | • va(n) layzhay. |
| • very dry wine. | • **vin brut.** | • va(n) brewt. |
| • a half-bottle. | • **une demi-bouteille.** | • ewn duhmee-bootehy. |
| • a carafe. | • **une carafe.** | • ewn kahrahf. |
| • a glass. | • **un verre.** | • uh(n) vehr. |
| • a liter. | • **un litre.** | • uh(n) leetr. |
| • another bottle. | • **encore une bouteille.** | • ah(n)kohr ewn bootehy. |
| • a local wine. | • **un vin du pays.** | • uh(n) va(n) dew payee. |
| • to taste some . . . | • **goûter un peu de . . .** | • gootay uh(n) puh duh . . . |
| • to see the wine list. | • **voir la carte des vins.** | • vwahr lah kahrt day va(n). |

## After-Dinner Drinks (Cognacs et liqueurs)

Here is a brief run-down of some of the more prominent after-dinner specialties. (You'll notice that many of them are priced much more reasonably in France than in the States.)

| | |
|---|---|
| **cognac** [kohnyahk] | the king of brandies, a wine-distilled drink from the region of Charentes. Courvoisier, Hennessy, Martel, and Remy-Martin are four distinct types of cognac. |
| **eau-de-vie** [oh-duh-vee] | distilled fruit brandies, somewhat stronger in taste. Many families make their own and drink them on special occasions. Popular *eaux-de-vie* include calvados, framboise, kirsch, and Poire William. |
| **liqueur** [leekuhr] | often sweetened and may be colored as well; some of the more well-known liqueurs include Bénédictine, Chambord, Chartreuse, Cointreau, crème de cassis, crème de menthe, and Grand Marnier. |

## SPECIAL DIETS

| | | |
|---|---|---|
| I'm on a diet. | **Je suis au régime.** | Zhuh swee zoh ray-zheem. |
| I'm on a special diet. | **Je suis au régime spécial.** | Zhuh swee zoh ray-zheem spaysyahl. |
| Do you have vegetarian dishes? | **Est-ce que vous avez des plats végétariens?** | Ehskuh voo zahvay day plah vayzhay-tahrya(n)? |
| I'm allergic to ___ . | **Je suis allergique à ___ .** | Zhuh swee zahlehrzheek ah ___ . |
| I can't eat . . . | **Je dois éviter . . .** | Zhuh dwah zayvee-tay . . . |
| • salt. | • **le sel.** | • luh sehl. |
| • fat. | • **le gras.** | • luh grah. |
| • sugar. | • **le sucre.** | • luh sewkr. |
| • flour. | • **la farine.** | • lah fahreen. |

89

| | | |
|---|---|---|
| I'm diabetic. | **Je suis diabétique.** | Zhuh swee deeyahbay-teek. |
| I'm looking for a kosher restaurant. | **Je cherche un restaurant kasher.** | Zhuh shehrsh uh(n) rehstohrah(n) kah-shehr. |
| I don't eat pork. | **Je ne mange pas la viande de porc.** | Zhuh nuh mah(n)zh pah lah vyah(n)d duh pohr. |
| I want to lose/gain weight. | **Je veux maigrir/ grossir.** | Zhuh vuh mehgreer/ grohseer. |

## READING THE MENU

Many restaurant menus feature English translations for the convenience of visitors from other countries. The following list of common menu terms should prove useful where translations are not provided.

| | | |
|---|---|---|
| **attente, 30 min.** | ahtahnt trahnt meenewt | 30 minutes for preparation |
| **au choix** | oh shwah | choice of . . . |
| **boisson comprise** | bwahsoh(n) koh(m)preez | drink included |
| **en saison** | ah(n) sayzohn | in season |
| **en sus** | oh(n) sews | extra charge |
| **garniture au choix** | gahrneetewr oh shwah | choice of vegetable |
| **menu à 60f** | muhnew ah swahsahnt frah(n) | 60-franc menu |
| **menu touristique** | muhnew tooreesteek | tourist menu (usually lower cost but fewer choices) |
| **plat du jour** | plah dew zhoor | special of the day |
| **pour deux personnes** | poor duh pehrsohn | for two people |

| selon arrivage | suhloh(n) ahreevahzh | when available |
| s.g. (selon gros-seur) | suhlohn grohsuhr | by weight |
| servi de 7h à 11h | sehrvee duh seht uhrah ohnz uhr | served from 7–11 A.M. |
| service compris | sehrvees koh(m)pree | service included |
| service non-compris | sehrvees noh(n)-koh(m)pree | service not included |
| supplément pour changement de garniture | sewplaymah(n) poor shah(n)zhmah(n) duh gahrneetewr | extra charge for change of vegetable |
| toutes nos viandes sont ser-vies avec une gar-niture | toot noh vyahnd soh(n) sehrvee ahvek ewn gahrneetewr | all our meat dishes come with a vegetable |
| TTC (toutes taxes comprises) | toot tahks koh(m)preez | all taxes included |

## THE BILL (L'ADDITION)

Since all French restaurants are required by law to post their menus where they can be seen before entering, the cost of the meal should come as no surprise. Further, French restaurants often include the gratuity, tax, and sometimes a house wine in the price of the meal. Credit cards are increasingly being accepted as a form of payment all over Europe. Even if service is included in the price, the French often leave a few francs extra, especially if the food or service was especially good.

| Waiter!/Miss! The check, please. | **Garçon!/Made-moiselle! L'addition, s'il vous plaît.** | Gahrsoh(n)!/Mahdmwahzehl! Lah-deesyoh(n), seel voo pleh. |
| Is service included? | **Est-ce que le service est compris?** | Ehskuh luh sehrvees ay koh(m)pree? |

| | | |
|---|---|---|
| What is this amount for? | **Que représente cette somme?** | Kuh ruhprayzah(n)t seht sohm? |
| Excuse me, I believe there is an error here. | **Excusez-moi, je crois qu'il y a une erreur ici.** | Ehkskewzay-mwah, zhuh krawh keel yah ewn ehruhr eesee. |
| Do you accept . . . | **Est-ce que vois acceptez . . .** | Ehskuh voo zahksehp-tay . . . |
| • this credit card? | • **cette carte de crédit?** | • seht kahrt duh kray-dee? |
| • travelers checks? | • **des chèques de voyage?** | • day shehk duh vwahyahzh? |
| This is for you. | **C'est pour vous.** | Seh poor voo. |
| The meal was excellent. | **Le repas était excellent.** | Luh ruhpah aytay ehksehlah(n). |

## COMPLAINTS (RÉCLAMATIONS)

Here is one section of the book we hope you will never have to use!

| | | |
|---|---|---|
| There must be some mistake. | **Je crois qu'il y a une erreur.** | Zhuh krwah keel yah ewn ehruhr. |
| I didn't order this. | **Je n'ai pas commandé cela.** | Zhuh neh pah kohmah(n)day suhlah. |
| Could I get something else? | **Est-ce que vous pourriez me changer ceci?** | Ehskuh voo pooryay muh shah(n)zhay suh-see? |
| This is too . . . | **C'est trop . . .** | Seh troh . . . |
| • rare (bloody). | • **saignant.** | • sehnyah(n). |
| • well done. | • **cuit.** | • kwee. |
| • salty. | • **salé.** | • sahlay. |
| • bitter. | • **amer.** | • ahmehr. |
| • sweet. | • **sucré.** | • sewkray. |
| This isn't clean. | **Ce n'est pas propre.** | Suh neh pah prohpr. |

| There's (a knife) missing. | **Il manque (un couteau).** | Eel mah(n)k (uh[n] kootoh). |
| This is cold. | **C'est froid.** | Seh frwah. |
| May I see the headwaiter, please? | **Je voudrais parler au maître-d'hôtel, s'il vous plaît.** | Zhuh voodreh pahrlay oh mehtr-dohtehl, seel voo pleh. |

# 7/PERSONAL CARE

## AT THE BARBERSHOP/BEAUTY PARLOR

| | | |
|---|---|---|
| Is there a barbershop/beauty parlor nearby? | **Est-ce qu'il y a un coiffeur/un salon de beauté près d'ici?** | Ehskeel yah uh(n) kwahfuhr/uh(n) sahloh(n) duh bohtay preh deesee? |
| Do I need an appointment? | **Est-ce que je dois prendre rendez-vous?** | Ehskuh zhuh dwah prah(n)dr rah(n)day-voo? |
| Can I get an appointment for today? | **Puis-je prendre rendez-vous pour aujourd'hui?** | Pweezh prah(n)dr rah(n)day-voo poor ohzhoordwee? |
| I need a haircut. | **J'ai besoin d'une coupe de cheveux.** | Zhay buhzwa(n) dewn koop duh shuhvuh. |
| Please leave it long here. | **Laissez-les longs ici, s'il vous plaît.** | Lehsay-lay loh(n) eesee, seel voo pleh. |
| Please cut it short. | **Je les veux courts, s'il vous plaît.** | Zhuh lay vuh koor, seel voo pleh. |
| Not too short! | **Pas trop court!** | Pah troh koor! |
| Cut a bit more off... <br> • here. <br> • in front. <br> • on the side. <br> • the neck. <br> • the back. <br> • the top. | **Coupex un peu plus...** <br> • **ici.** <br> • **devant.** <br> • **sur les côtés.** <br> • **sur la nuque.** <br> • **derrière.** <br> • **dessus.** | Koopay uh(n) puh plews... <br> • eesee. <br> • duhvah(n). <br> • sewr lay kohtay. <br> • sewr lah newk. <br> • dehryehr. <br> • dehsew. |
| It's fine like that. | **C'est bien comme ça.** | Seh byeh(n) kohm sah. |

| I'd like . . . | Je voudrais . . . | Zhuh voodreh . . . |
|---|---|---|
| • a razor cut. | • une coupe au rasoir. | • ewn koop oh rahzwahr. |
| • a shampoo. | • un shampooing. | • uh(n) shah(m)pwa(n). |
| • a set. | • une mise en pli. | • ewn meez ah(n) plee. |
| • a permanent. | • une per- manente. | • ewn pehr- mahnah(n)t. |
| • a manicure. | • une manucure. | • ewn mahnewkewr. |
| • a touch-up. | • une retouche. | • ewn ruhtoosh. |
| • a facial. | • un massage facial. | • uh(n) mahsahzh fah- syahl. |
| • a blow dry. | • un brushing. | • uh(n) bruhsheeng. |
| • a color rinse. | • un shampooing colorant. | • uh(n) shah(m)pwa(n) kohlohrah(n). |

| Make the part . . . | Faites la raie . . . | Feht lah reh . . . |
|---|---|---|
| • on the right. | • à droite. | • ah drwaht. |
| • on the left. | • à gauche. | • ah gohsh. |
| • down the middle. | • au milieu. | oh meelyuh. |

| No hairspray, please. | Pas de laque, s'il vous plaît. | Pah duh lahk, seel voo pleh. |
|---|---|---|

| Could I see a color chart? | Puis-je voir une échelle de teintes? | Pwee-zh vwahr ewn ayshehl duh ta(n)t? |
|---|---|---|

| I prefer . . . | Je préfère . . . | Zhuh prayfehr . . . |
|---|---|---|
| • a lighter shade. | • une teinte plus claire. | • ewn ta(n)t plew klehr. |
| • a darker shade. | • une teinte plus foncée. | • ewn ta(n)t plew foh(n)say. |
| • light blond. | • blond (clair). | • bloh(n) (klehr). |
| • brunette. | • brun. | • bruh(n). |

| I'd like a shave. | Je voudrais me faire raser. | Zhuh voodray muh fehr rahzay. |
|---|---|---|

| Trim my . . . | Rafraîchissez- moi . . . | Rahfrehsheesay mwah . . . |
|---|---|---|
| • mustache. | • la moustache. | • lah moostahsh. |
| • beard. | • la barbe. | • lah bahrb. |

95

## LAUNDRY/DRY CLEANING

| Where is the nearest . . . | Où est ___ la plus proche? | Oo eh ___ lah plew prohsh? |
|---|---|---|
| • laundry? | • la blanchisserie | • lah blah(n)sheesree |
| • dry cleaners? | • la teinturerie | • lah ta(n)tewruhree |
| • laundromat? | • la laverie automatique | • lah lahvree ohtohmahteek |

| I have some clothes to be . . . | J'ai des vêtements à faire . . . | Zheh day vehtmah(n) ah fehr . . . |
|---|---|---|
| • washed. | • laver. | • lahvay. |
| • dry cleaned. | • nettoyer à sec. | • nehtwahyay ah sehk. |
| • ironed. | • repasser. | • ruhpahsay. |
| • pressed. | • repasser à la vapeur. | • ruhpahsay ah lah vahpuhr. |
| • mended. | • réparer. | • raypahray. |

| I need them . . . | Il me les faut . . . | Eel muh lay foh . . . |
|---|---|---|
| • tomorrow. | • demain. | • duhma(n) |
| • the day after tomorrow. | • après-demain. | • ahpreh-duhma(n). |
| • in a week. | • dans une semaine. | • dah(n) zewn suhmehn. |

| When will they be ready? | Quand est-ce qu'ils seront prêts? | Kah(n) tehskeel suhroh(n) preh? |
|---|---|---|

| I'm leaving tomorrow. | Je pars demain. | Zhuh pahr duhma(n). |
|---|---|---|

| This isn't mine. | Ce n'est pas à moi. | Suh neh pah zah mwah. |
|---|---|---|

| There is a shirt missing. | Il y a une chemise qui manque. | Eel yah ewn shuhmeez kee mah(n)k. |
|---|---|---|

| Can you get this stain out? | Pouvez-vous faire partir cette tache? | Poovay-voo fehr pahrteer seht tahsh? |
|---|---|---|

96

| Can you sew on this button? | Pouvez-vous coudre ce bouton? | Poovay-voo koodr suh bootoh(n)? |
|---|---|---|
| I have . . . | J'ai . . . | Zheh . . . |
| • two shirts. | • deux chemises. | • duh shuhmeez. |
| • five underpants. | • cinq slips. | • sa(n) sleep. |
| • a suit. | • un complet. | • uh(n) koh(m)play. |
| • eight pairs of socks. | • huit paires de chaussettes. | • whee pehr duh shohseht. |
| • several handkerchiefs. | • plusieurs mouchoirs. | • plewzyuhr mooshwahr. |
| • two ties. | • deux cravates. | • duh krahvaht. |
| • a sweater. | • un chandail. | • uh(n) shah(n)dahy. |
| • two pairs of pants. | • deux pantalons. | • duh pah(n)tahloh(n). |
| • a bathing suit. | • un maillot de bain. | • uh(n) mahyoh duh ba(n). |
| • three blouses. | • trois blouses. | • trwah blooz. |

# 8/HEALTH CARE
## DOCTORS/MEDICAL SERVICES

It is a good idea to check with your health insurance company to find out what accident and illness expenses overseas are covered by your current policy.

Many doctors in France, Switzerland, Belgium, and of course Quebec speak English, especially in the larger cities. The American embassies or consulates are often helpful in locating English-speaking doctors. The telephone number of the American consulate in Paris is 42.96.12.02. Paris boasts the well-respected American Hospital (tel: 46.37.72.00) with a mostly bilingual staff.

## DIALOGUE: CHEZ LE MÉDECIN (AT THE DOCTOR'S)

| | | |
|---|---|---|
| Médecin: | **Qu'est-ce que vous avez, madame?** | Kehskuh voo zahvay, mahdahm? |
| Touriste: | **Je ne sais pas exactement . . . Je ne me sens pas bien. J'ai mal à la tête.** | Zhuh nuh seh pah ehgzahktuhmah(n) . . . Zhuh nuh muh sah(n) pah byeh(n). Zheh mahl ah lah teht. |
| Médecin: | **Avez-vous des nausées?** | Ahvay-voo day nohzay? |
| Touriste: | **Oui, j'ai vomi ce matin.** | Wee, zheh vohmeeh suh mahta(n). |
| Médecin: | **Depuis quand êtes-vous malade?** | Duhpwee kah(n) eht voo mahlahd? |
| Touriste: | **Depuis dimanche; c'est-à-dire, depuis trois jours.** | Duhpwee deemah(n)sh; seht-ah-deer, duhpwee trwah zhoor. |
| Doctor: | What's the matter? | |
| Tourist: | I don't know exactly. . . I'm not feeling well. I have a headache. | |

98

| Doctor: | Are you nauseated? |
| Tourist: | Yes. I threw up this morning. |
| Doctor: | How long have you been ill? |
| Tourist: | Since Sunday; that is for three days. |

## PATIENT/DOCTOR EXPRESSIONS
### Before the Visit

| Could you call me a doctor? | **Pouvez-vous m'appeler un médecin?** | Poovay-voo mahplay uh(n) maydsa(n)? |
| Where is the doctor's office? | **Où est le cabinet du médecin?** | Oo eh luh kahbeenay dew maydsa(n)? |
| I need a doctor who speaks English. | **J'ai besoin d'un médecin qui parle anglais.** | Zheh buhzwa(n) duh(n) maydsa(n) kee pahrl ah(n)gleh. |
| When can I see the doctor? | **Quand pourrai-je voir le médecin?** | Kah(n) poorehzh vwahr luh maydsa(n)? |
| Could the doctor see me here? | **Le médecin peut-il venir me voir ici?** | Luh maydsa(n) puhteel vuhneer muh vwahr eesee? |
| Can I have an appointment for... | **Puis-je avoir un rendez-vous pour...** | Pweezh ahvwahr uh(n) rah(n)day-voo poor... |
| • today? | • **aujourd'hui?** | • ohzhoordwee? |
| • tomorrow? | • **demain?** | • duhma(n)? |
| • as soon as possible? | • **aussitôt que possible?** | • ohseetoh kuh poh-seebl? |
| What are the doctor's visiting hours? | **Quelles sont les heures de visite du médecin?** | Kehl soh(n) lay zuhr duh veezeet dew maydsa(n)? |
| I need... | **Il me faut...** | Eel muh foh... |
| • a general practitioner. | • **un généraliste.** | • uh(n) zhaynayrah-leest. |
| • a pediatrician. | • **un pédiatre.** | • uh(n) paydyahtr. |

99

| • a gynecologist. | • un **gynécologue**. | • uh(n) zheenay-kohlohg. |
| • an eye doctor. | • un **oculiste**. | • uh(n) nohkewleest. |

## Talking to the Doctor

| I don't feel well. | **Je ne me sens pas bien.** | Zhuh nuh muh sah(n) pah byeh(n). |
| I'm sick. | **Je suis malade.** | Zhuh swee mahlahd. |
| I don't know what I've got. | **Je ne sais pas ce que j'ai.** | Zhuh nuh say pah suh kuh zheh. |
| I have a fever. | **J'ai de la fièvre.** | Zheh duh lah fyehvr. |
| I don't have a temperature. | **Je n'ai pas de fièvre.** | Zhuh neh pah duh fyehvr. |
| I'm nauseated. | **J'ai des nausées.** | Zheh day nohzay. |
| I'm feeling dizzy. | **J'ai des vertiges.** | Zheh day vehrteezh. |
| I can't sleep. | **Je ne peux pas dormir.** | Zhuh nuh puh pah dohrmeer. |
| I threw up. | **J'ai vomi.** | Zheh vohmee. |
| I'm constipated. | **Je suis constipé(e).** | Zhuh swee koh(n)steepay. |
| I have . . . | **J'ai . . .** | Zheh . . . |
| • asthma. | • **de l'asthme.** | • duh lahsm. |
| • a bite. | • **une morsure.** | • ewn mohrsewr. |
| • bruises. | • **des contusions.** | • day koh(n)tew-zyoh(n). |
| • a burn. | • **une brûlure.** | • ewn brewlewr. |
| • something in my eye. | • **quelque chose dans l'oeil.** | • kehlkuh shohz dah(n) luhy. |
| • a cold. | • **un rhume.** | • uh(n) rewm. |
| • a cough. | • **la toux.** | • lah too. |
| • cramps. | • **des crampes.** | • day krah(m)p. |
| • a cut. | • **une coupure.** | • ewn koopewr. |
| • diarrhea. | • **la diarrhée.** | • lah dyahray. |
| • a headache. | • **mal à la tête.** | • mahl ah lah teht. |
| • a lump. | • **une grosseur.** | • ewn grohsuhr. |

100

| • rheumatism. | • **des rhuma-tismes.** | • day rhewmahteezm. |
| • a sore throat. | • **mal à la gorge.** | • mahl ah lah gohrzh. |
| • a sting. | • **une piqûre.** | • ewn peekewr. |
| • a stomach ache. | • **mal à l'estomac.** | • mahl ah lehstohmah. |
| • sunstroke. | • **une insolation.** | • ewn a(n)sohlah-syoh(n). |
| • a swelling. | • **une enflure.** | • ewn ah(n)flewr. |
| • an upset stomach. | • **une indigestion.** | • ewn a(n)deezhehsty-oh(n). |
| My ___ hurt(s). | **J'ai mal . . .** | Zheh mahl . . . |
| • head | • **à la tête.** | • ah lah teht. |
| • stomach | • **à l'estomac.** | • ah lehstohmah. |
| • neck | • **au cou.** | • oh koo. |
| • feet | • **aux pieds.** | • oh pyay. |
| I'm allergic to penicillin. | **Je suis allergique à la pénicilline.** | Zhuh swee ahlehrzheek ah lah pehneeseeleen. |
| Here is the medicine I take. | **Voici le médi-cament que je prends.** | Vwahsee luh maydee-kahmah(n) kuh zhuh prah(n). |
| I've had this pain for two days. | **J'ai cette douleur depuis deux jours.** | Zheh seht dooluhr duhpwee duh zhoor. |
| I had a heart attack four years ago. | **J'ai eu une crise cardiaque il y a quatre ans.** | Zheh ew ewn kreez kahrdyahk eel yah kahtr ah(n). |
| I'm four months pregnant. | **Je suis enceinte de quatre mois.** | Zhuh swee zah(n)sa(n)t duh kahtr mwah. |
| I have menstrual cramps. | **J'ai des règles douleureuses.** | Zheh day rehgl dooluhruhz. |

## Parts of the Body

| ankle (left/right) | **la cheville (gauche/droite)** | lah shuhveey (gohsh/drwaht) |
| appendix | **l'appendice** | lahpa(n)dees |

| arm | le bras | luh brah |
| artery | l'artère | lahrtehr |
| back | le dos | luh doh |
| bladder | la vessie | lah vehsee |
| bone | l'os | lohs |
| bowels | les intestins | lay za(n)tehsta(n) |
| breast | le sein | luh sa(n) |
| buttocks | les fesses | lay fehs |
| calf | le mollet | luh mohlay |
| chest | la poitrine | lah pwahtreen |
| ear | l'oreille | lohrehy |
| an eye | un oeil | uh(n) nuhy |
| eyes | les yeux | lay zyuh |
| face | la figure | lah feegewr |
| finger | le doigt | luh dwah |
| foot | le pied | luh pyay |
| forehead | le front | luh froh(n) |
| gland | la glande | lah glah(n)d |
| hair | les cheveux | lay shuhvuh |
| hand | la main | lah ma(n) |
| head | la tête | lah teht |
| heart | le coeur | luh kuhr |
| hip | la hanche | lah ah(n)sh |
| jaw | la mâchoire | lah mahshwahr |
| joint | l'articulation | lahrteekewlahsyoh(n) |
| kidneys | les reins | lay ra(n) |
| knee | le genou | luh zhuhnoo |
| leg | la jambe | lah zhah(m)b |
| lip | la lèvre | lah lehvr |
| liver | le foie | luh fwah |
| lungs | les poumons | lay poomoh(n) |
| mouth | la bouche | lah boosh |
| muscle | le muscle | luh mewskl |
| nail | l'ongle | loh(n)gl |
| neck | le cou | luh koo |
| nose | le nez | luh nay |
| penis | le pénis | luh paynees |
| ribs | les côtes | lay koht |
| shoulder | l'épaule | laypohl |
| skin | la peau | lah poh |

| spine | **la colonne vertébrale** | lah kohlohn vehrtay-brahl |
| stomach | **l'estomac** | lehstohmah |
| teeth | **les dents** | lay dah(n) |
| thigh | **la cuisse** | lah kwees |
| throat | **la gorge** | lah gohrzh |
| thumb | **le pouce** | luh poos |
| toe | **l'orteil** | lohrtehy |
| tongue | **la langue** | lah lah(n)g |
| tonsils | **les amygdales** | lay zahmeedahl |
| vagina | **le vagin** | luh vahzha(n) |
| vein | **la veine** | lah vehn |
| wrist | **le poignet** | luh pwahnyay |

## What the Doctor Says

| **Déshabillez-vous.** | Dayzahbeeyay-voo. | Get undressed. |
| **Déshabillez-vous jusqu'à la ceinture.** | Dayzahbeeyay-voo zhewskah lah sa(n)tewr. | Undress to the waist. |
| **Etendez-vous ici.** | Aytah(n)day-voo z'ee-see. | Lie down here. |
| **Ouvrez la bouche.** | Oovray lah boosh. | Open your mouth. |
| **Toussez!** | Toosay! | Cough! |
| **Respirez à fond.** | Rehspeeray ah foh(n). | Breathe deeply. |
| **Montrez-moi où vous avez mal.** | Moh(n)tray-mwah oo voo zahvay mahl. | Show me where it hurts. |
| **Tirez la langue.** | Teeray lah lah(n)g. | Stick out your tongue. |
| **Habillez-vous.** | Ahbeeyay-voo. | Get dressed. |
| **Depuis quand éprouvez-vous ces douleurs?** | Duhpwee kah(n) ay-prouvay voo say dooluhr? | How long have you had these pains? |
| **C'est . . .** | Seh . . . | It's . . . |
| • **déboité.** | • daybwahtay. | • dislocated. |

| | | |
|---|---|---|
| • cassé. | • kahsay. | • broken. |
| • foulé. | • foolay. | • sprained. |
| • grave. | • grahv. | • serious. |
| • pas grave. | • pah grahv. | • not serious. |
| • infecté. | • a(n)fehktay. | • infected. |

| | | |
|---|---|---|
| **Il faut vous faire . . .** | Eel foh voo fehr. . . | You'll need to get . . . |
| • une radio. | • ewn rahdyoh. | • an x-ray. |
| • une piqûre. | • ewn peekewr. | • an injection. |

| | | |
|---|---|---|
| **Je vais vous donner un calmant.** | Zhuh veh voo dohnay uh(n) kahlmah(n). | I'm going to give you a painkiller. |

| | | |
|---|---|---|
| **Vous devriez . . .** | Voo duhvreeay. . . | You need to . . . |
| • aller à l'hôpital. | • ahlay ah lohpeetahl. | • go to the hospital. |
| • voir un spécialiste. | • vwahr uh(n) spaysyahleest. | • see a specialist. |

| | | |
|---|---|---|
| **Je vais prendre votre . . .** | Zhuh vay prah(n)dr vohtr. . . | I'm going to take your. . . |
| • température. | • tah(m)payrahtewr. | • temperature. |
| • tension. | • tah(n)syoh(n). | • blood pressure. |

| | | |
|---|---|---|
| **Vous avez . . .** | Voo zahvay. . . | You have . . . |
| • une appendicite. | • ewn ahpa(n)deeseet. | • appendicitis. |
| • une fracture. | • ewn frahktewr. | • a broken bone. |
| • une gastrite. | • ewn gahstreet. | • gastritis. |
| • la grippe. | • lah greep. | • the flu. |
| • une intoxication alimentaire. | • ewn a(n)tohkseekahsyoh(n) ahleemah(n)tehr. | • food poisoning. |
| • une maladie vénérienne. | • ewn mahlahdee vaynayryehn. | • veneral disease. |
| • la cystite. | • lah seesteet. | • cystitis. |
| • une pneumonie. | • ewn pnuhmohnee. | • pneumonia. |
| • la rougeole. | • lah roozhohl. | • measles. |
| • le sida. | • luh seedah. | • AIDS. |

| | | |
|---|---|---|
| **Il me faut un prélèvement de . . .** | Eel muh foh uh(n) praylehvmah(n) duh . . . | I need a sample of . . . |
| • votre sang. | • vohtr sah(n). | • your blood. |

| | | |
|---|---|---|
| • vos selles. | • voh sehl. | • your stool. |
| • votre urine. | • vohtr ewreen | • your urine. |

## Patient Questions

| | | |
|---|---|---|
| Is it serious? | C'est grave? | Seh grahv? |
| Is it contagious? | C'est contagieux? | Seh koh(n)tahzhyuh? |
| How long should I stay in bed? | Jusqu'à quand dois-je garder le lit? | Zhewskah kah(n) dwahzh gahrday luh lee? |
| What exactly is wrong with me? | Qu'est-ce que j'ai exactement? | Kehskuh zhay ehg-zahk-tuh-mah(n)? |
| How frequently do I take this medication? | Combien de fois par jour est-ce que je prends ce médicament? | Koh(m)bya(n) duh fwah pahr zhoor ehskuh zhuh prah(n) suh maydeekah-mah(n)? |
| Do I need to see you again? | Est-ce que je dois vous revoir? | Ehskuh zhuh dwah voo ruhvwahr? |
| Do I need a prescription? | Est-ce que j'ai besoin d'une ordonnance? | Ehskuh zhay buhzwa(n) dewn ohr-dohnah(n)s? |
| When can I start traveling again? | Quand est-ce que je pourrai poursuivre mon voyage? | Kah(n) tehskuh zhuh pooray poorsweevr moh(n) vwahyahzh? |
| Can you give me a prescription for... | Pourriez-vous me prescrire . . . | Pooryay-voo muh prehskreer... |
| • a painkiller. | • un calmant. | • uh(n) kahlmah(n). |
| • a tranquilizer. | • un tranquilisant. | • uh(n) trah(n)kee-leezah(n). |
| • a sleeping pill. | • un somnifère. | • uh(n) sohmneefehr. |
| Are these pills or suppositories? | Ce sont des pillules ou des suppositoires? | Suh soh(n) day peelewl oo day sewpoh-zeetwahr? |

HEALTH CARE

105

| English | French | Pronunciation |
|---|---|---|
| Can I have a bill for my insurance? | **Puis-je avoir une quittance pour mon assurance?** | Pweezh ahvwahr ewn keetah(n)s poor mohn ahsewrah(n)s? |
| Could you fill out this medical form? | **Pourriez-vous remplir cette feuille maladie?** | Pooryay-voo rah(m)pleer seht fuhy mahlahdee? |

## AT THE HOSPITAL

| English | French | Pronunciation |
|---|---|---|
| Where is the nearest hospital? | **Où est l'hôpital le plus proche?** | Oo eh lohpeetahl leh plew prohsh? |
| Call an ambulance! | **Faites venir une ambulance!** | Feht vuhneer ewn ah(m)bewlah(n)s! |
| Help me! | **Aidez-moi!** | Ehday-mwah! |
| Get me to a hospital! | **Emmenez-moi à l'hôpital!** | Ah(m)mnay-mwah ah lohpeetahl! |
| I need first aid fast! | **J'ai besoin de premiers soins; c'est urgent!** | Zheh buhzwa(n) duh pruhmyay swa(n); seh tewrzhah(n)! |
| I was in an accident. | **J'étais dans un accident.** | Zhayteh dah(n) zuh(n) nahkseedah(n). |
| I cut . . . | **Je me suis coupé . . .** | Zhuh muh swee koopay . . . |
| • my hand. | • **la main.** | • lah ma(n). |
| • my leg. | • **la jambe.** | • lah zhah(m)b. |
| • my face. | • **le visage.** | • luh veezahzh. |
| I can't move . . . | **Je ne peux pas bouger . . .** | Zhuh nuh puh pah boozhay . . . |
| • my finger. | • **le doigt.** | • luh dwah. |
| • my leg. | • **la jambe.** | • lah zhah(m)b. |
| • my neck. | • **le cou.** | • luh koo. |
| He/she hurt his/her head. | **Il/(elle) s'est blessé(e) à la tête.** | Eel/(ehl) seh blehsay ah lah teht. |
| His ankle is . . . | **Sa cheville est . . .** | Sah shveey eh . . . |
| • broken. | • **cassée.** | • kahsay. |

106

| English | French | Pronunciation |
|---|---|---|
| • twisted. | • **tordue.** | • tohrdew. |
| • swollen. | • **enflée.** | • ah(n)flay. |
| She's bleeding heavily. | **Elle saigne abondamment.** | Ehl sehnyuh ahboh(n)dahmah(n). |
| He's unconscious. | **Il s'est évanoui.** | Eel seh tayvahnwee. |
| He/she burned himself/herself. | **Il (elle) s'est brûlé(e).** | Eel (ehl) seh brewlay. |
| I ate something poisonous. (I got food poisoning.) | **J'ai eu une intoxication alimentaire.** | Zhay ew ewn a(n)tohkseekahsyoh(n) ahleemah(n)tehr. |
| When can I leave? | **Quand pourrai-je partir?** | Kah(n) poorayzh pahrteer? |
| When will the doctor come? | **Quand est-ce que le médecin va passer?** | Kah(n) tehskuh luh maydsa(n) vah pahsay? |
| I can't . . . | **Je ne peux pas . . .** | Zhuh nuh puh pah . . . |
| • eat. | • **manger.** | • mah(n)zhay. |
| • drink. | • **boire.** | • bwahr. |
| • sleep. | • **dormir.** | • dohrmeer. |
| Where's the nurse? | **Où est l'infirmière?** | Oo eh la(n)feermyehr? |
| What are the visiting hours? | **Quelles sont les heures de visite?** | Kehl soh(n) lay zuhr duh veezeet? |

## THE DENTIST

| English | French | Pronunciation |
|---|---|---|
| Do you know a dentist? | **Connaissez-vous un dentiste?** | Kohnehsay-voo uh(n) dah(n)teest? |
| It's an emergency. | **C'est très urgent.** | Seh treh zewrzhah(n). |
| I'm in a lot of pain. | **J'ai très mal.** | Zheh treh mahl. |
| My gums are bleeding. | **Les gencives saignent.** | Lay zhah(n)seev sehnyuh. |

| I've lost a filling. | **J'ai perdu un plombage.** | Zheh pehrdew uh(n) ploh(m)bahzh. |
|---|---|---|
| I broke a tooth. | **Je me suis cassé(e) une dent.** | Zhuh muh swee kahsay ewn dah(n). |
| This tooth hurts. | **Cette dent me fait mal.** | Seht dah(n) muh feh mahl. |
| I don't want to have it extracted. | **Je ne veux pas la faire extraire.** | Zhuh nuh vuh pah lah fehr ehkstrehr. |
| Can you fill it . . . | **Pouvez-vous l'obturer. . .** | Poovay-voo lohbtewray. . . |
| • with gold? | • **avec de l'or?** | • ahvehk duh lohr? |
| • with silver? | • **avec de l'argent?** | • ahvehk duh lahrzhah(n)? |
| • temporarily? | • **provisoirement?** | • prohveezwahrmah(n)? |
| I want a local anesthetic. | **Je veux une anesthésie locale.** | Zhuh vuh zewn ahneh-stayzee lohkahl. |
| ___ is broken. | **___ est cassé.** | ___ eh kahsay. |
| • My denture | • **Mon dentier** | • Moh(n) dah(n)tyay |
| • My bridge | • **Mon bridge** | • Moh(n) breedzh |
| • My crown | • **Ma couronne** | • Mah koorohn |
| Can you fix it? | **Pouvez-vous le/la réparer?** | Poovay-voo luh/lah raypahray? |
| How much do I owe? | **Combien vous dois-je?** | Koh(m)byeh(n) voo dwahzh? |

## What the Dentist Says

| **Vous avez . . .** | Voo zahvay. . . | You have . . . |
|---|---|---|
| • **une infection.** | • ewn a(n)fehksyoh(n). | • an infection. |
| • **une dent carriée.** | • ewn dah(n) kahryay. | • a rotten tooth. |
| • **un abcès.** | • uh(n) ahbseh. | • an abscess. |
| **Ça vous fait mal?** | Sah voo feh mahl? | Does that hurt? |
| **Il faut extraire cette dent.** | Eel foh ehkstrehr seht dah(n). | That tooth must come out. |

| Vous devrez revenir... | Voo dehvray ruhvneer... | You'll need to come back... |
| • demain. | • duhma(n). | • tomorrow. |
| • dans quelques jours. | • dah(n) kehlkuh zhoor. | • in a few days. |
| • la semaine prochaine. | • lah smehn prohshehn. | • next week. |

## THE OPTICIAN

If you wear glasses or contact lenses, it's a good idea to bring an extra pair and to have your prescription with you in case of loss.

| I broke... | J'ai cassé... | Zheh kahsay... |
| • a lens. | • un verre. | • uh(n) vehr. |
| • the frame. | • la monture. | • lah moh(n)tewr. |

| I lost... | J'ai perdu... | Zheh pehrdew... |
| • my glasses. | • mes lunettes. | • may lewneht. |
| • a contact lens. | • un verre de contact. | • uh(n) vehr duh koh(n)tahkt. |

| Can they be replaced right away? | Est-ce qu'il est possible de les remplacer tout de suite? | Ehs keel eh pohseebl duh lay rah(m)plahsay tood sweet? |

| I'd like soft/hard contact lenses. | Je voudrais des verres de contact souples/durs. | Zhuh voodreh day vehr duh koh(n)tahkt soopl/dewr. |

| Here's the prescription. | Voilà l'ordonnance. | Vwahlah lohrdohnah(n)s. |

| When can I come and get them? | Quand pourrai-je venir les chercher? | Kah(n) poorehzh vuhneer lay shehrshay? |

| I need sunglasses. | Il me faut des lunettes de soleil. | Eel muh foh day lewneht duh sohlehy. |

## AT THE PHARMACY

You can recognize a pharmacy by the green cross in the window. The address of the all-night pharmacy is posted on the door or window of every pharmacy in town. The typical French pharmacy is more specialized than its counterpart in the United States, dealing primarily with prescription and over-the-counter drugs and other health products. You will find household and toilet products at the *droguerie* [drohgree] or the *hypermarché* [eepehrmahrshay].

| Is there an all-night pharmacy near here? | **Y-a-til une pharmacie de garde près d'ici?** | Yah teel ewn fahrmahsee duh gahrd preh deesee? |
|---|---|---|
| I need something for... | **Il me faut quelque chose contre ...** | Eel muh foh kehlkuh shohz koh(n)tr... |
| • a cold. | • **le rhume.** | • luh rewm. |
| • constipation. | • **la constipation.** | • lah koh(n)steepahsyoh(n). |
| • a cough. | • **la toux.** | • lah too. |
| • diarrhea. | • **la diarrhée.** | • lah dyahray. |
| • fever. | • **la fièvre.** | • lah fyehvr. |
| • hay fever. | • **le rhume des foins.** | • luh rewm day fwa(n). |
| • headache. | • **le mal de tête.** | • luh mahl duh teht. |
| • an insect bite. | • **les piqûres d'insecte.** | • lay peekewr da(n)sehkt. |
| • sunburn. | • **le coup de soleil.** | • luh koo duh sohlay. |
| • travel (motion) sickness. | • **le mal du voyage.** | • luh mahl dew vwahyahzh. |
| • an upset stomach. | • **les indigestions.** | • lay za(n)deezhehstyoh(n). |
| I'd like ... | **Je voudrais ...** | Zhuh voodreh ... |
| • some alcohol. | • **de l'alcool.** | • duh lahlkohl. |
| • an analgesic. | • **un analgésique.** | • uh(n) nahnahlzhayzeek. |
| • an antiseptic. | • **un antiseptique.** | • uh(n) nah(n)teesehpteek. |
| • some aspirin. | • **de l'aspirine.** | • duh lahspeereen. |
| • a bandage. | • **un bandage.** | • uh(n) bah(n)dahzh. |
| • some Band-aids. | • **du sparadrap.** | • dew spahrahdrah. |
| • some contact lens solution. | • **de la solution de verres de contact.** | • duh lah sohlewsyoh(n) duh vehr duh koh(n)tahkt. |

110

| English | French | Pronunciation |
|---|---|---|
| • some contraceptives. | • **des contra-ceptifs.** | • day koh(n)trahsehp-teef. |
| • some cotton. | • **de l'ouate.** | • duh lwaht. |
| • some cough drops. | • **des pastilles contre la toux.** | • day pahsteey koh(n)tr lah too. |
| • a disinfectant. | • **un désinfectant.** | • uh(n) dayza(n)-fehktah(n). |
| • some ear drops. | • **des gouttes pour les oreilles.** | • day goot poor lay zohrehy. |
| • some eye drops. | • **des gouttes pour les yeux.** | • day goot poor lay zyuh. |
| • some gauze. | • **de la gaze.** | • duh lah gahz. |
| • some insect spray. | • **une bombe insecticide.** | • ewn boh(m)b a(n)sehkteeseed. |
| • some iodine. | • **de la teinture d'iode.** | • duh lah ta(n)tewr dyohd. |
| • a laxative. | • **un laxatif.** | • uh(n) lahksahteef. |
| • some nose drops. | • **des gouttes nasales.** | • day goot nahzahl. |
| • some pills. | • **des pilules.** | • day peelewl. |
| • some sanitary napkins. | • **des serviettes hygiéniques.** | • day sehrvyeht eezhy-ayneek. |
| • some sleeping pills. | • **des somnifères.** | • day sohmneefehr. |
| • some suppositories. | • **des supposi-toires.** | • day sewpoh-zeetwahr. |
| • some tablets. | • **des comprimés.** | • day koh(m)preemay. |
| • some tampons. | • **des tampons.** | • day tah(m)poh(n). |
| • a thermometer. | • **un thermomètre.** | • uh(n) tehrmohmehtr |
| • some vitamins. | • **des vitamines.** | • day veetahmeen. |

It's urgent!

**C'est urgent!**

Seh tewrzhah(n)!

111

# 9/ON THE ROAD
## CAR RENTALS

France has an excellent system of superhighways (*autoroutes* [ohtohroot]) that offer rapid, convenient access to major cities from Paris. Some roadside stops (*haltes routières* [ahlt rootyehr]) are veritable resorts, with high-class restaurants, supermarkets, hotels, and cafés.

You may use your currently valid American driver's license to rent a car abroad. If you are to be renting for a month or more, an International Driver's License may be required. They are available at a nominal charge from AAA before you leave home.

Many of the major automobile rental companies have branches in France, Belgium and Switzerland, including Hertz and Avis. Fly-drive packages not only allow you to have a confirmed reservation before you leave home but offer some attractive deals as well. Local, independent car-rental agencies sometimes boast lower prices than the international firms, but they may not accept credit cards, in which case you'll need to pay a hefty deposit in cash. Beware the advertised low daily rate; it is for the smallest subcompact (which may not be available) and does not usually include taxes or insurance.

If you are planning to rent a car for three weeks or longer, there is a way around the high rates of auto rentals. The alternative is leasing, technically known as the "Financed Purchase-Repurchase Plan." You get a brand-new, factory-fresh car, with no extra charges for collision coverage, and no TVA to pay. There are some real bargains on smaller Renaults. The minimum rental (lease) is 22 days. The longer you keep the car, the cheaper the per-day and per-week rate, on an unlimited mileage basis. For information, contact European Delivery Services, Renault, Inc., 650 First Avenue, New York, NY 10016-3214.

## DIALOGUE: À L'AGENCE DE LOCATION DE VOITURES
(AT THE CAR RENTAL AGENCY)

| Client: | **Bonjour. Je voudrais louer une voiture pas chère.** | Boh(n)zhoor. Zhuh voodreh looway ewn vwahtewr pah shehr. |
| Employée: | **Très bien, monsieur. Il nous reste une Toyota Starlet climatisée.** | Treh byeh(n), muhsyuh. Eel noo rehst ewn Toyohtah Starleht kleemahteezay. |
| Client: | **Est-ce que je pourrais l'avoir pour trois jours?** | Ehskuh zhuh pooreh lahvwahr poor trwah zhoor? |
| Employée: | **Certainement, monsieur. Et le kilométrage illimité est compris dans le prix.** | Sehrta(n)mah(n), muhsyuh. Ay luh keelohmuhtrahzh eeleemeetay ay koh(m)pree dah(n) luh pree. |
| Client: | **D'accord, c'est parfait. Je la prends.** | Dakohr, say pahrfay. Zhuh lah prah(n). |
| Employée: | **Très bien. Votre passeport et votre permis de conduire, s'il vous plaît.** | Treh byeh(n). Vohtr pahspohr ay vohtr pehrmee duh koh(n)dweer, seel voo pleh. |

. . . . . . . . . . . . . . . . . . . . . . . . . . . . . . . . . . . . . . . . . . . . .

| Customer: | Hello. I'd like to rent an inexpensive car. |
| Employee: | Very well, sir. We still have a Toyota Starlet with air-conditioning left. |
| Customer: | Could I have it for three days? |
| Employee: | Certainly, sir. And unlimited mileage is included in the price. |
| Customer: | Perfect! I'll take it. |
| Employee: | Very good, sir. Passport and driver's license, please. |

113

| Is there a car rental agency in this town? | **Y a-t-il une agence de location de voitures dans cette ville?** | Yahteel ewn ahzhah(n)s duh lohkahsyoh(n) duh vwahtewr dah(n) seht veel? |
| I'd like to rent . . . | **Je voudrais louer. . .** | Zhuh voodreh looay. . . |
| • a small car. | • **une petite voiture.** | • ewn puhteet vwahtewr. |
| • a mid-size car. | • **une voiture moyenne.** | • ewn vwahtewr mwahyehn. |
| • a large car. | • **une grande voiture.** | • ewn grah(n)d vwahtewr. |
| • the least expensive car. | • **la voiture la moins chère.** | • lah vwahtewr lah mwa(n) shehr. |
| • a car with automatic transmission. | • **une voiture automatique.** | • ewn vwahtewr ohtohmahteek. |
| Do you have unlimited mileage? | **Avez-vous le kilométrage illimité?** | Ahvay-voo luh keelohmehtrazh eeleemeetay? |
| I'd like full insurance coverage. | **Je voudrais l'assurance tous risques.** | Zhuh voodreh lahsewrah(n)s too reesk. |
| How much is the rate . . . | **C'est combien le tarif . . .** | Say koh(m)byehn luh tahreef . . . |
| • per day? | • **à la journée?** | • ah lah zhoornay? |
| • per week? | • **à la semaine?** | • ah lah smehn? |
| • per kilometer? | • **au kilomètre?** | • oh keelohmehtr? |
| Do you accept this credit card? | **Acceptez-vous cette carte de crédit?** | Ahksehptay-voo seht kahrt duh kraydee? |
| Do you need my driver's license? | **Avez-vous besoin de mon permis de conduire?** | Ahvay-voo buhzwa(n) duh moh(n) pehrmee duh koh(n)dweer? |

114

| Can I rent it here and return it in ___ ? | **Puis-je la louer ici et la rendre à ___ ?** | Pweezh lah looay ee-see ay lah rah(n)dr ah ___ ? |

## DRIVING

If you haven't done it before, you may be hesitant to drive in a foreign country. You can reduce your anxiety by getting a good roadmap (Michelin's recently published road atlas of France is available from Crown Publishers, Inc.). Prepare your itinerary in advance and allow for plenty of time to sightsee along the way.

Parking in cities is usually plentiful. Aside from parking lots (*des parking* [day pahrkeeng]) and meters (*des parcomètres* [day pahrkohmehtr]), you may park anywhere in the blue zone (*zone bleue* [zohn bluh]) simply by posting a parking disc (*disque de stationnement* [deesk duh stahsyohnmah(n)]) in your windshield set to show your arrival and departure times. These discs may be obtained at gas stations, hotels, garages, tourist offices, etc. at no cost.

| Excuse me, how do I get to ___ ? | **Pardon, comment aller à ___ ?** | Pahrdoh(n), kohmah(n) ahlay ah ___ ? |
| Is this the road to ___ ? | **Est-ce bien la route de ___ ?** | Ehs byeh(n) lah root duh ___ ? |
| How far is it to ___ ? | **Nous sommes à quelle distance de ___ ?** | Noo sohm zah kehl deestah(n)s duh ___ ? |
| Where can I get a roadmap of ___ ? | **Où puis-je obtenir une carte routière de ___ ?** | Oo pweezh ohbtuh-neer ewn kahrt roo-tyehr duh ___ ? |
| Do I . . . | **Est-ce que je dois . . .** | Ehskuh zhuh dwah . . . |
| • go straight? | • **aller tout droit?** | • ahlay too drwah? |
| • turn right? | • **tourner à droite?** | • toornay ah drwaht? |
| • turn left? | • **tourner à gauche?** | • toornay ah gohsh? |
| • make a U-turn? | • **faire demi-tour?** | • fehr duhmee-toor? |

115

| I want to go to ___; what do I do at the next intersection? | **Je veux aller à ___; qu'est-ce que je dois faire au prochain carrefour?** | Zhuh vuh zahlay ah ___; kehskuh zhuh dwah fehr oh proh-sha(n) kahrfoor? |
| Where can I park? | **Où puis-je me garer?** | Oo pweezh muh gahray? |
| Is there a parking lot nearby? | **Y a-t-il un parking près d'ici?** | Yahteel uh(n) pahrkeeng preh dee-see? |

## DISTANCES AND LIQUID MEASURES

As you are no doubt aware, distances are expressed in kilometers and liquid measures (gas and oil, for example) in liters. Unless you are a whiz at mental calculating, the switch from one system to another can be hard to get used to. The following conversion formulas and charts should help.

**MILES/KILOMETERS**

1 kilometer (*km*) = .62 miles
1 mile = 1.51 km
(1,51 km)

| Kilometers | Miles |
|---|---|
| 1 | 0.62 |
| 5 | 3.1 |
| 8 | 5.0 |
| 10 | 6.2 |
| 15 | 9.3 |
| 20 | 12.4 |
| 50 | 31.0 |
| 75 | 46.5 |
| 100 | 62.0 |

**GALLONS/LITERS**

1 liter (*l*) = .26 gallon
1 gallon = 3.75 liters
(3,75 *l*)

| Liters | Gallons |
|---|---|
| 10 | 2.6 |
| 15 | 3.9 |
| 20 | 5.2 |
| 30 | 7.8 |
| 40 | 10.4 |
| 50 | 13.0 |
| 60 | 15.6 |
| 70 | 18.2 |

## THE SERVICE STATION

| Where is the nearest service station? | **Où est la station-service la plus proche?** | Oo eh lah stahsyoh(n)-sehrvees lah plew prohsh? |
| Fill it with . . . | **Faites le plein . . .** | Feht luh pla(n) . . . |
| • regular. | • **de l'ordinaire.** | • duh lohrdeenehr. |
| • super. | • **du super.** | • dew sewpehr. |
| • diesel. | • **du gas-oil.** | • dew gahz-wahl. |
| Give me 20 litres of regular. | **Donnez-moi vingt litres d'ordinaire.** | Dohnay-mwah va(n) leetr dohrdeenehr. |
| Give me 20 francs of regular. | **Donnez-moi pour vingt francs de l'ordinaire.** | Dohnay-mwah poor va(n) frah(n) duh lohrdeenehr. |
| Please check . . . | **Voulez-vous bien vérifier. . .** | Voolay-voo byeh(n) vayreefyay. . . |
| • the battery. | • **la batterie.** | • lah bahtree. |
| • the brake fluid. | • **le liquide des freins.** | • luh leekeed day fra(n). |
| • the carburetor. | • **le carburateur.** | • luh kahrbewrahtuhr. |
| • the tire pressure. | • **la pression des pneus.** | • lah prehsyoh(n) day pnuh. |
| • the water. | • **l'eau.** | • loh. |
| ___ needs to be changed. | **Il faut changer. . .** | Eel foh shah(n)zhay. . . |
| • The oil. | • **l'huile.** | • lweel. |
| • The spark plugs. | • **les bougies.** | • les boozhee. |
| • The tire. | • **le pneu.** | • luh pnuh. |
| My car has broken down. | **Ma voiture est en panne.** | Mah vwahtewr eh tah(n) pahn. |
| Can you repair it? | **Pouvez-vous la réparer?** | Poovay-voo lah ray-pahray? |
| Do you have the part? | **Avez-vous la pièce de rechange?** | Ahvay-voo lah pyehs duh ruhshah(n)zh? |
| I've run out of gas. | **Je suis en panne d'essence.** | Zhuh swee zah(n) pahn dehsah(n)s. |

117

| It won't start. | **Elle ne démarre pas.** | Ehl nuh daymahr pah. |
| I have a flat tire. | **J'ai un pneu crevé.** | Zheh uh(n) pnuh kruh-vay. |
| The battery's dead | **La batterie est à plat.** | Lah bahtree eh tah plah. |
| Can you check the battery? | **Pourriez-vous vérifier la batterie?** | Pooryay-voo vay-reefyay lah bahtree? |
| It's overheating. | **Le moteur chauffe.** | Luh mohtuhr shohf. |
| Can you tow me? | **Pouvez-vous la remorquer?** | Poovay-voo lah ruhmohrkay. |
| I have a problem with . . . | **J'ai un problème avec . . .** | Zheh uh(n) prohblehm ahvehk . . . |
| • the carburetor. | • **le carburateur.** | • luh kahrbewrahtuhr. |
| • the directional signal. | • **le clignotant.** | • luh kleenyohtah(n). |
| • the gears. | • **l'engrenage.** | • lah(n)gruhnahzh. |
| • the brakes. | • **les freins.** | • lay fra(n). |
| • the headlights. | • **les phares.** | • lay fahr. |
| • the ignition. | • **l'allumage.** | • lahlewmahzh. |
| • the radiator. | • **le radiateur.** | • luh rahdyahtuhr. |
| • the starter. | • **le démarreur.** | • luh daymahruhr. |
| • the transmission. | • **la transmission.** | • lah trah(n)smee-syoh(n). |
| I have no tools. | **Je n'ai pas d'outils.** | Zhuh neh pah dooteey. |
| Do you have . . . | **Avez-vous . . .** | Ahvay voo . . . |
| • a flashlight? | • **une lampe de poche?** | • ewn lah(m)p duh pohsh? |
| • a jack? | • **un cric?** | • uh(n) kreek |
| • pliers? | • **des pinces?** | • day pa(n)s? |
| • a screwdriver? | • **un tournevis?** | • uh(n) toornuhvees? |
| How long will it take? | **Combien de temps faut-il compter?** | Koh(m)byeh(n) duh tah(m) foh teel koh(m)tay? |

| I need it today. | **Il me la faut aujourd'hui.** | Eel muh lah foh ohzhoordwee. |

## ROAD SIGNS

| | |
|---|---|
| **Accôtements non stabilisés** | Soft Shoulders |
| **Allumez vos phares** | Headlights On |
| **Attachez-vous vos ceintures** | Fasten Your Seatbelts |
| **Autoroute** | Highway |
| **Camping interdit** | No Camping |
| **Cédez le passage** | Yield Right of Way |
| **Centre ville** | Downtown |
| **Chantier** | Construction |
| **Chaussée défoncée** | Bad Surface |
| **Chaussée glissante** | Slippery Road |
| **Chaussée rétrécie** | Road Narrows |
| **Chute de pierres** | Falling Rocks |
| **Circuit touristique** | Scenic Route |
| **Côté de stationnement** | Parking This Side |
| **Défense d'entrer** | No Trespassing |
| **Dépannage** | Emergency Road Repairs |
| **Descente dangereuse** | Caution: Steep Hill |
| **Déviation** | Detour |
| **Douane** | Customs |
| **Feux de circulation** | Traffic Light Ahead |
| **File de droite** | Right Lane |
| **File de gauche** | Left Lane |
| **Impasse** | Dead End |
| **Interdit aux piétons** | No Pedestrians |
| **Ne roulez pas trop près** | No Tailgating |
| **Nids de poule** | Potholes |
| **Parking** | Parking Lot |
| **Passage à niveau** | Railroad Crossing |
| **Passage clouté** | Pedestrian Crossing |
| **Péage** | Toll |
| **Poids lourds** | Trucks |
| **Priorité à droite** | Yield to the Right |
| **Propriété privée** | Private Property |
| **Ralentir** | Slow |

*(Continued on page 122)*

**ONE WAY**

**MAIN ROAD**

**PARKING**

**SUPERHIGHWAY**

**YIELD**

**GAS**
(10 km ahead)

**DANGER AHEAD**

**DANGEROUS DESCENT**

**BUMPS**

**ROAD NARROWS**

**LEVEL (RAILROAD) CROSSING**

**TWO-WAY TRAFFIC**

**SLIPPERY ROAD**

**CAUTION—SHARP CURVES**

**PEDESTRIAN CROSSING**

**NO ENTRY FOR MOTOR VEHICLES**

**DANGEROUS INTERSECTION AHEAD**

**STOP**

**NO ENTRY**

**MINIMUM SPEED** (km/hr)

**SPEED LIMIT** (km/hr)

**DIRECTION TO BE FOLLOWED**

**OVERHEAD CLEARANCE** (meters)

**ROTARY**

**NO PASSING**

**END OF NO PASSING ZONE**

**END OF RESTRICTION**

**NO LEFT TURN**

**NO U-TURN**

**NO PARKING**

| | |
|---|---|
| **Rappel 70** | Reminder: Speed Limit is 70 km/h |
| **Réservé aux autobus** | Buses Only |
| **Sens unique** | One Way |
| **Serrez à droite** | Keep Right |
| **Sortie d'autoroute** | Highway Exit |
| **Sortie de camions** | Caution: Truck Exit |
| **Stationnement interdit** | No Parking |
| **Stationnement jours impairs** | Parking Permitted Odd Days of Month |
| **Stationnement jours pairs** | Parking Permitted Even Days of Month |
| **Toutes directions** | Through Traffic |
| **Travaux** | Construction |
| **Verglas** | Icy Road |
| **Virages** | Caution: Curves |
| **Voie sans issue** | No Through Way |
| **Zone bleue** | Parking Disc Required |

# 10/COMMUNICATIONS

## DIALOGUE: AU TÉLÉPHONE (ON THE TELEPHONE)

| | | |
|---|---|---|
| Mme. Robert: | **Allô.** | Ahloh. |
| Jean Guyon: | **Allô. Ici Jean Guyon.** | Ahloh. Eesee Zhah(n) Gheeyoh(n). |
| Mme. Robert: | **Bonjour, monsieur. Je voudrais parler à M. Roger, s'il vous plaît.** | Boh(n)zhoor, muhsyuh. Zhuh voodreh pahrlay ah Muhsyuh Rohzhay, seel voo pleh. |
| Jean Guyon: | **Ne quittez pas . . . Je suis désolé, mais il n'est pas là.** | Nuh keetay pah . . . Zhuh swee dayzohlay, meh eel neh pah lah. |
| Mme. Robert: | **Quand sera-t-il de retour?** | Kah(n) suhrah teel duh ruhtoor? |
| Jean Guyon: | **Vers quinze heures.** | Vehr ka(n)z uhr. |
| Mme. Robert: | **Alors, pourriez-vous lui dire de me rappeler? C'est de la part de Mme. Robert.** | Ahlohr, pooryay-voo lwee deer duh muh rahpehlay. Seh duh lah pahr duh Mahdahm Rohbehr. |
| Jean Guyon: | **Très bien. Je lui ferai le message. Au revoir, madame.** | Treh byeh(n). Zhuh lwee fuhray luh mehsahzh. Ow rvwahr, mahdahm. |
| Mme. Robert: | **Merci. Au revoir, monsieur.** | Mehrsee. Oh rvwahr, muhsyuh. |

. . . . . . . . . . . . . . . . . . . . . . . . . . . . . . . . . . . .

| | |
|---|---|
| Mrs. Robert: | Hello? |
| Jean Guyon: | Hello. Jean Guyon speaking. |
| Mrs. Robert: | Hello. I'd like to speak with Mr. Roger, please. |
| Jean Guyon: | Hold the line . . . I'm sorry, but he's not here. |

123

| | | |
|---|---|---|
| Mrs. Robert: | When will he be back? | |
| Jean Guyon: | Around three P.M. | |
| Mrs. Robert: | Well, could you tell him to return my call? This is Mrs. Robert. | |
| Jean Guyon: | Very well. I'll give him the message. Goodbye. | |
| Mrs. Robert: | Thanks. Goodbye. | |

## TELEPHONES

Pay phones on the street in France have gone through a metamorphosis. Recently the phone company installed new units, and they work like a dream; now thay have put in a state-of-the-art system where you no longer need coins but insert a plastic computerized card to place a call. You can buy a card at a post office or *tabac* [tahbah]—the nearest point of sale is indicated on all phone booths (look for the sign *PTT*—Post-Telephone-Telegraph). This entitles you to so many *units* (not calls). So, if you only want to make one or two calls, it's not worth it. Of course, you can still use coins in phone booths.

International calls can be placed from virtually any phone booth, and international operators will be able to assist you in English. Direct dialing to the U.S. is possible from the newer public phones. Simply dial 19 + 1 + area code + number.

Some of the older phones—in cafés, for instance—still use tokens (*jetons* [zhuhtoh(n)]) instead of coins. You may purchase a token at the counter.

| | | |
|---|---|---|
| Where can I make a phone call? | **Où puis-je téléphoner?** | Oo pweezh taylayfoh-nay? |
| Is there a phone booth here? | **Y a-t-il une cabine téléphonique ici?** | Yahteel ewn kahbeen taylayfohneek eesee? |
| Are tokens needed? | **Faut-il des jetons?** | Foh-teel day zhuhtoh(n)? |

| Do you have a phone directory? | **Avez-vous un annuaire téléphonique?** | Ahvay-voo zuh(n) nahnwehr taylayfohneek? |
| What do I dial to get the international operator? | **Quel numéro faut-il composer pour avoir le service international?** | Kehl newmayroh fohteel koh(m)pohzay poor ahvwahr luh sehrvees a(n)tehrnahsyohnahl? |
| I'd like to buy some tokens. | **Je voudrais acheter des jetons.** | Zhuh voodreh ahshtay day zhuhtoh(n). |
| I'd like 42.23.67.43 in Nice. | **Je voudrais le quarante-deux, vingt-trois, soixante-sept, quarante-trois à Nice.** | Zhuh voodreh luh kahrah(n)t-duh, va(n)-trwah, swahsah(n)t-seht, kahrah(n)t-trwah ah Nees. |
| I'd like to call . . . | **Je voudrais téléphoner. . .** | Zhuh voodreh taylayfohnay. . . |
| • overseas. | **• à l'étranger.** | • ah laytrah(n)zhay. |
| • person-to-person. | **• avec préavis.** | • ahvehk prayahvee. |
| • collect. | **• en P.C.V.** | • ah(n) pay say vay. |
| My number is ___ . | **Mon numéro est . . .** | Moh(n) newmayroh eh . . . |
| What is the area code for ___ ? | **Quel est l'indicatif de ___ ?** | Kehl eh la(n)deekahteef duh ___ ? |
| How do I get the operator? | **Que fait-on pour avoir l'opérateur?** | Kuh fehtoh(n) poor ahvwahr lohpayrahtuhr? |
| I was cut off. | **J'ai été coupé(e).** | Zhay aytay koopay. |
| To whom am I speaking? | **Qui est à l'appareil?** | Kee eh tah lahpahray? |
| Speak more slowly, please. | **Parlez plus lentement, s'il vous plaît.** | Pahrlay plew lah(n)tuhmah(n), seel voo pleh. |

| Could you telephone for me? | **Voulez-vous bien téléphoner pour moi?** | Voolay-voo byeh(n) taylayfohnay poor mwah? |
| I'd like to speak to... | **Je voudrais parler à...** | Zhuh voodreh pahrlay ah... |
| Please leave this message: | **Laissez ce message, s'il vous plaît:** | Lehsay suh mehsazh, seel voo pleh: |
| Give me long-distance, please. | **Donnez-moi l'Inter, s'il vous plaît.** | Dohnay-mwah la(n)tehr, seel voo pleh. |

## What You May Hear

| **C'est de la part de qui?** | Seh duh lah pahr duh kee? | Who's calling? |
| **Ne quittez pas.** | Nuh keetay pah. | Hold the line. |
| **On ne répond pas.** | Oh(n) nuh raypoh(n) pah. | They don't answer. |
| **Vous vous êtes trompé de numéro.** | Voo voo zeht troh(m)pay duh new-mayroh. | You got a wrong number. |
| **Puis-je prendre un message?** | Pweezh prah(n)dr uh(n) mehsahzh? | Can I take a message? |
| **Pourriez-vous rappeler plus tard?** | Pooryay-voo rahplay plew tahr? | Could you call back later? |
| **La ligne est occupée.** | Lah leenyeh tohkew-pay. | The line is busy. |
| **On vous demande au téléphone.** | Oh(n) voo duhmah(n)d oh taylay-fohn. | You have a call. |
| **Quel numéro demandez-vous?** | Kehl newmayroh duhmah(n)day-voo? | What number do you want? |

## POST OFFICE AND MAIL

Hours are usually 8 A.M. to noon and 2 P.M. to 6:30 or 7 P.M., although the main post office in Paris does not close. On weekends, the post office usually opens Saturday mornings only. Stamps can be purchased at the post office or the tobacco shop (*bureau de tabac*).

As for getting mail sent to Paris, your best bet is likely to be American Express, 11 Rue Scribe, right next to the Opéra. Service is free to card members and customers (you qualify if you use their traveler's checks); otherwise there's a small service charge.

| | | |
|---|---|---|
| I'm looking for the post office. | **Je cherche un bureau de poste.** | Zhuh shehrsh uh(n) bewroh duh pohst. |
| Where's the nearest mailbox? | **Où est la boîte aux lettres la plus proche?** | Oo eh lah bwaht oh lehtr lah plew prohsh? |
| I'd like to mail a letter. | **Je voudrais poster une lettre.** | Zhuh voodreh pohstay ewn lehtr. |
| How much is it for . . . | **C'est combien pour . . .** | Seh koh(m)byeh(n) poor . . . |
| • a letter (to the U.S.)? | • **une lettre (aux Etats-Unis)?** | • ewn lehtr (oh zaytah-zewnee)? |
| • a postcard? | • **une carte postale?** | • ewn kahrt pohstahl? |
| • a registered letter? | • **une lettre recommandée?** | • ewn lehtr ruhkohmah(n)day? |
| • this package? | • **ce colis?** | • suh kohlee? |
| • a special delivery letter? | • **une lettre par express?** | • ewn lehtr pahr ehks-prehs? |
| Which window is it for . . . | **C'est quel guichet pour . . .** | Seh kehl gheeshay poor . . . |
| • general delivery? | • **la poste restante?** | • lah pohst rehs-tah(n)t? |
| • stamps? | • **les timbres?** | • lay ta(m)br? |
| • money orders? | • **les mandats-poste?** | • lay mah(n)dah-pohst? |

| Is there mail for me? | **Y a-t-il du courier pour moi?** | Yahteel dew kooryay poor mwah? |
| I need stamps for . . . | **Il me faut des timbres pour . . .** | Eel muh foh day ta(m)br poor . . . |
| • five postcards to the United States. | • **cinq cartes postales pour les Etats-Unis.** | • sa(n) kahrt pohstahl poor lay zahtay-zewnee. |
| • two air-letters. | • **deux aéro-grammes.** | • duh zah-ehrohgrahm. |

## TELEGRAMS

There is usually a special window at the Post Office for sending telegrams.

| Which window is it for telegrams? | **C'est quel guichet pour les télégrammes?** | Seh kehl gheeshay poor lay taylaygrahm? |
| May I send a telegram? | **Puis-je envoyer un télégramme?** | Pweezh ah(n)vwah-yay u(h)n taylay-grahm? |
| How much is it per word? | **C'est combien le tarif par mot?** | Say koh(m)byehn luh tahreef pahr moh? |
| When will it get there? | **Quand arrivera-t-il?** | Kah(n) tahreevrah-teel? |
| I'd like a telegram form. | **Je voudrais un formulaire pour un télégramme.** | Zhuh voodreh uh(n) fohrmewlehr poor uh(n) taylaygrahm. |

## WIRING CASH FROM THE UNITED STATES

If you need additional cash while in Paris, it can easily be wired via Western Union from the States.

Holders of American Express cards can also cash checks drawn on their American bank at the American Express office in Paris.

Don't forget that your major credit cards will be honored in most establishments in France, thus cutting down on the need for taking along large amounts of cash on your trip.

## THE MEDIA

In Paris, you can get newspapers and magazines from all over the world. Among the English-language newspapers, look for *The International Herald Tribune, The Wall Street Journal,* and *The Christian Science Monitor. Passion* is an English-language publication sold at kiosks. It is perfect for the American who wants to be *au courant* [oh coorah(n)] or *branché* [brah(n)shay] in Paris, offering timely information about things to do. Watching French television is a good way to practice your comprehension. Many hotels offer English-language television by satellite if you happen to be a little homesick.

### Books and Newspapers

| Do you have . . . | **Avez-vous des . . .** | Ahvay voo day . . . |
|---|---|---|
| • newspapers in English? | • **journeaux en anglais?** | • zhoornoh zah(n) nah(n)glay? |
| • magazines in English? | • **magazines en anglais?** | • mahgahzeen zah(n) nah(n)glay? |
| • books in English? | • **livres en anglais** | • leevr zah(n) nah(n)glay? |

### Radio and Television (Radio et Télévision)

| Is there a(n) ___ station? | **Est-ce qu'il y a une station . . .** | Ehs keel yah ewn stah-syoh(n) . . . |
|---|---|---|
| • English-speaking | • **en anglais?** | • ah(n) nah(n)glay? |
| • music | • **musicale?** | • moozeekahl? |
| • news | • **d'informations?** | • da(n)fohrmahsyoh(n)? |
| • weather | • **météorologique?** | • maytayohrohlohzheek? |
| What is | **Quelle est** | Kehl eh |
| • the number on the dial? | • **la fréquence?** | • lah fraykah(n)s? |
| • the television channel? | • **la chaîne?** | • lah shehn? |

| What time is the program? | **À quelle heure commence l'émission?** | Ah kehl uhr kohmah(n)s laymeesyoh(n)? |
| Is there an English-speaking TV channel? | **Est-ce qu'il y a une chaîne en anglais?** | Eskeel yah ewn shehn ah(n) nah(n)gleh? |
| Do you have a TV guide? | **Est-ce que vous avez un programme?** | Ehskuh voo zahvay uh(n) prohgrahm? |
| Do they have international news in English? | **Est-ce qu'ils ont des informations internationales en anglais?** | Ehskeel zoh(n) day za(n)fohrmahsyoh(n) a(n)tehrnahsyohnahl ah(n) nah(n)gleh? |
| When is the weather forecast? | **A quelle heure est la météo?** | Ah kehl uhr ay lah maytayoh? |

# 11/SEEING THE SIGHTS
## PLACES OF INTEREST

Before your trip, we recommend reading about the countries you plan to visit. In addition to guidebooks, your travel agent or national tourist offices offer the information that will help you plan a sightseeing itinerary. Ask at your hotel for a guide to the city and activities of the week. You may also be able to obtain information about bus tours and places of interest to visit.

## DIALOGUE: AU MUSÉE (AT THE MUSEUM)

| | | |
|---|---|---|
| Sheila: | **Vous savez je m'intéresse beaucoup à l'histoire de l'art.** | Voo sahvay zhuh ma(n)tayrehs bohkoo ah leestwahr duh lahr. |
| Pierre: | **Moi aussi! Quelle période préférez-vous?** | Mwah ohsee! Kehl payreeyohd prayfayray-voo? |
| Sheila: | **J'adore les impressionnistes. Tenez! Regardez! Voilà un tableau impressionniste. Qui en est le peintre?** | Zhahdohr lay za(m)prehsyohneest. Tuhnay! Ruhgahrday! Vwahlah uh(n) tahbloh a(m)prehsyohneest. Kee ah(n) neh luh pa(n)tr? |
| Pierre: | **C'est un tableau de Monet.** | Say tuh(n) tahbloh duh Mohnay. |
| Sheila: | **Ah, oui. En quelle année l'a-t-il terminé?** | Ah, wee. Ah(n) kehl ahnay lahteel tehrmeenay? |
| Pierre: | **Attendez un moment. Je vais voir. . . . en 1898.** | Ahtah(n)day zuh(n) mohmah(n). Zhuh vay vwahr. . . . ah(n) meel weet sah(n), kahtruh-va(n)-deezweet. |

. . . . . . . . . . . . . . . . . . . . . . . . . . . . . . . . . . . . .

Sheila: You know, I'm very interested in art history.

Pierre: Me too! What period do you like the best?

| Sheila: | I love the Impressionists. Look! There's an Impressionist painting. Who's the painter? |
| Pierre: | It's a painting by Monet. |
| Sheila: | Oh, yes. What year did he complete it? |
| Pierre: | Just a moment. I'll look. . . . in 1898. |

## SIGHTSEEING

| English | French | Pronunciation |
|---|---|---|
| What is worth seeing in town? | **Quelles sont les curiosités de la ville?** | Kehl soh(n) lay kewry-ohzeetay duh lah veel? |
| How far is it from here? | **C'est à quelle distance d'ici?** | Seh tah kehl deestah(n)s deesee? |
| Where is the tourist office? | **Où se trouve l'office du tourisme?** | Oo suh troov lohfees dew tooreezm? |
| Can you tell me about . . . | **Pouvez-vous me renseigner sur . . .** | Poovay-voo muh rah(n)sehnyay sewr . . . |
| • guided tours? | • **les visites guidées?** | • lay veezeet ghee-day? |
| • excursions? | • **les excursions?** | • lay zehkskewr-syoh(n)? |
| Are there English-speaking guides? | **Y a-t-il des guides qui parlent anglais?** | Yahteel day gheed kee pahrl ah(n)gleh? |
| We'd like a guide . . . | **Nous voudrions un guide . . .** | Noo voodreeoh(n) zuh(n) gheed . . . |
| • for a day. | • **pour une journée.** | • poor ewn zhoornay. |
| • for an afternoon. | • **pour un après-midi.** | • poor uh(n) nahpray-meedee. |
| When does the excursion begin? | **A quelle heure commence l'excursion?** | Ah kehl uhr kohmah(n)s lehkskewr-syoh(n)? |

| English | French | Pronunciation |
|---|---|---|
| Is breakfast (lunch, dinner) included? | **Est-ce que le petit déjeuner (le déjeuner, le dîner) est compris?** | Ehskuh luh ptee day-zhuhnay (luh dayzhuh-nay, luh deenay) eh koh(m)pree? |
| How much is the excursion, everything included? | **A combien revient l'excursion tout compris?** | Ah koh(m)byeh(n) ruh-vyeh(n) lehkskewr-syoh(n) too koh(m)pree? |
| When do we return to the hotel? | **A quelle heure revient-on à l'hôtel?** | Ah kehl uhr ruhvya(n)-toh(n) ah lohtehl? |
| Where do the tours start from? | **D'où partent les visites?** | Doo pahrt lay veezeet? |
| I'd like to see . . . | **J'aimerais voir. . .** | Zhehmreh vwahr. . . |
| • the aquarium. | • **l'aquarium.** | • lahkwahryuhm. |
| • the art galleries. | • **les galéries d'art.** | • lay gahlree dahr. |
| • the botanical gardens. | • **le jardin botanique.** | • luh zhahrda(n) bohtahneek. |
| • the business district. | • **le quartier des affaires.** | • luh kahrtyay day zahfehr. |
| • the castle. | • **le château.** | • luh shahtoh. |
| • the catacombs. | • **les catacombes.** | • lay kahtahkoh(m)b. |
| • the cathedral. | • **la cathédrale.** | • lah kahtaydrahl. |
| • the caves. | • **les grottes.** | • lay groht. |
| • the cemetery. | • **le cimetière.** | • luh seemtyehr. |
| • the central square. | • **la place principale.** | • lah plahs pra(n)-seepahl. |
| • the chapel. | • **la chapelle.** | • lah shahpehl. |
| • the church. | • **l'église.** | • laygleez. |
| • the citadel. | • **la citadelle.** | • lah seetahdehl. |
| • the convent. | • **le couvent.** | • luh koovah(n). |
| • the courthouse. | • **le palais de justice.** | • luh pahleh duh zhewstees. |
| • downtown. | • **le centre ville.** | • luh sah(n)truh veel. |
| • the exhibition center. | • **le centre d'exposition.** | • luh sah(n)tr dehks-pohzeesyoh(n). |
| • the factories. | • **les usines.** | • lay zewzeen. |

133

| English | French | Pronunciation |
|---|---|---|
| • the flea market. | • **le marché aux puces.** | • luh mahrshay oh pewss. |
| • the fortress. | • **la forteresse.** | • lah fohrtuhrehs. |
| • the fountains. | • **les fontaines.** | • lay foh(n)tehn. |
| • the grave of ___ . | • **la tombe de ___ .** | • lah toh(m)b duh ___ . |
| • the harbor. | • **le port.** | • luh pohr. |
| • historic sites. | • **les sites historiques.** | • lay seet eestohreek. |
| • the library. | • **la bibliothèque.** | • lah beebleeohtehk. |
| • the market. | • **le marché.** | • luh mahrshay. |
| • the monastery. | • **le monastère.** | • luh mohnahstehr. |
| • the mosque. | • **la mosquée.** | • lah mohskay. |
| • the museums. | • **les musées.** | • lay mewzay. |
| • the old city. | • **la vieille ville.** | • lah vyay veel. |
| • the opera house. | • **l'opéra.** | • lohpayrah. |
| • the park. | • **le parc.** | • luh pahrk. |
| • the planetarium. | • **le planétarium.** | • luh plahnaytahry-uhm. |
| • the public gardens. | • **le jardin public.** | • luh zhahrda(n) pewbleek. |
| • the royal palace. | • **le palais royal.** | • luh pahlay rwahyahl. |
| • the ruins. | • **les ruines.** | • lay rween. |
| • the shopping district. | • **le quartier commerçant.** | • luh kahrtyay kohmehrsah(n). |
| • the stadium. | • **le stade.** | • luh stahd. |
| • the statue of ___ . | • **la statue de ___ .** | • lah stahtew duh ___ . |
| • the stock exchange. | • **la bourse.** | • lah boors. |
| • the synagogue. | • **la synagogue.** | • lah seenahgohg. |
| • the tower. | • **la tour.** | • lah toor. |
| • the town hall. | • **l'hôtel de ville.** | • lohtehl duh veel. |
| • the university. | • **l'université.** | • lewneevehrseetay. |
| • the zoo. | • **le jardin zoologique.** | • luh zhahrda(n) zoh-ohlohzheek. |
| Would you take our picture? | **Voudriez-vous nous prendre en photo?** | Voodreeyay-voo noo prah(n)dr ah(n) fohtoh? |
| One more shot! | **Encore une!** | Ah(n)kohr ewn! |
| Smile! | **Souriez!** | Sooryay! |

## PARIS FOR FREE

Like many other great cities the world over, Paris offers an exciting array of cultural and recreational attractions that are absolutely free of charge. The following list is merely a sampling; consult the newspapers and weekly city guides for additional ideas.

**Jazz**   Two evenings a week at 8:30 P.M., the Museum of Modern Art offers free jazz in its auditorium. 11 Avenue du Président Wilson. Métro: Alma Marceau.

**Museums**   Paris's national museums are open free of charge to the public one day a week. For the *Louvre*, Sunday is the free day, while the other museums (Musée d'Art et d'Essai, Musée d'Arts et Traditions Populaires, Grand Palais, Musée Guimet, Monument Français) offer a free day on Wednesdays.

Museums of the City of Paris are free on Sundays and at all times for those under seven or over sixty-five. Municipal museums include le Carnavalet, le Musée de la Mode et des Costumes, and le Petit Palais.

Beaubourg, the innovative and architecturally daring museum also known as le Centre Georges Pompidou, offers free entry at all times.

**Bastille Day**   If you are fortunate enough to be in Paris on July 14, don't miss the big parade on the Champs-Élysées. Later on there is a choice of spectacular fireworks displays at Montmartre, le Parc Montsouris, and le Palais de Chaillot. The evening before the national holiday, traditional popular dancing takes place in neighborhoods all over the city and of course at the Bastille!

**In the Suburbs of Paris**   La Galerie des Glaces de Versailles, the famous Hall of Mirrors at Versailles, is free to the public on Wednesday. The king's chambers are also included in the guided tour. A special treat on the first and third Sunday of each month, from May to September, is the breathtaking fountain display called les Grandes Eaux. This show is always free of charge.

Métro to Pont de Sevres, where you can board bus no. 171 for Versailles.

Fontainebleau may be visited free of charge on Wednesdays. It is less than an hour's train trip from the Gare de Lyon in Paris.

## AT THE MUSEUM

| When does the museum open (close)? | A quelle heure ouvre (ferme) le musée? | Ah kehl uhr oovr (fehrm) luh mewzay? |
|---|---|---|
| How much is it . . . | Quel est le tarif . . . | Kehl eh luh tahreef . . . |
| • for an adult? | • pour un adulte? | • poor uh(n) nahdewlt? |
| • for a child? | • pour un enfant? | • poor uh(n) nah(n)-fah(n)? |
| • for seniors? | • pour les personnes âgées? | • poor lay pehrsohn zahzhay? |
| Do you have a guidebook in English? | Avez-vous un guide en anglais? | Ahvay-voo uh(n) geed ah(n) nah(n)gleh? |
| Can I take pictures? | Puis-je prendre des photos? | Pweezh prah(n)dr day fohtoh? |
| Where can I get reproductions? | Où puis-je acheter des repro-ductions? | Oo pweezh ahshtay day ruhprohdewk-syoh(n)? |
| I'm interested . . . | Je m'intéresse . . . | Zhuh ma(n)tayrehs . . . |
| • in antiques. | • aux antiquités. | • oh zah(n)teekeetay. |
| • in anthropology. | • à l'anthro-pologie. | • ah lah(n)trohpohl-ohzhee. |
| • in archaeology. | • à l'archéologie. | • ah lahrkay-ohlohzhee. |
| • in ___ art. classical medieval modern | • à l'art . . . classique médiéval moderne | • ah lahr . . . klahseek maydyayvahl mohdehrn |

| Renaissance | de la Renaissance | duh lah Ruhnay-sah(n)s |
| surrealistic | surréaliste | sewrayahleest |
| • in ceramics. | • à la céramique. | • ah lah sayrahmeek. |
| • in fine arts. | • aux beaux-arts. | • oh boh-zahr. |
| • in furniture. | • aux meubles. | • oh muhbl. |
| • in geography. | • à la géographie. | • ah lah zhayohgrah-fee. |
| • in geology. | • à la géologie. | • ah lah zhay-ohlohzhee. |
| • in handicrafts. | • à l'artisanat. | • ah lahrteezahnah. |
| • in history. | • à l'histoire. | • ah leestwahr. |
| • in natural history. | • à l'histoire naturelle. | • ah leestwahr nah-tewrehl. |
| • in pottery. | • à la poterie. | • ah lah pohtree. |
| • in sculpture. | • à la sculpture. | • ah lah skewltewr. |
| • in zoology. | • à la zoologie. | • ah lah zoh-ohlohzhee. |

## Saving Money on Paris Museums

For a small charge, you may purchase a card called *carte*, which provides entry to over sixty museums and monuments in the Paris area. The card also entitles you to a small discount on items such as books and catalogs sold in museum shops. The card may be purchased at any of the participating museums (the Louvre, the Rodin museum, the Catacombes, etc.) or at any branch of the Crédit Agricole bank.

## IN THE COUNTRY

| Can you tell me how to get to ___? | Pouvez-vous m'indiquer le chemin pour ___ ? | Poovay-voo ma(n)-deekay luh shma(n) poor ___? |
| Where are the most beautiful land-scapes? | Où sont les plus beaux paysages? | Oo soh(n) lay plew boh payeezahzh? |

## Word List

| | | |
|---|---|---|
| bridge | **le pont** | luh poh(n) |
| cliff | **la falaise** | lah fahlehz |
| corniche | **la corniche** | lah kohrneesh |
| farm | **la ferme** | lah fehrm |
| field | **le champ** | luh shah(m) |
| flowers | **les fleurs** | lay fluhr |
| foliage | **le feuillage** | luh fuhyahzh |
| forest | **la forêt** | lah fohreh |
| garden | **le jardin** | luh zhahrda(n) |
| gorge | **la gorge** | lah gohrzh |
| hill | **la colline** | lah kohleen |
| inn | **l'auberge** | lohbehrzh |
| lake | **le lac** | luh lahk |
| meadow | **le pré** | luh pray |
| mountain | **la montagne** | lah moh(n)tahnyuh |
| mountain pass | **le col** | luh kohl |
| national park | **le parc national** | luh pahrk nahsyohnahl |
| peak | **le sommet** | luh sohmay |
| pond | **l'étang** | laytah(n) |
| river | **le fleuve,** | luh fluhv, |
| | **la rivière** | lah reevyehr |
| road | **la route** | lah root |
| scenic route | **le circuit** | luh seerkwee tooreesteek |
| | **touristique** | |
| sea | **la mer** | lah mehr |
| spring | **la source** | lah soors |
| stream | **le ruisseau** | luh rweesoh |
| swamp | **le marais** | luh mahreh |
| valley | **la vallée** | lah vahlay |
| village | **le village** | luh veelahzh |
| vineyard | **le vignoble** | luh veenyohbl |
| waterfall | **la chute d'eau** | lah shewt doh |

## RELIGIOUS SERVICES

Travelers to France often report back that a highlight of their trip was attending a religious service at a church or synagogue and observing the similarities and differences in devotional practice, music, and ceremonies.

Since France is predominantly Roman Catholic, churches and cathedrals abound all over the country. Don't forget that most of the great cathedrals that are part of the traveler's circuit are also fully functioning churches and can be more fully appreciated by attending one of the regular masses. A schedule of services is posted on the main entrance of each church.

In Paris and other large cities, Protestant churches and synagogues can be located easily by looking in the yellow pages under *Eglises,* or ask at the local *Syndicat d'initiative* (tourist office).

Jewish visitors may well be interested in exploring the old Jewish section in the *Marais* or attending services at one of the local synagogues. Information on sites of special interest to Jewish travelers is obtainable from Air France.

| I'd like to see . . . | **Je voudrais voir. . .** | Zhuh voodreh vwahr. . . |
|---|---|---|
| • a Catholic church. | • **une église Catholique.** | • ewn aygleez kahtoh-leek. |
| • a mosque. | • **une mosquée.** | • ewn mohskay. |
| • a Protestant church. | • **une église Protestante.** | • ewn aygleez Proh-tehstah(n)t. |
| • a synagogue. | • **une synagogue.** | • ewn seenahgohg. |
| When does the mass (service) begin? | **A quelle heure commence la messe (le culte)?** | Ah kehl uhr kohmah(n)s lah mehs (luh kewlt)? |
| I'm looking for an English-speaking . . . | **Je cherche un ___ qui parle anglais.** | Zhuh shehrsh uh(n) ___ kee pahrl ah(n)gleh. |
| • minister. | • **pasteur** | • pahstuhr |
| • priest. | • **prêtre** | • prehtr |
| • rabbi. | • **rabbin** | • rahba(n) |

# 12/SHOPPING

Stores generally open at 9:00 A.M. and close for the day between 6:00 and 7:00 P.M. Monday through Saturday. Most stores still close for an hour or two at lunchtime, so check the *heures d'ouverture* [uhr doovehrtewr] (business hours) sign on the door if you plan on shopping around midday. Department stores usually remain open throughout the day, however.

Sunday hours vary quite a bit, with many stores closed for the day and others open for at least a few hours. Most food stores remain open on Sunday until noon. Some shops close one other day during the week, most frequently on Monday.

The big city-wide sales in Paris take place in mid-January and in July (and run through much of August). Then, windows everywhere proclaim *Soldes* [sohld] and *Occasion* [ohkahzyoh(n)], meaning clearance sales and the opportunity to save money.

## DIALOGUE: AU MAGASIN DE VÊTEMENTS POUR HOMMES
### (AT THE MEN'S CLOTHING STORE)

| | | |
|---|---|---|
| Cliente: | **Bonjour, monsieur. Je voudrais une chemise pour mon mari.** | Boh(n)zhoor, muhsyuh. Zhuh voodreh ewn shuh-meez poor moh(n) mahree. |
| Vendeur: | **Bonjour, madame. Nous avons un grand choix de che-mises . . . Aimez-vous ce style?** | Boh(n)zhoor, mahdahm. Noo zahvoh(n) uh(n) grah(n) shwah duh shuh-meez . . . Ehmay-voo suh steel? |
| Cliente: | **Oui, mais je n'aime pas la couleur. L'avez-vous en bleu?** | Wee, meh zhuh nehm pah lah kooluhr. Lahvay-voo ah(n) bluh? |
| Vendeur: | **Oui. Connaissez-vous sa taille?** | Wee. Kohnehsay-voo sah tahy? |

| Cliente: | **Oui. Quarante, je crois.** | Wee. Kahrah(n)t, zhuh krwah. |
| Vendeur: | **Eh bien, voilà.** | Ay byeh(n), vwahlah. |
| Cliente: | **Parfait! Voulez-vous bien l'emballer, s'il vous plaît?** | Pahrfeh! Voolay-voo byeh(n) lah(m)bahlay, seel voo pleh? |

. . . . . . . . . . . . . . . . . . . . . . . . . . . . . . . . . . . . . . . . .

| Customer: | Hello. I'd like a shirt for my husband. |
| Salesman: | Hello. We have a large selection of shirts . . . Do you like this style? |
| Customer: | Yes, but I don't care for the color. Do you have it in blue? |
| Salesman: | Yes. Do you know his size? |
| Customer: | Yes. I think it's a 40.* |
| Salesman: | Here it is. |
| Customer: | Perfect! Could you wrap it for me, please? |

*See clothing size conversion charts (pages 151–152) for translating American to French sizes.

## TYPES OF STORES

I'm looking for. . .
- an antique shop.
- an art gallery.

- an automatic cash machine.
- a bakery.

- a bank.
- a barbershop.
- a beauty parlor.

**Je cherche . . .**
- **un antiquaire.**
- **une galerie d'art.**

- **un guichet automatique.**
- **une boulangerie.**

- **une banque.**
- **un coiffeur.**
- **un salon de beauté.**

Zhuh shehrsh . . .
- uh(n) nah(n)teekehr.
- ewn gahlree dahr.

- uh(n) gheeshay ohtohmahteek.
- ewn boolah(n)zhree.

- ewn bah(n)k.
- uh(n) kwahfuhr.
- uh(n) sahloh(n) duh bohtay.

141

| | | |
|---|---|---|
| • a bookstore. | • **une librairie.** | • ewn leebrehree. |
| • a butcher shop. | • **une boucherie.** | • ewn booshree. |
| • a camera store. | • **un magasin de photos.** | • uh(n) mahgaza(n) duh fohtoh. |
| • a candy store. | • **une confiserie.** | • ewn koh(n)feezree. |
| • a cheese store. | • **une fromagerie.** | • ewn frohmahzhree. |
| • a clothing store for men/women/ children. | • **un magasin de vêtements pour hommes/ femmes/ enfants.** | • uh(n) mahgaza(n) duh vehtmah(n) poor ohm/fahm/ ah(n)fah(n). |
| • a dairy store. | • **une laiterie.** | • ewn lehtree. |
| • a delicatessen. | • **une charcuterie.** | • ewn shahrkewtree. |
| • a dentist. | • **un dentiste.** | • uh(n) dah(n)teest. |
| • a department store. | • **un grand magasin.** | • uh(n) grah(n) mahgaza(n). |
| • a discount store. | Examples of inexpensive variety store chains include **Monoprix** [Mohnohpree], **Prisunic** [Preezewneek], and **Uniprix** [Ew-neepree]. | |
| • a drugstore. | • **une pharmacie.** | • ewn fahrmahsee. |
| • a drycleaners. | • **une teinturerie.** | • ewn ta(n)tewruhree. |
| • a fish store. | • **une poisson-nerie.** | • ewn pwahsohnree. |
| • a flower shop. | • **une fleuriste.** | • ewn fluhreest. |
| • a furniture store. | • **un magasin d'ameublement.** | • uh(n) mahgaza(n) dahmuhbluhmah(n). |
| • a grocery. | • **une épicerie/un magasin d'alimentation.** | • ewn aypeesree/uh(n) mahgaza(n) dah-leemah(n)tahsyoh(n). |
| • a hardware store. | • **une quin-caillerie.** | • ewn ka(n)kahyuhree. |
| • a health food store. | • **un magasin de diététique.** | • uh(n) mahgaza(n) duh deeyaytayteek. |
| • a household goods store. | • **une droguerie.** | • ewn drohgree. |
| • a jeweler. | • **une bijouterie.** | • ewn beezhootree. |
| • a laundromat. | • **une laverie automatique.** | • ewn lahvree ohtohmahteek. |
| • a leather goods store. | • **une maro-quinerie.** | • ewn mahrohkeenree. |

142

| | | |
|---|---|---|
| • a library. | • **une biblio- thèque.** | • ewn beebleeyohtehk. |
| • a laundry. | • **une blanchisserie.** | • ewn blah(n)sheesree. |
| • a liquor store. | • **un magasin de vins et spiritueux.** | • uh(n) mahgahza(n) duh va(n) ay speereetwuh. |
| • a market. | • **un marché.** | • uh(n) mahrshay. |
| • a newsstand. | • **un kiosque à journaux.** | • uh(n) kyohsk ah zhoornoh. |
| • an optician. | • **un opticien.** | • uh(n) nohpteesya(n). |
| • a pastry shop. | • **une pâtisserie.** | • ewn pahteesree. |
| • a photographer. | • **un photo- graphe.** | • uh(n) fohtohgrahf. |
| • a police station. | • **un poste de police.** | • uh(n) pohst duh poh- lees. |
| • a post office. | • **un bureau de poste.** | • uh(n) bewroh duh pohst. |
| • a produce shop. | • **un primeur.** | • uh(n) preemuhr. |
| • a record store. | • **un magasin de disques.** | • uh(n) mahgahza(n) duh deesk. |
| • a shoemaker. | • **un cordonnier.** | • uh(n) kohrdohnyay. |
| • a shoe store. | • **un magasin de chaussures.** | • uh(n) mahgahza(n) duh shohsewr. |
| • a shopping center. | • **un centre commercial.** | • uh(n) sah(n)tr kohmehrsyahl. |
| • a souvenir shop. | • **un magasin de souvenirs.** | • uh(n) mahgahza(n) duh soovneer. |
| • a sporting goods store. | • **un magasin d'articles de sport.** | • uh(n) mahgahza(n) dahrteekl duh spohr. |
| • a stationer. | • **une papeterie.** | • ewn pahpehtree. |
| • a supermarket. | • **un supermarché.** | • uh(n) sewpehr- mahrshay. |
| • a tailor. | • **un tailleur.** | • uh(n) tahyuhr. |
| • a tobacconist. | • **un bureau de tabac.** | • uh(n) bewroh duh tahbah. |
| • a toy shop. | • **un magasin de jouets.** | • uh(n) mahgahza(n) duh zhooay. |
| • a travel agency. | • **une agence de voyage.** | • ewn ahzhah(n)s duh vwahyahzh. |

143

SHOPPING

| • a veterinarian. | • **un vétérinaire.** | • uh(n) vaytayreenehr. |
| • a watchmaker. | • **une horlogerie.** | • ewn ohrlohzhree. |

## SOUVENIR AND GIFT SHOPPING

France is a shopper's paradise, especially for such luxury items as perfume, lace, handbags, designer clothes, crystal, pottery, kitchen utensils, art prints, and tablecloths. Every region of the country also specializes in fine crafts products that can often be purchased directly from the producer. Check for signs indicating a nearby *atelier* (workshop).

For those who prefer or need to do most of their shopping in one location, the best bet would be the *Grands magasins* in Paris. Two of the foremost are *Galeries Lafayette* and *Au Printemps*, side by side behind the *Opéra*. They stock just about anything one might want to buy in Paris. Note that American visitors are entitled to a refund of the TVA, or *taxes de valeur ajoutée* (value-added tax), on purchases of 1200 francs or more at any single store. Discounts range from 13 to 23 percent, depending on the type of goods. You must have a passport for the forms to be filled out. Present the completed forms at the airport customs counter prior to checking in with your luggage. You may have to show merchandise to the officers. Forms will be stamped, processed, and mailed to the store. A refund will be sent to you a few weeks later or credited to your charge card account.

Belgium is known for its linen, diamond markets, lace products, glassware, and crystal. Be sure not to overlook the many gourmet food items, especially Belgian chocolate, condiments, and candy.

Switzerland also boasts an array of distinctive high-quality products that are perfect gifts for the folks back home. Swiss watches and clocks, fondu sets, ceramics, embroidery, and wood products are a few of the most popular items. And is there any need to remind you of Swiss chocolate and cheeses?

144

# GENERAL SHOPPING EXPRESSIONS

| Where can I find ___? | **Où puis-je trouver ___?** | Oo pweezh troovay ___? |
|---|---|---|
| When do you close? | **A quelle heure fermez-vous?** | Ah kehl uhr fehrmay-voo? |
| Can you help me? | **Pouvez-vous m'aider?** | Poovay-voo mehday? |
| I'm just browsing. | **Je ne fais que regarder.** | Zhuh nuh feh kuh ruhgahrday. |

Can you show me . . .

**Pouvez-vous me montrer . . .**

Poovay-voo muh moh(n)tray . . .

| • this? | • **ceci?** | • suhsee? |
|---|---|---|
| • that? | • **cela?** | • suhlah? |
| • the one in the window? | • **celui de la vitrine?** | • suhlwee duh lah vee-treen? |
| • something less costly? | • **quelque chose de moins cher?** | • kehlkuh shohz duh mwa(n) shehr? |
| • something better? | • **quelque chose de meilleur?** | • kehlkuh shohz duh mehyuhr? |
| • something darker? | • **quelque chose de plus foncé?** | • kehlkuh shohz duh plew foh(n)say? |
| • something lighter? (color) | • **quelque chose de plus clair?** | • kehlkuh shohz duh plew klehr? |
| • something lighter? (weight) | • **quelque chose de plus léger?** | • kehlkuh shohz duh plew layzhay? |
| • something bigger/ smaller? | • **quelque chose de plus grand/ petit?** | • kehlkuh shohz duh plew grah(n)/ puhtee? |
| • a different color? | • **une autre couleur?** | • ewn ohtr kooluhr? |
| • a different style? | • **un autre style?** | • uh(n) nohtr steel? |

I'd like a gift for. . .

**Je voudrais un cadeau pour . . .**

Zhuh voodreh uh(n) kahdoh poor . . .

| • an adult. | • **un adulte.** | • uh(n) nahduhlt. |
|---|---|---|
| • a child. | • **un enfant.** | • uh(n) nah(n)fah(n). |
| • a girl of seventeen. | • **une jeune fille de dix-sept ans.** | • ewn zhuhn feey duh dee-seht ah(n). |

| | | |
|---|---|---|
| • a boy of fifteen. | • **un garçon de quinze ans.** | • uh(n) gahrsoh(n) duh ka(n)z ah(n). |
| I prefer something . . . | **Je préfère quelque chose . . .** | Zhuh prayfehr kehlkuh shohz . . . |
| • locally made. | • **de fabrication locale.** | • duh fahbreekah-syoh(n) lohkahl. |
| • handmade. | • **fait main.** | • feh ma(n). |
| • more practical. | • **de plus pratique.** | • duh plew prahteek. |
| • more typical. | • **de plus typique.** | • duh plew teepeek. |
| Show me your selection . . . | **Montrez-moi votre choix . . .** | Moh(n)tray-mwah vohtr shwah . . . |
| • of antiques. | • **d'antiquités.** | • dah(n)teekeetay. |
| • of cut crystal. | • **de cristal taillé.** | • duh kreestahl tahyay. |
| • of jewelry. | • **de bijoux.** | • duh beezhoo. |
| • of lace. | • **de dentelle.** | • duh dah(n)tehl. |
| • of leather goods. | • **d'objets en cuir.** | • dohbzhay ah(n) kweer. |
| • of perfume. | • **de parfums.** | • duh pahrfuh(m). |
| How much is this . . . | **Combien coûte ceci . . .** | Koh(m)byeh(n) koot suhsee . . . |
| • in dollars? | • **en dollars?** | • ah(n) dohlahr? |
| • in francs? | • **en francs?** | • ah(n) frah(n)? |
| Can you write down the price (for me)? | **Pouvez-vous m'écrire le prix?** | Poovay voo maykreer luh pree? |
| I don't want to spend more than ___ dollars/francs. | **Je ne veux pas dépenser plus de ___ dollars/francs.** | Zhuh nuh vuh pah daypah(n)say plew duh ___ dohlahr/frah(n). |
| I'll take it. | **Je le prends.** | Zhuh luh prah(n). |
| I'll take two. | **J'en prends deux.** | Zhah(n) prah(n) duh. |
| Can I pay . . . | **Puis-je payer . . .** | Pweezh payay . . . |
| • in dollars? | • **en dollars?** | • ah(n) dohlahr? |
| • with traveler's checks? | • **avec des chèques de voyage?** | • ahvehk day shehk duh vwahyahzh? |

146

| English | French | Pronunciation |
|---|---|---|
| • with a credit card? | • **avec une carte de crédit?** | • ahvehk ewn kahrt duh kraydee? |
| Can you . . . | **Pouvez-vous . . .** | Poovay-voo. . . |
| • order it? | • **le commander?** | • luh kohmah(n)day? |
| • send it to me? | • **me l'envoyer?** | • muh lah(n)vwahyay? |
| • deliver it to this address? | • **le livrer à cette adresse?** | • luh leevray ah seht ahdrehs? |
| Is it out of stock? | **Votre stock est épuisé?** | Vohtr stohk eh taypweezay? |
| Do I have to pay the value-added tax? | **Dois-je payer la TVA?** | Dwahzh payay lah tay vay ah? |
| I'd like my money back. | **Je voudrais me faire rembourser.** | Zhuh voodreh muh fehr rah(m)boorsay. |
| Here's my receipt. | **Voici le reçu.** | Vwahsee luh ruhsew. |
| Can I exchange this? | **Puis-je échanger ceci?** | Pweezh ayshah(n)zhay suhsee? |
| May I have a bag? | **Un sac, s'il vous plaît.** | Uh(n) sahk, seel voo pleh. |
| That will be all. | **Ce sera tout.** | Suh suhruh too. |
| It's a gift; can you wrap it? | **C'est pour offrir; pouvez-vous l'emballer?** | Seh poor ohfreer; poovay-voo lah(m)bahlay? |

## CLOTHING

| English | French | Pronunciation |
|---|---|---|
| I'd like to buy. . . | **Je voudrais acheter. . .** | Zhuh voodreh zahshtay. . . |
| • a bathrobe. | • **un peignoir de bain.** | • uh(n) pehnwahr duh ba(n). |
| • a bathing cap. | • **un bonnet de bain.** | • uh(n) bohnay de ba(n). |
| • a bathing suit. | • **un maillot de bain.** | • uh(n) mahyoh duh ba(n). |
| • a belt. | • **une ceinture.** | • ewn sa(n)tewr. |
| • a blouse. | • **un chemisier.** | • uh(n) shuhmeezyay. |

147

| | | |
|---|---|---|
| a bra. | un soutien-gorge. | uh(n) sootya(n)-gohrzh. |
| a cap. | une casquette. | ewn kahskeht. |
| a coat. | un manteau. | uh(n) mah(n)toh. |
| a dress. | une robe. | ewn rohb. |
| a dressing gown. | un peignoir. | uh(n) pehnwahr. |
| an evening dress. | une robe de soir. | ewn rohb duh swahr. |
| gloves. | des gants. | day gah(n). |
| a handbag/ pocketbook. | un sac à main. | uh(n) sahk ah ma(n). |
| a handkerchief. | un mouchoir. | uh(n) mooshwahr. |
| a hat. | un chapeau. | uh(n) shahpoh. |
| a jacket. | un veston. | uh(n) vehstoh(n). |
| jeans. | des jeans. | day dzheen. |
| an overcoat. | un pardessus. | uh(n) pahrduhsew. |
| overalls. | une salopette. | ewn sahlohpeht. |
| panties. | des pantalons de femme. | day pahntahloh(n) duh fahm. |
| pants. | un pantalon. | uh(n) pahntahloh(n). |
| pantyhose. | un collant. | uh(n) kohlah(n). |
| a turtleneck pullover. | un pullover à col roulé. | uh(n) pewlohvehr ah kohl roolay. |
| a V-neck pullover. | un pullover à col V. | uh(n) pewlohvehr ah kohl vay. |
| pajamas. | un pyjama. | uh(n) peezhahmah. |
| a raincoat. | un imperméable. | uh(n) na(n)pehrmay-ahbl. |
| a scarf. | un foulard. | uh(n) foolahr. |
| a long-sleeved shirt. | une chemise à manches longues. | ewn shuhmeez ah mah(n)sh loh(n)g. |
| a short-sleeved shirt. | une chemisette. | ewn shuhmeezeht. |
| a sleeveless shirt. | une chemise sans manches. | ewn shuhmeez sah(n) mah(n)sh . |
| shoes (a pair). | une paire de chaussures. | ewn pehr duh shohsewr. |
| shorts. | un short. | uh(n) shohrt. |
| a skirt. | une jupe. | ewn zhewp. |
| a slip. | un jupon. | uh(n) zhewpoh(n). |
| socks. | des chaussettes. | day shohseht. |

148

| | | |
|---|---|---|
| • a sports jacket. | • **une veste de sport.** | • ewn vehst duh spohr. |
| • stockings. | • **des bas.** | • day bah. |
| • a suit (man's). | • **un complet.** | • uh(n) koh(m)play. |
| • a suit (woman's). | • **un tailleur.** | • uh(n) tahyuhr. |
| • suspenders. | • **des bretelles.** | • day bruhtehl. |
| • a sweater. | • **un chandail.** | • uh(n) shah(n)dahy. |
| • a tie. | • **une cravate.** | • ewn krahvaht. |
| • tights. | • **un collant.** | • un(n) kohlah(n). |
| • an umbrella. | • **un parapluie.** | • uh(n) pahrahplwee. |
| • an undershirt. | • **un maillot de corps.** | • uh(n) mahyoh duh kohr. |
| • underwear. | • **des sous-vêtements.** | • day soo-vehtmah(n). |
| • a vest. | • **un gilet.** | • uh(n) zheelay. |

| | | |
|---|---|---|
| Can I try it on? | **Puis-je l'essayer?** | Pweezh lehsayay? |
| Do you do alterations? | **Pouvez-vous le/la retoucher?** | Poovay-voo luh/lah ruhtooshay? |
| Do you have a skirt that's . . . | **Avez-vous une jupe . . .** | Ahvay voo ewn zhewp. . . |
| • longer? | • **plus longue?** | • plew loh(n)gh? |
| • shorter? | • **plus courte?** | • plew koort? |
| • bigger? | • **plus grande?** | • plew grah(n)d? |
| • smaller? | • **plus petite?** | • plew puhteet? |
| I wear size 42. | **Je porte du quarante-deux.** | Zhuh pohrt dew kahrah(n)t-duh. |

## Colors and Patterns

| | | |
|---|---|---|
| I think you would look nice in . . . | **Je vous voir très bien en . . .** | Zhuh voo vwah(r) tray byeh(n) ah(n) . . . |
| • beige. | • **beige.** | • behzh. |
| • black. | • **noir.** | • nwahr. |
| • blue. | • **bleu.** | • bluh. |
| • brown. | • **brun.** | • bruh(n). |
| • gray. | • **gris.** | • gree. |
| • green. | • **vert.** | • vehr. |
| • orange. | • **orange.** | • ohrah(n)zh. |
| • pink. | • **rose.** | • rohz. |
| • purple. | • **violet.** | • vyohlay. |

149

| | | |
|---|---|---|
| • red. | • rouge. | • roozh. |
| • silver. | • argenté. | • ahrzhah(n)tay. |
| • white. | • blanc. | • blah(n). |
| • yellow. | • jaune. | • zhohn. |

| | | |
|---|---|---|
| I prefer something . . . | Je préfère quelque chose . . . | Zhuh prayfehr kehlkuh shohz . . . |
| • lighter. | • de plus clair. | • duh plew klehr. |
| • darker. | • de plus foncé. | • duh plew foh(n)say. |
| • in a solid color. | • de couleur unie. | • duh kooluhr ewnee. |
| • with stripes. | • à rayures. | • ah rayewr. |
| • with polka dots. | • à pois. | • ah pwah. |
| • in plaid. | • d'écossais. | • daykohseh. |
| • checked. | • à carreaux. | • ah kahroh. |

## Materials

| | | |
|---|---|---|
| I don't like this material. Do you have anything in . . . | Je n'aime pas ce tissu. Avez-vous quelque chose en . . . | Zhuh nehm pah suh teesew. Ahvay voo kehlkuh shohz ah(n) . . . |
| • corduroy? | • velours côtelé? | • vuhloor kohtlay? |
| • cotton? | • coton? | • kohtoh(n)? |
| • crepe? | • crêpe? | • krehp? |
| • denim? | • toile? | • twahl? |
| • flannel? | • flanelle? | • flahnehl? |
| • gabardine? | • gabardine? | • gahbahrdeen? |
| • lace? | • dentelle? | • dah(n)tehl? |
| • leather? | • cuir? | • kweer? |
| • linen? | • lin? | • la(n)? |
| • nylon? | • nylon? | • neeloh(n)? |
| • poplin? | • popeline? | • pohpleen? |
| • satin? | • satin? | • sahta(n)? |
| • silk? | • soie? | • swah? |
| • suede? | • daim? | • da(m)? |
| • velvet? | • velours? | • vuhloor? |
| • wool? | • laine? | • lehn? |

## Shoes

| | | |
|---|---|---|
| I'd like a pair of . . . | Je voudrais une paire de . . . | Zhuh voodreh ewn pehr duh . . . |

| | | |
|---|---|---|
| • boots. | • **bottes.** | • boht. |
| • flats. | • **chaussures à talons plats.** | • shohsewr ah tahloh(n) plah. |
| • high heels. | • **chaussures à talons hauts.** | • shohsewr ah tahlon(n) oh. |
| • sandals. | • **sandales.** | • sah(n)dahl. |
| • shoes. | • **chaussures.** | • shohsewr. |
| • slippers. | • **pantoufles.** | • pah(n)toofl. |
| • sneakers. | • **tennis.** | • tehnees. |
| They fit me well. | **Elles me vont bien.** | Ehl muh voh(n) byeh(n). |
| They don't fit. | **Elles ne me vont pas.** | Ehl nuh muh voh(n) pah. |
| They're too... | **Elles sont trop...** | Ehl soh(n) troh... |
| • big. | • **grandes.** | • grah(n)d. |
| • small. | • **petites.** | • puhteet. |
| • wide. | • **larges.** | • lahrzh. |
| • narrow. | • **étroites.** | • aytrwaht. |
| I don't know my size. | **Je ne sais pas ma pointure.** | Zhuh nuh say pah mah pwa(n)tewr. |
| I wear size ___. | **Je chausse du ___.** | Zhuh shohs dew ___. |
| I'd like the same in brown. | **Je voudrais les mêmes en brun.** | Zhuh voodreh lay mehm ah(n) bruh(n). |

## WOMEN'S CLOTHING SIZES

| Coats, dresses, suits, skirts, slacks | | | | | | | |
|---|---|---|---|---|---|---|---|
| U.S. | 4 | 6 | 8 | 10 | 12 | 14 | 16 |
| France | 36 | 38 | 40 | 42 | 44 | 46 | 48 |

| Blouses/Sweaters | | | | | | |
|---|---|---|---|---|---|---|
| U.S. | 32/6 | 34/8 | 36/10 | 38/12 | 40/14 | 42/16 |
| France | 38/2 | 40/3 | 42/4 | 44/5 | 46/6 | 48/7 |

| Shoes | | | | | | | | | | | | |
|---|---|---|---|---|---|---|---|---|---|---|---|---|
| U.S. | 4 4½ | 5 5½ | 6 6½ | 7 7½ | 8 8½ | 9 9½ | 10 |
| Europe | 35 35 | 36 36 | 37 37 | 38 38 | 39 39 | 40 40 | 41 |

## MEN'S CLOTHING SIZES

**Suits/Coats**

| U.S. | 34 | 36 | 38 | 40 | 42 | 44 | 46 | 48 |
|------|----|----|----|----|----|----|----|----|
| France | 44 | 46 | 48 | 50 | 52 | 54 | 56 | 58 |

**Sweaters**

| U.S. | XS/36 | S/38 | M/40 | L/42 | XL/44 |
|------|-------|------|------|------|-------|
| France | 42/2 | 44/3 | 46–48/4 | 50/5 | 52–54/6 |

**Shirts**

| U.S. | 14 | 14½ | 15 | 15½ | 16 | 16½ | 17 | 17½ | 18 |
|------|----|-----|----|-----|----|-----|----|-----|----|
| France | 36 | 37 | 38 | 39 | 40 | 41 | 42 | 43 | 44 |

**Slacks**

| U.S. | 30 | 31 | 32 | 33 | 34 | 35 | 36 | 37 | 38 | 39 |
|------|----|----|----|----|----|----|----|----|----|----|
| France | 38 | 39–40 | 41 | 42 | 43 | 44–45 | 46 | 47 | 48–49 | 50 |

**Socks**

| U.S. | 9½ | 10 | 10½ | 11 | 11½ | 12 | 13 |
|------|----|----|-----|----|-----|----|----|
| France | 36–37 | 38–39 | 40–41 | 42–43 | 44–45 | 46–47 | 48–49 |

**Shoes**

| U.S. | 7 | 7½ | 8 | 8½ | 9 | 9½ | 10 | 10½ | 11 |
|------|----|----|----|----|----|----|----|-----|----|
| Europe | 39 | 40 | 41 | 42 | 43 | 43 | 44 | 44 | 45 |

## THE JEWELRY STORE (LA BIJOUTERIE)

| Would you show me . . . | **Montrez-moi . . .** | moh(n)tray-mwah . . . |
|---|---|---|
| • an alarm clock? | • **un réveil?** | • uh(n) rayvehy? |
| • a bracelet? | • **un bracelet?** | • uh(n) brahslay? |
| • a brooch? | • **une broche?** | • ewn brohsh? |
| • a chain? | • **une chaînette?** | • ewn shehneht? |
| • cufflinks? | • **des boutons de manchettes?** | • day bootoh(n) duh mah(n)sheht? |
| • some earrings? | • **des boucles d'oreilles?** | • day bookl dohrehy? |
| • a gem? | • **une pierre précieuse?** | • ewn pyehr pray-syuhz? |

152

| | | |
|---|---|---|
| • a jewelry box? | • **un coffret à bijoux?** | • uh(n) kohfray ah beezhoo? |
| • a necklace? | • **un collier?** | • uh(n) kohlyay? |
| • a pin? | • **une épingle?** | • ewn aypa(n)yl? |
| • a ring? | • **une bague?** | • ewn bahg? |
| • an engagement ring? | • **une bague de fiançailles?** | • ewn bahg duh fyah(n)sahy? |
| • a wedding ring? | • **une alliance?** | • ewn ahlyah(n)s? |
| • a tie-pin? | • **une épingle à cravate?** | • ewn aypa(n)gl ah krahvaht? |
| • a watch? | • **une montre?** | • ewn moh(n)tr? |
| digital | **digitale** | deezheetahl |
| quartz | **à quartz** | a kwahrts |

| | | |
|---|---|---|
| Do you have something . . . | **Avez-vous quelque chose . . .** | Ahvay-voo kehlkuh shohz . . . |
| • gold? | • **en or?** | • ah(n) nohr? |
| solid gold | **en or massif** | ah(n) nohr mahseef |
| gold-plated | **en plaqué or** | ah(n) plahkay ohr |
| • platinum? | • **en platine?** | • ah(n) plahteen? |
| • silver? | • **en argent?** | • ah(n) nahrzhah(n)? |

| | | |
|---|---|---|
| Can you repair this? | **Pouvez-vous réparer ceci?** | Poovay-voo raypahray suhsee? |
| This is how many karats? | **C'est combien de carats?** | Say koh(m)bya(n) duh kahrah? |
| What is this made out of? | **En quoi est-ce?** | Ah(n) kwah ehs? |

| | | |
|---|---|---|
| It's . . . | **C'est . . .** | Seht . . . |
| • an amethyst. | • **une améthyste.** | • ewn ahmayteest. |
| • copper. | • **en cuivre.** | • ah(n) kweevr. |
| • coral. | • **en corail.** | • ah(n) kohrahy. |
| • crystal. | • **en cristal.** | • ah(n) kreestahl. |
| • a diamond. | • **un diamant.** | • uh(n) dyahmah(n). |
| • an emerald. | • **une émeraude.** | • ewn aymrohd. |
| • ivory. | • **en ivoire.** | • ah(n) neevwahr. |
| • jade. | • **un jade.** | • uh(n) zhahd. |
| • onyx. | • **un onyx.** | • uh(n) nohneeks. |
| • a pearl. | • **une perle.** | • ewn pehrl. |
| • a ruby. | • **un rubis.** | • uh(n) rewbee. |

153

| • a sapphire. | • un saphir. | • uh(n) sahfeer. |
| • a topaz. | • une topaze. | • ewn tohpahz. |

## THE RECORD STORE (LE MAGASIN DE DISQUES)

| Do you have any ___ | Avez-vous des ___ | Ahvay-voo day ___ |
| • records by Debussy? | • disques de Debussy? | • deesk duh Duhbew-see? |
| • cassettes? | • cassettes? | • kahseht? |
| • compact discs? | • disques compacts? | • deesk koh(m)pahkt? |

| Is there a section for. . . | Y a-t-il un rayon où l'on trouve . . . | Yahteel uh(n) rah-yoh(n) oo loh(n) troov. . . |
| • American music? | • de la musique américaine? | • duh lah mewzeek ah-mayreekehn? |
| • classical music? | • de la musique classique? | • duh lah mewzeek klahseek? |
| • folk music? | • de la musique folklorique? | • duh lah mewzeek fohklohreek? |
| • jazz? | • du jazz? | • dew ''jazz''? |
| • musical comedy? | • des comédies musicales? | • day kohmaydee mewzeekahl? |
| • music of the region? | • de la musique du pays? | • duh lah mewzeek dew payee? |
| • opera? | • de l'opéra? | • duh lohpayrah? |
| • pop music? | • de la musique pop? | • duh lah mewzeek pohp? |

## THE PHOTO SHOP (LE MAGASIN DE PHOTOS)

| Do you sell . . . | Vendez-vous . . . | Vah(n)day-voo. . . |
| • cameras? | • des appareils photos? | • day zahpahrehy fohtoh? |
| • automatic cameras? | • des appareils automatiques? | • day zahpahray ohtohmahteek? |
| • movie cameras? | • des caméras? | • day kahmayrah? |
| • filters? | • des filtres? | • day feeltr? |
| • batteries? | • des piles? | • day peel? |

- light meters?
- lens caps?
- lenses?
- telephoto lenses?
- wide-angle lenses?
- film?

I'd like a roll of . . .

- color film.
- black and white film.
- film for a 35mm camera.
- 20 exposures.
- 36 exposures.
- slide film.
- print film.
- film this size.
- film this ASA number.
- film for artificial light.
- film for natural light.

How much is it to develop a roll of film of this type?

I'd like . . .
- 2 prints of each one.
- an enlargement.

- des cellules photoélectriques?
- des capuchons d'objectif?
- des objectifs?
- des téléobjectifs?
- des grand angulaires?
- des pellicules?

Je voudrais une pellicule . . .
- en couleur.
- en noir et blanc.
- pour un appareil 35mm.
- de 20 poses.
- de 36 poses.
- pour diapositives.
- pour épreuves.
- de ce format.
- de ce chiffre ASA.
- pour lumière artificielle.
- pour lumière naturelle.

Combien coûte le développement d'une pellicule de ce genre?

Je voudrais . . .
- deux épreuves de chacune.
- un agrandissement.

- day sehlewl fohtoh-aylehktreek?
- day kahpewshoh(n) dohbzhehkteef?
- day zohbzhehkteef?
- day taylay-ohbzhehkteef?
- day grah(n)-tah(n)gewlehr?
- day pehleekewl?

Zhuh voodreh ewn pehleekewl . . .
- ah(n) kooluhr.
- ah(n) nwahr ay blah(n).
- poor uh(n) nahpahray trah(n)t sa(n) meeleemehtr.
- duh va(n) pohz.
- duh trah(n)t-see pohz.
- poor deeahpoh-zeeteev.
- poor aypruhv.
- duh suh fohrmah.
- duh suh sheefr ah ehs ah.
- poor lewmyehr ahr-teefeesyehl.
- poor lewmyehr nahtewrehl.

Koh(m)byeh(n) koot luh dayvehlohpmah(n) dewn pehleekewl duh suh zhah(n)r?

Zhuh voodreh . . .
- duh zaypruhv duh shahkewn.
- uh(n) nagrah(n)dees-mah(n).

155

| | | |
|---|---|---|
| • prints with a glossy finish. | • **des épreuves sur papier brillant.** | • day zaypruhv sewr pahpyay breeyah(n). |
| • prints with a matte finish. | • **des épreuves sur papier mat.** | • day zaypruhv sewr pahpyay maht. |
| When will they be ready? | **Quand seront-elles prêtes?** | Kah(n) suhroh(n)-tehl preht? |
| I'm having a problem with . . . | **J'ai un petit problème avec . . .** | Zheh uh(n) ptee prohblehm ahvehk . . . |
| • the flash. | • **le flash.** | • luh flahsh. |
| • the focus. | • **la mise au point.** | • lah meez oh pwa(n). |
| • the shutter. | • **l'obturateur.** | • lohbtewrahtuhr. |
| • the winding mechanism. | • **le levier d'avancement.** | • luh luhvyay dahvah(n)smah(n). |
| Do you do camera repairs? | **Réparez-vous les appareils photos?** | Raypahray-voo lay zahpahrehy fohtoh? |

## ELECTRICAL APPLIANCES

Make sure you check the voltage when buying or bringing in electrical appliances, since 220 volts AC is the rule all over the Continent. You will thus need a transformer to use U.S. equipment, as well as auxiliary adapter plugs.

| | | |
|---|---|---|
| What is the voltage? | **Quel est le voltage?** | Kehl eh luh vohltahzh? |
| I need batteries for this. | **Il me faut des piles pour ceci.** | Eel muh foh day peel poor suhsee. |
| It's broken; can you fix it? | **C'est cassé; pouvez-vous le réparer?** | Seh kahsay; poovay-voo luh raypahray? |
| I'd like . . . | **Je voudrais . . .** | Zhuh voodreh . . . |
| • a bulb. | • **une ampoule.** | • ewn ah(m)pool. |
| • a cassette recorder. | • **un magnéto-phone à cassette.** | • uh(n) mahnyay-tohfohn ah kahseht. |
| • a clock radio. | • **un radio-réveil.** | • uh(n) rahdyoh-rayvehy. |

| | | |
|---|---|---|
| • a hair dryer. | • **un sèche-cheveux.** | • uh(n) sehsh-shuhvuh. |
| • a travel iron. | • **un fer à repasser de voyage.** | • uh(n) fehr ah ruhpahsay duh vwahyahzh. |
| • a lamp. | • **une lampe.** | • ewn lah(m)p. |
| • a plug. | • **une fiche.** | • ewn feesh. |
| • a radio (portable). | • **un poste de radio (portatif).** | • uh(n) pohst duh rahdyoh (pohrtahteef). |
| • a record player. | • **un tourne-disque.** | • uh(n) toornuh-deesk. |
| • a shaver. | • **un rasoir électrique.** | • uh(n) rahzwahr aylehktreek. |
| • a tape recorder. | • **un magnéto-phone.** | • uh(n) mahnyay-tohfohn. |
| • a black and white TV. | • **un téléviseur noir et blanc.** | • uh(n) taylayveezuhr nwahr ay blah(n). |
| • a color TV. | • **un téléviseur couleur.** | • uh(n) taylayveezuhr kooluhr. |
| • a transformer. | • **un transformateur.** | • uh(n) trah(n)sfohr-mahtuhr. |
| • a VCR. | • **un magnétoscope.** | • uh(n) manyay-tohskohp. |

## BOOKS, MAGAZINES, AND PAPER GOODS

In France, bookstores (*les libraries* [lay leebrayree]) are usually limited to selling popular and scholarly books and manuals. Writing supplies are found at the stationery store (*la papeterie* [lah pahpehtree]). Your best bet for newspapers and magazines are the outdoor *kiosques* [keeohsk] or the numerous *bureaux de tabac* [bewroh duh tahbah]. For your convenience, we have included items from all of these categories in the section below.

When in Paris, you may enjoy a visit to Shakespeare & Co. (the name appropriated from the famous bookshop owned and operated by Sylvia Beach, a friend of Hemingway and a patron of James Joyce, fifty-plus years ago), an American bookstore on Rue de la Bûcherie; it's run by an expatriate on the Paris scene since 1946.

| I'm looking for... | Je cherche... | Zhuh shehrsh... |
|---|---|---|
| • a bookstore. | • une librairie. | • ewn leebrehree. |
| • a stationer. | • une papeterie. | • ewn pahpehtree. |
| • a newsstand. | • un kiosque à journaux. | • uh(n) kyohsk ah zhoornoh. |

| Where are... | Où sont... | Oo soh(n)... |
|---|---|---|
| • books in English? | • les livres en anglais? | • lay leevr ah(n) nah(n)gleh? |
| • magazines in English? | • les magazines en anglais? | • lay mahgahzeen ah(n) nah(n)gleh? |
| • newspapers in English? | • les journaux en anglais? | • lay zhoornoh ah(n) nah(n)gleh? |

| Here is... | Voici... | Vwahsee... |
|---|---|---|
| • the title. | • le titre. | • luh teetr. |
| • the author. | • l'auteur. | • lohtuhr. |

| Do you have it in paperback? | L'avez-vous en livre de poche? | Lahvay-voo ah(n) leevr duh pohsh? |
|---|---|---|

| I'd like... | Je voudrais... | Zhuh voodreh... |
|---|---|---|
| • a ballpoint pen. | • un stylo à billes. or un bic | • uh(n) steeloh ah beey. uh(n) beek |
| • a book on ___. | • un livre sur ___. | • uh(n) leevr sewr ___ |
| • a calendar. | • un calendrier. | • uh(n) kahlah(n)-dreeay. |
| • crayons. | • des crayons de couleur. | • day krayoh(n) duh kooluhr. |
| • a dictionary English-French | • un dictionnaire anglais-français | • uh(n) deeksyohnehr ah(n)gleh-frah(n)seh |
| • envelopes. | • des enveloppes. | • day zah(n)vuhlohp. |
| • an eraser. | • une gomme. | • ewn gohm. |
| • glue. | • de la colle. | • duh lah kohl. |
| • a travel guide. | • un guide de voyage. | • uh(n) gheed duh vwahyahzh. |
| • ink. | • de l'encre. | • duh lah(n)kr. |
| • labels. | • des étiquettes. | • day zayteekeht. |
| • a map. | • une carte. | • ewn kahrt. |
| city map | un plan de ville | uh(n) plah(n) duh veel |
| road map | une carte routière | ewn kahrt rootyehr |

| | | |
|---|---|---|
| • a marker. | • **un crayon feutre.** | • uh(n) krayoh(n) fuhtr. |
| • a notebook. | • **un cahier.** | • uh(n) kahyay. |
| • paper. | • **du papier.** | • dew pahpyay. |
| • paperclips. | • **des trombones.** | • day troh(m)bohn. |
| • a pen. | • **une plume.** | • ewn plewm. |
| • a pencil. | • **un crayon.** | • uh(n) krayoh(n). |
| • a pencil sharpener. | • **un taille-crayon.** | • uh(n) tahy-krayoh(n). |
| • a pocket calculator. | • **une calculatrice de poche.** | • ewn kahlkewlahtrees duh pohsh. |
| • a ruler. | • **une règle.** | • ewn rehgl. |
| • scotch tape. | • **du scotch.** | • dew skohtsh. |
| • a stapler. | • **une agrafeuse.** | • ewn ahgrahfuhz. |
| • staples. | • **des agrafes.** | • day zahgrahf. |
| • stationery. | • **du papier à lettres.** | • dew pahpyay ah lehtr. |
| • thumbtacks. | • **des punaises.** | • day pewnehz. |
| • a typewriter. | • **une machine à écrire.** | • ewn mahsheen ah aykreer. |
| • a typewriter ribbon. | • **un ruban de machine à écrire.** | • uh(n) rewbah(n) duh mahsheen ah ay-kreer. |
| • typing paper. | • **du papier à machine.** | • dew pahpyay ah mahsheen. |
| • a writing pad. | • **un bloc.** | • uh(n) blohk. |

## THE TOBACCO SHOP (LE TABAC)

In France, the sale of tobacco products is strictly controlled by—and is a monopoly of—the state. The red cone in cafés and bars indicates a state-approved tobacco outlet. (Incidentally, the final *c* in tabac is not pronounced, an exception to the *careful* rule on page 7.)

| | | |
|---|---|---|
| Give me a pack of cigarettes, please. | **Donnez-mois un paquet de cigarettes, s'il vous plaît.** | Dohnay mwah uh(n) pahkay duh seegahreht, seel voo play. |

| Do you have . . . | Avez-vous . . . | Ahvay-voo . . . |
|---|---|---|
| • American cigarettes? | • des cigarettes américaines? | • day seegahreht ah-mayreekehn? |
| • chewing gum? | • du chewing-gum? | • dew shooing-guhm? |
| • chocolate? | • du chocolat? | • dew shohkohlah? |
| • cigarette cases? | • des étuis à cigarettes? | • day zaytwee ah seegahreht? |
| • filtered cigarettes? | • des cigarettes avec filtre? | • day seegahreht ahvehk feeltr? |
| • French cigarettes? | • des cigarettes françaises? | • day seegahreht frah(n)sehz? |
| • king-size cigarettes? | • des cigarettes long format? | • day seegahreht loh(n) fohrmah? |
| • lighters? | • des briquets? | • day breekay? |
| • lighter fluid? | • de l'essence à briquet? | • duh lehsah(n)s ah breekay? |
| • matches? | • des allumettes? | • day zahlewmeht? |
| • mild cigarettes? | • des cigarettes douces? | • day seegahreht doos? |
| • pipe tobacco? | • du tabac à pipe? | • dew tahbah ah peep? |
| • strong cigarettes? | • des cigarettes fortes? | • day seegahreht fohrt? |
| • unfiltered cigarettes? | • des cigarettes sans filtre? | • day seegahreht sah(n) feeltr? |

## TOILETRIES

Perfume and cosmetics are available at many major department stores. You can also find them at a *parfumerie* [pahrfewmree]. Other toiletries may be found at a *droguerie* [drohgree] or at the newer *drugstores*, which resemble their U.S. counterparts more closely.

| Do you have . . . | Avez-vous . . . | Ahvay-voo . . . |
|---|---|---|
| • after-shave lotion? | • de la lotion après-rasage? | • duh lah lohsyoh(n) ahpreh-rahzahzh? |
| • bobby pins? | • des épingles à cheveux? | • day zaypa(n)gl ah shuhvuh? |

160

| | | |
|---|---|---|
| • a brush? | • **une brosse?** | • ewn brohs? |
| • bubble bath? | • **du bain de mousse?** | • dew ba(n) duh moos? |
| • cleansing cream? | • **une crème démaquillante?** | • ewn krehm daymahkeeyah(n)t? |
| • a comb? | • **un peigne?** | • uh(n) pehnyuh? |
| • a deodorant? | • **un déodorant?** | • uh(n) day-ohdohrah(n)? |
| • curlers? | • **des bigoudis?** | • day beegoodee? |
| • emery boards? | • **des limes à ongles?** | • day leem ah oh(n)gl? |
| • eye liner? | • **un eye liner?** | • uh(n) nahy lahynehr? |
| • an eyebrow pencil? | • **un crayon pour les yeux?** | • uh(n) krayoh(n) poor lay zyuh? |
| • eye shadow? | • **du fard à paupières?** | • dew fahr ah poh-pyehr? |
| • face powder? | • **de la poudre?** | • duh lah poodr? |
| • hairspray? | • **de la laque?** | • duh lah lahk? |
| • hand cream? | • **de la crème pour les mains?** | • duh lah krehm poor lay ma(n)? |
| • lipstick? | • **du rouge à lèvres?** | • dew roozh ah lehvr? |
| • make-up? | • **du maquillage?** | • dew mahkeeyahzh? |
| • mascara? | • **du cosmétique pour les cils?** | • dew kohzmayteek poor lay seel? |
| • a mirror? | • **un miroir?** | • uh(n) meerwahr? |
| • moisturizing cream? | • **de la crème hydratante?** | • duh lah krehm ee-drahtah(n)t? |
| • nail clippers? | • **un coupe-ongles?** | • uh(n) koop-oh(n)gl? |
| • nail polish? | • **du vernis à ongles?** | • dew vehrnee ah oh(n)gl? |
| • nail polish remover? | • **du dissolvant?** | • dew deesohlvah(n)? |
| • perfume? | • **du parfum?** | • dew pahrfuh(m)? |
| • prophylactics? | • **des prophylactiques?** | • day proh-feelahkteek? |
| • a razor? | • **un rasoir?** | • uh(n) razwahr? |
| • razor blades? | • **des lames de rasoir?** | • day lahm duh rahzwahr? |
| • rouge? | • **du fard?** | • dew fahr? |

| | | |
|---|---|---|
| • safety pins? | • **des épingles de sûreté?** | • day zaypa(n)gl duh sewrtay? |
| • sanitary napkins? | • **des serviettes hygiéniques?** | • day sehrvyeht eezhyayneek? |
| • scissors? | • **des ciseaux?** | • day seezoh? |
| • setting lotion? | • **du fixatif?** | • dew feeksahteef? |
| • shaving cream? | • **de la crème à raser?** | • duh lah krehm ah rahzay? |
| • soap? | • **du savon?** | • dew sahvoh(n)? |
| • suntan lotion? | • **du crème solaire?** | • dew krehm sohlehr? |
| • suntan oil? | • **de l'huile solaire?** | • duh lweel sohlehr? |
| • talcum powder? | • **du talc?** | • dew tahlk? |
| • tampons? | • **des tampons?** | • day tah(m)poh(n)? |
| • tissues? | • **des mouchoirs en papier?** | • day mooshwahr ah(n) pahpyay? |
| • toilet paper? | • **du papier hygiénique?** | • dew pahpyay eezhyayneek? |
| • toilet water? | • **de l'eau de toilette?** | • duh loh duh twahleht? |
| • a toothbrush? | • **une brosse à dents?** | • ewn brohs ah dah(n)? |
| • toothpaste? | • **de la pâte dentifrice?** | • duh lah paht dah(n)-teefrees? |
| • towels? | • **des serviettes?** | • day sehrvyeht? |
| • tweezers? | • **des pinces à épiler?** | • day pa(n)s ah aypeelay? |

## FOOD SHOPPING

The most famous food store of all is Fauchon, 26 Place de la Madeleine. E. Dehillerin, 18–20 Rue Coquillière, on the edge of Les Halles, is the world's number-one source for professional kitchenware, a veritable museum of utensils. Everything you always wanted for cooking and didn't know where to find is here, crammed into this traditional corner store.

If you want to pick up some provisions at a grocery store or at the small specialty shops, remember to bring along a large sturdy shopping bag to carry everything, as American-style bags are not always provided. Be prepared to pack the bag yourself after paying.

## Measures and Containers

| I'd like . . . | Je voudrais . . . | Zhuh voodreh . . . |
|---|---|---|
| • a kilo of potatoes. | • un kilo de pommes de terre. | • uh(n) keeloh duh pohm duh tehr. |
| • a can of peas. | • une boîte de petit pois. | • ewn bwaht duh puh-tee pwah. |
| • a jar of coffee. | • un bocal de café. | • uh(n) bohkahl duh kahfay. |
| • a dozen eggs. | • une douzaine d'oeufs. | • ewn doozehn duh. |
| • five slices of cheese. | • cinq tranches de fromage. | • sa(n) trah(n)sh duh frohmahzh. |
| • a piece of cheese. | • un morceau de fromage. | • uh(n) mohrsoh duh frohmahzh. |
| • a liter of mineral water. | • un litre d'eau minérale. | • uh(n) leetr doh meenayrahl. |
| • a box of chocolates. | • une boîte de chocolats. | • ewn bwaht duh shohkohlah. |
| • a bottle of milk. of juice. | • une bouteille de lait. de jus. | • ewn bootehy duh leh. duh zhew. |
| • 200 grams of flour. | • deux cents grammes de farine. | • duh sah(n) grahm duh fahreen. |

## Additional Items

| • a bottle of soda | • une bouteille de soda | • ewn bootehy duh sohdah |
| • some butter | • du beurre | • dew buhr |

163

| | | |
|---|---|---|
| • some cookies | • **des biscuits** | • day beeskwee |
| • cold cuts | • **de la charcuterie** | • duh lah shahrkewtree |
| | | |
| • ham | • **du jambon** | • dew zhah(m)boh(n) |
| • ice cream | • **de la glace** | • duh lah glahs |
| • a lemon | • **un citron** | • uh(n) seetroh(n) |
| • mustard | • **de la moutarde** | • duh lah mootahrd |
| • oranges | • **des oranges** | • day zohrah(n)zh |
| • pears | • **des poires** | • day pwahr |
| • pepper | • **du poivre** | • dew pwahvr |
| • potato chips | • **des chips** | • day sheep |
| • salt | • **du sel** | • dew sehl |
| • sausage | • **des saucisses** | • day sohsees |
| • sugar | • **du sucre** | • dew sewkr |
| • tea | • **du thé** | • dew tay |
| • yoghurt | • **du yaourt** | • dew yah-oort |

## Bread

| | | |
|---|---|---|
| Give me . . . | **Donnez-moi . . .** | Dohnay-mwah . . . |
| a croissant. | **un croissant.** | uh(n) krwahsah(n). |
| a brioche. | **une brioche.** | ewn breeyohsh. |
| a chocolate roll. | **un pain au chocolat.** | uh(n) pa(n) oh shohkohlah. |
| a roll. | **un petit pain.** | uh(n) puhtee pa(n). |
| (types of French bread) | **une ficelle.** **une flûte.** **une baguette.** **un pain.** | ewn feesehl. ewn flewt. ewn bahgeht. uh(n) pa(n). |
| • a white bread. | • **un pain de mie.** | • uh(n) pa(n) duh mee. |
| • a rye bread. | • **un pain de seigle.** | • uh(n) pa(n) duh sehgl. |
| • six rolls. | • **six petits pains.** | • see puhtee pa(n). |
| • a whole wheat bread. | • **un pain complet.** | • uh(n) pa(n) koh(m)-play. |

One inch = 2.54 centimeters.
One centimeter = .39 inch.

|        | in.   | feet  | yards |
|--------|-------|-------|-------|
| 1 mm.  | 0.039 | 0.003 | 0.001 |
| 1 cm.  | 0.39  | 0.03  | 0.01  |
| 1 dm.  | 3.94  | 0.32  | 0.10  |
| 1 m.   | 39.40 | 3.28  | 1.09  |

.39 (# of centimeters) = (# of inches)
2.54 (# of inches) = (# of centimeters)

|        | mm.   | cm.   | m.    |
|--------|-------|-------|-------|
| 1 in.  | 25.4  | 2.54  | 0.025 |
| 1 ft.  | 304.8 | 30.48 | 0.304 |
| 1 yd.  | 914.4 | 91.44 | 0.914 |

(32 meters = 35 yards)

## WEIGHTS AND MEASURES

**Metric Weight**     **U.S.**
1 gram (g)            0.035 ounce
28.35 grams           1 ounce
100 grams             3.5 ounces
454 grams             1 pound
1 kilogram (kilo)     2.2 pounds

**Liquids**           **U.S.**
1 liter (l)           4.226 cups
1 liter               2.113 pints
1 liter               1.056 quarts
3.785 liters          1 gallon

**Dry Measures**      **U.S.**
1 liter               0.908 quart
1 decaliter           1.135 pecks
1 hectoliter          2.837 bushels

165

# 13/ACTIVITIES AND ENTERTAINMENT
## SPORTS

Sports are a way of life in France—in fact, a *passionate* way of life, from both the participant's and the spectator's sides.

For the latter experience, one need only be on hand for the finish of the three-week Tour de France bicycle race as it reaches the Champs Élysées in late August. All Paris turns itself inside out for the occasion, a kind of Bastille Day without the parades and dancing in the streets.

Just a few points lower on the enthusiasm scale for spectators are days at the Paris racetracks with betting on the horses. One could easily say no visit to Paris is complete without an afternoon at the races, preferably at Longchamps, considered the world's most beautiful racetrack, in a splendid Seine-side setting in the Bois de Boulogne. Also in the Bois is Auteuil, the city's steeplechase track.

Other spectator sports in the Paris area are polo at Pelouse de Bagatelle in the Bois de Boulogne, Sundays in summer, and tennis (national and international tournaments) at Stade Roland-Garros. Farther afield are auto races (24 Hours of Le Mans). Tickets are available through the Automobile Club de France, 8 Place de la Concorde.

Participatory sports in the Paris area include tennis. Information on courts is available from La Ligue de Tennis de Paris, 74 Rue de Rome 75008, tel. 45.22.22.08, and FFT (Fédération Française de Tennis), at Roland Garros, Avenue Gordon Bennet, 75016, tel. 47.43.96.81. At the latter, queries in English are welcome.

For horseback riding call the Fédération Equestre Française, 164 Rue du Faubourg St-Honoré, 75008, tel. 42.25.11.22. There are also seasonal sports in different parts of France, such as fishing, hunting, and skiing. For all these, the French Government Tourist Office has detailed information.

## DIALOGUE: LA NATATION (SWIMMING)

| Jean-Pierre: | **Qu'est-ce qu'il fait chaud!** | Kehs keel fay shoh! |
|---|---|---|
| Mary Ann: | **Oui! Si on allait se baigner?** | Wee! See oh(n) nahlay suh behnyay? |
| Jean-Pierre: | **Bonne idée! Qu'est-ce que tu préfères: la mer ou la piscine?** | Bohn eeday! Kehskuh tew prayfehr: lah mehr oo lah peeseen? |
| Mary Ann: | **J'adore la mer! Mais . . . y a-t-il des courants dange-reux?** | Zhahdohr lah mehr! Meh . . . yahteel day koo-rah(n) dah(n)zhuhruh? |
| Jean-Pierre: | **Mais, non! La mer est plutôt calme par ici.** | May noh(n)! Lah mehr ay plewtoh kahlm pahr eesee. |
| Mary Ann: | **Tant mieux! D'ac-cord, rendez-vous sur la plage dans cinq minutes!** | Tah(n) myuh. Dakohr, rah(n)day-voo sewr lah plahzh dah(n) sa(n) meenewt! |
| Jean-Pierre: | **Entendu! Et n'ou-blie pas ton huile de bronzage!** | Ah(n)tah(n)dew! Ay nooblee pah toh(n) nweel duh broh(n)zahzh! |

- - - - - - - - - - - - - - - - - - - - - - - - - - - - - -

| Jean-Pierre: | It's so hot out! |
|---|---|
| Mary Ann: | Yes. What do you say we go swimming? |
| Jean-Pierre: | Good idea! Which do you prefer: the beach or the pool? |
| Mary Ann: | I love the sea! But . . . are there any danger-ous currents? |
| Jean-Pierre: | No! The sea is pretty calm around here. |
| Mary Ann: | So much the better! Okay, see you on the beach in five minutes. |
| Jean-Pierre: | Right! And don't forget your suntan lotion! |

## PARTICIPATORY SPORTS

### Swimming

#### The Beach

| English | French | Pronunciation |
|---|---|---|
| Where are the best beaches? | Où se trouvent les meilleures plages? | Oo suh troov lay meh-yuhr plahzh? |
| How do we get there? | Comment y va-t-on? | Kohmah(n) ee vahtoh(n)? |
| Is it a private or public beach? | Est-ce une plage privée ou publique? | Ehs ewn plahzh pree-vay oo pewbleek? |
| Where is the life guard? | Où est le maître nageur? | Oo eh luh mehtr nahzhuhr? |
| Ouch! The sand is hot. But the water is cool. | Aïe! Le sable est chaud. Mais l'eau est fraîche. | Ahy! Luh sahbl ay shoh. May loh ay frehsh. |
| Are there dangerous currents? | Y a-t-il des courants dangereux? | Yahteel day koorah(n) dah(n)zhuhruh? |
| No, there are only small waves. | Non, il n'y a que des petites vagues. | Nohn, eel neeyah kuh day puhteet vahg. |
| I'd like to rent . . . | Je voudrais louer. . . | Zhuh voodreh looway. . . |
| • a beach chair. | • une chaise longue. | • ewn shehz loh(n)g. |
| • a beach towel. | • une serviette de plage. | • ew sehrvyeht duh plahzh. |
| • a cabana. | • une cabine. | • ewn kahbeen. |
| • a rowboat. | • une barque à rames. | • ewn bahrk ah rahm. |
| • a sailboard. | • une planche à voile. | • ewn plah(n)sh ah vwahl. |
| • a sailboat. | • un voilier. | • uh(n) vwahlyay. |

| | | |
|---|---|---|
| • skin-diving equipment. | • **un équipement de plongée sous-marine.** | • uh(n) naykeep-mah(n) duh ploh(n)zhay soo-mahreen. |
| • umbrella. | • **un parasol.** | • uh(n) pahrahsohl. |
| • surfboard. | • **une planche de surf.** | • ewn plah(n)sh duh sewrf. |
| • waterskis. | • **des skis nautiques.** | • day skee nohteek. |
| Don't forget to bring . . . | **N'oubliez pas d'apporter. . .** | Noobleeyay pah dahportay . . . |
| • sunglasses. | • **des lunettes de soleil.** | • day lewneht duh soh-lehy. |
| • suntan lotion. | • **de la crème solaire.** | • duh lah krehm sohlehr. |

## Poolside

| | | |
|---|---|---|
| Where is the pool? | **Où se trouve la piscine?** | Oo suh troov lah pee-seen? |
| Is the pool . . . | **Est-ce une piscine . . .** | Ehs ewn peeseen . . . |
| • outdoors? | • **en plein air?** | • ah(n) plehn ehr? |
| • indoors? | • **couverte?** | • koovehrt? |
| • heated? | • **chauffée?** | • shohfay? |
| When does the pool open/close? | **A quelle heure ouvre/ferme la piscine?** | Ah kehl uhr oovr/fehrm lah peeseen? |

## Other Active Sports

| | | |
|---|---|---|
| I like (to play) . . . | **Je pratique . . .** | Zhuh prahteek . . . |
| • basketball. | • **le basket.** | • luh bahskeht. |
| • boxing. | • **la boxe.** | • lah bohks. |
| • cycling. | • **le cyclisme.** | • luh seekleezm. |
| • deep-sea diving. | • **la plongée sous-marine.** | • lah ploh(n)zhay soo-mahreen. |
| • rugby. | • **le rugby.** | • luh rewgbee. |
| • running. | • **le footing.** | • luh footeeng. |
| • skiing (downhill). | • **le ski alpin.** | • luh skee ahlpa(n). |

169

| | | |
|---|---|---|
| • skiing (cross-country). | • **le ski de fond.** | • luh skee duh foh(n). |
| • swimming. | • **la natation.** | • lah nahtahsyoh(n). |
| • tennis. | • **le tennis.** | • luh tehnees. |
| • volleyball. | • **le volley.** | • luh vohlay. |

Note: Two popular American sports that are not played much in France, Belgium, or Switzerland are baseball and football. The French word *le football* [luh footbohl] always refers to soccer. Say *le football américain* [ahmehreeka(n)] when referring to U.S.-style football. Baseball is, not surprisingly, *le baseball* (lah baysbohl).

| | | |
|---|---|---|
| Where can I find . . . | **Où y a-t-il . . .** | Oo yahteel . . . |
| • a tennis court? | • **un court de tennis?** | • uh(n) koor duh tehnees? |
| • a pool? | • **une piscine?** | • ewn peeseen? |
| • a racket? | • **une raquette?** | • ewn rahkeht? |
| • a golf course? | • **un terrain de golf?** | • uh(n) tehra(n) duh gohlf? |
| • a skating rink? | • **une patinoire?** | • ewn pahteenwahr? |
| How much is it . . . | **Quel est le tarif . . .** | Kehl eh luh tahreef . . . |
| • per hour? | • **à l'heure?** | • ah luhr? |
| • per day? | • **à la journée?** | • ah lah zhoornay? |
| Would you like to play. . . | **Voulez-vous jouer au . . .** | Voolay-voo zhooay oh . . . |
| • tennis? | • **tennis?** | • tehnees? |
| • golf? | • **golf?** | • gohlf? |
| We need to buy some balls. | **Il faut qu'on achète des balles.** | Eel foh koh(n) nah-sheht day bahl. |
| You play very well. | **Vous jouez très bien.** | Voo zhooay treh byeh(n). |
| He plays fairly well. | **Il joue assez bien.** | Eel zhoo ahsay byeh(n) |
| I don't play well. | **Je ne joue pas bien.** | Zhuh nuh zhoo pah byeh(n). |

| What's the score? | **Quel est le score?** | Kehl eh luh skohr? |
| Who's winning? | **Qui gagne?** | Kee gahnyuh? |

## Skiing

| Would you like to go skiing? | **Voulez-vous faire du ski?** | Voolay-voo fehr dew skee? |
| What is the best ski area? | **Quelle est la meilleure station de ski?** | Kehl eh lah mehyuhr stahsyoh(n) duh skee? |
| I like Val d'Isere | **J'aime bien Val d'Isere.** | Zhehm byeh(n) Vahl Deezehr. |
| Are there slopes for... | **Y a-t-il des pistes pour...** | Yahteel day peest poor... |
| • beginners? | • **débutants?** | • daybewtah(n)? |
| • intermediates? | • **skieurs moyens?** | • skeeuhr mwahya(n)? |
| • experts? | • **experts?** | • ehkspehr? |
| I'm going to take a lesson. | **Je vais prendre une leçon.** | Zhuh vay prah(n)dr ewn luhsoh(n). |
| What are the conditions like now? | **Quelles sont les conditions en ce moment?** | Kehl soh(n) lay koh(n)-deesyoh(n) ah(n) suh mohmah(n)? |
| There's lots of snow. | **Il y a beaucoup de neige.** | Eel yah bohkoo duh nehzh. |
| Where are the lifts? | **Où sont les téléskis?** | Oo soh(n) lay taylay-skee? |
| How much is the lift? | **Combien coûte le trajet?** | Koh(m)byeh(n) koot luh trahzheh? |
| I'd like to rent... | **Je voudrais louer...** | Zhuh voodreh looay... |
| • ski equipment | • **un équipement de ski.** | • uh(n) naykeep-mah(n) duh skee. |
| • skis. | • **des skis.** | • day skee. |
| • ski boots. | • **des chaussures de ski.** | • day shohsewr duh skee. |
| • poles. | • **des bâtons.** | • day bahtoh(n) |

171

## CAMPING

Camping is a highly popular pastime in France and cuts across the divisions of class and geography. The well-organized system reflects the French passion for classification and evaluation. Campsites receive from one to four stars according to the quality of the facilities. Reservations in summer are a must. *Le camping sauvage* [luh kah(m)peeng sohvahzh], i.e., unofficial camping "in the wild," is common, but you must ask the landowner first.

| I'm looking for a campsite with . . . | **Je cherche un camping avec . . .** | Zhuh shehrsh uh(n) kah(m)peeng ahvehk . . . |
|---|---|---|
| • drinking water. | • **de l'eau potable.** | • duh loh pohtahbl. |
| • toilets. | • **des toilettes.** | • day twahleht. |
| • electricity. | • **de l'électricité.** | • duh lay-lehktreeseetay. |
| • a grocery. | • **une épicerie.** | • ewn aypeesree. |
| • a pool. | • **une piscine.** | • ewn peeseen. |
| • showers. | • **des douches.** | • day doosh. |
| • butane gas. | • **du butane.** | • dew bewtahn. |
| What does it cost for one night? | **Quel est le tarif pour une nuit?** | Kehl eh luh tahreef poor ewn nwee? |
| Can we camp here? | **Pouvons-nous camper ici?** | Poovoh(n)-noo kah(m)-pay eesee? |
| Is there room for a trailer? | **Y a-t-il de la place pour une cara-vane?** | Yahteel duh lah plahs poor ewn kahrahvahn? |

## SPECTATOR SPORTS

| Let's go to the sports stadium! | **Allons au stade!** | Ahloh(n) zoh stahd! |
|---|---|---|
| I'd like to see . . . | **J'aimerais voir. . .** | Zhehmreh vwahr. . . |
| • a tennis match. | • **un match de tennis.** | • uh(n) mahtsh duh tehnees. |
| • horse racing. | • **une course de chevaux.** | • ewn koors duh shuhvoh. |

172

| • a soccer match. | • **un match de football.** | • uh(n) mahtsh duh footbohl. |
| • a boxing match. | • **un match de boxe.** | • uh(n) mahtsh duh bohks. |
| How much do tickets cost? | **Combien coûtent les billets?** | Koh(m)byeh(n) koot lay beeyay? |
| When does the match begin? | **A quelle heure commence le match?** | Ah kehl uhr kohmah(n)s luh mahtsh? |
| Who's playing? | **Qui joue?** | Kee zhoo? |
| Who won? | **Qui a gagné?** | Kee ah gah(n)yay? |
| What are the teams? | **Quelles sont les équipes?** | Kehl soh(n) lay zay-keep? |

## CULTURAL DIVERSIONS
### Movies

Parisians adore movies, and not just great art films but real junk flicks as well. Foreign films play in different versions in different theaters, either dubbed or in the original language with French subtitles. The latter is indicated by the letters *v.o. (version originale* [vehrsyoh(n) ohreezheenahl]). Cost: over $5. Prices are sharply reduced on Monday afternoons. Tip the usher who shows you to your seat (even in an empty house) two francs.

The easiest way to find out what's playing at Paris theaters is to pick up one of the weekly entertainment guides such as *Pariscope*. Here you will find complete listings and times for all movie and legitimate theaters in Paris, along with brief synopses of prominent recent films.

| Let's go to the movies! | **Allons au cinéma!** | Ahloh(n) zoh seenay-mah! |
| What's playing? | **Qu'est-ce qu'on joue?** | Kehs koh(n) zhoo? |
| What kind of film is it? | **Quel genre de film est-ce?** | Kehl zhah(n)r duh feelm ehs? |

173

| Is it in French or English? | **Est-ce en français ou en anglais?** | Ehs ah(n) frah(n)seh oo ah(n) nah(n)gleh? |
| Is it dubbed? | **Est-ce doublé?** | Ehs dooblay? |
| I prefer to see . . . | **Je préfère voir. . .** | Zhuh prehfehr vwahr. . . |
| • the v.o. (original version) with subtitles. | • **la version originale avec soustitres.** | • lah vehrsyoh(n) ohreezheenahl ahvehk sooteetr. |
| • a comedy. | • **une comédie.** | • ewn kohmaydee. |
| • science fiction. | • **un film de science-fiction.** | • uh(n) feelm duh seeah(n)s feek-syoh(n). |
| • a musical comedy. | • **une comédie musicale.** | • ewn kohmaydee mu-zeekahl. |
| • a drama. | • **un drame.** | • uh(n) drahm. |
| • a political film. | • **un film politique.** | • uh(n) feelm poh-leeteek. |
| • a war film. | • **un film de guerre.** | • uh(n) feelm duh ghehr. |
| • a love story. | • **une histoire d'amour.** | • ewn eestwahr dah-moor. |
| • a western. | • **un western.** | • uh(n) wehstehrn. |
| When does the show start? | **A quelle heure commence le spectacle?** | Ah kehl uhr kohmah(n)s luh spehktahkl? |
| How much are the tickets? | **Combine coûtent les places?** | Koh(m)bya(n) koot lay plahs? |
| What theater is showing the new film by ___ with ___? | **Dans quel cinéma passe le nouveau film de ___ avec ___?** | Dah(n) kehl seenay-mah pahs luh noovoh feelm duh ___ ahvehk ___? |

## Theater, Opera, Concert Hall, Ballet

For those who speak or understand French, there is an incredible variety of theater available in Paris, with important efforts in major cities such as Lyon, Strasbourg, Bordeaux, and Marseille. For summer theater at its best, check out the July Festival de théâtre d'Avignon, in the south of France. For variety, innovation, and quality of performance, it is one of the best theater festivals in the world. In addition to the established theatrical groups, such as *La Comédie française,* look for appearances by Third World troupes based in France and by the wildly innovative experimental groups. The daily press in Paris lists schedules and programs.

You should be aware that theaters, like so many establishments in France, are closed in August. During the rest of the year, you will find a nonstop parade of the world's greatest orchestras, soloists, dancers, and opera companies. Reservations are recommended.

| | | |
|---|---|---|
| What's on at the theaters? | **Qu'est-ce qu'on joue au théâtre?** | Kehs koh(n) zhoo oh tayahtr? |
| What kind of play is it? | **Quel genre de pièce est-ce?** | Kehl zhah(n)r duh pyehs ehs? |
| It's an avant-garde play. | **C'est une pièce avant-garde.** | Seh tewn pyehs ahvah(n)-gahrd. |
| Who wrote it? | **Qui l'a écrite?** | Kee lah aykreet? |
| Are there tickets for tonight? | **Y a-t-il des places pour ce soir?** | Yahteel day plahs poor suh swahr? |
| How much are the least expensive seats? | **Combien coûtent les places les moins chères?** | Koh(m)bya(n) koot lay plahs lay mwa(n) shehr? |
| I'd like . . . | **Je voudrais . . .** | Zhuh voodreh . . . |
| • an orchestra seat. | • **une place à l'orchestre.** | • ewn plahs ah lohrkehstr. |
| • a balcony seat. | • **une place au balcon.** | • ewn plahs oh bahlkoh(n). |
| • two tickets for the Saturday matinee. | • **deux billets pour samedi en matinée.** | • duh beeyay poor sahmdee ah(n) mahteenay. |
| • two seats in the balcony not too far back. | • **deux places au balcon pas trop loin.** | • duh plahs oh bahlkoh(n) pah troh lwa(n). |

175

ACTIVITIES

| A program, please. | **Un programme, s'il vous plaît.** | Uh(n) prohgrahm, seel voo pleh. |
|---|---|---|
| I'd like to see . . . | **J'aimerais voir. . .** | Zhehmreh vwahr. . . |
| • a concert. | • **un concert.** | • uh(n) koh(n)sehr. |
| • a classical music concert. | • **un concert de musique classique.** | • uh(n) koh(n)sehr duh muzeek klahseek. |
| • a jazz concert. | • **un concert de jazz.** | • uh(n) koh(n)sehr duh dzhahz. |
| • an opera. | • **un opéra.** | • uh(n) nohpayrah. |
| • a ballet. | • **un ballet.** | • uh(n) bahlay. |
| What's playing tonight at the opera? | **Qu'est-ce qu'on joue ce soir à l'opéra?** | Kehs koh(n) zhoo suh swahr ah lohpayrah? |
| Who's . . . | **Qui . . .** | Kee . . . |
| • playing? | • **joue?** | • zhoo? |
| • singing? | • **chante?** | • shah(n)t? |
| • dancing? | • **danse?** | • dah(n)s? |
| • the conductor? | • **est le chef d'orchestre?** | • eh luh shehf dohrkehstr? |
| Do we need a reservation? | **Faut-il réserver?** | Fohteel rayzehrvay? |

## CLUBS, DISCOS, AND CABARET

Renowned for its exciting night life, Paris offers everything from sophisticated political satire to bawdy extravaganzas. Jazz is especially popular, with both traditional and contemporary fare widely appreciated. Paris is a late town; many shows do not begin until ten P.M.

| I'd like to go to . . . | **Je voudrais aller dans . . .** | Zhuh voodreh ahlay dah(n) . . . |
|---|---|---|
| • a disco. | • **une disco-thèque.** | • zewn deeskohtehk. |
| • a nightclub. | • **une boîte de nuit.** | • zewn bwaht duh nwee. |
| • a jazz club. | • **un club de jazz.** | • zuh(n) kluhb duh dzhahz. |

176

| I'd like to go dancing. | **Je voudrais aller danser.** | Zhuh voodray zahlay dah(n)say. |
| There's a small cover charge. | **Il y a un prix d'entrée minime.** | Eel yah uh(n) pree dah(n)tray meeneem. |
| Would you like to dance? | **Voulez-vous danser?** | Voolay-voo dah(n)say? |
| Is there a floor show? | **Y a-t-il un spectacle de cabaret?** | Yahteel uhn spehktahkl duh kahbahray? |

## TRAVELING WITH CHILDREN IN PARIS

Children can have a ball in Paris, where they will find amusement parks, aquariums, marionette shows, museums, playgrounds, and zoos.

Babysitting services are available from the following organizations, which will send a student at an hourly rate. If sitting goes beyond midnight (last Metro service), there's an extra charge for taxi fare home for the sitter.

- American College in Paris, 31 Avenue Bosquet, 75007. Tel. 45.55.91.73.
- Baby Sitting, 18 Rue Tronchet, 75008. Tel. 46.37.51.24.
- Gard'Enfants, 3 Rue de Duras, 75008. Tel. 47.42.30.99.
- Kid Service, 17 Rue Molière, 75001. Tel. 42.96.04.18.
- Medical Students Association, 105 Blvd. de l'Hôpital, 75013. Tel 45.86.19.44 or 45.86.19.42.

A favorite, conveniently located kiddy hangout is Jardin du Luxembourg, which has a pond to sail boats, a playground, and marionette and puppet shows. Playgrounds and ponds are also in the Tuileries Gardens and the Champ de Mars, at the foot of the Eiffel Tower. Other puppet shows are in the Champ de Mars and in Jardin des Champs-Élysées, Avenue Gabriel.

There's a Musée des Enfants at 11 Avenue President Wilson, open from 10 A.M. to 5:45 P.M. except Mondays; an aquarium in the Trocadero Gardens; and a zoo in the Jardin des Plantes, 3

Quai St-Bernard, on the Left Bank of the Seine, not far from Notre Dame.

A far more famous and extensive zoo (Parc Zoologique de Paris) is in the Vincennes Forest at the eastern edge of the city. There are playgrounds, another zoo, and an amusement park in the Bois de Boulogne, on the western rim of Paris. In fact, the Jardin d'Acclimatation de Paris in the Bois de Boulogne could be considered a total world of amusements, rides, distractions, and sports for the young.

## PARIS COOKING SCHOOLS

Learn how to make the perfect soufflé or a tasty coq-au-vin at the following world-renowned schools:

**La Varenne,** Ecole de Cuisine, 34 Rue St-Dominique, 75007. Tel. 46.05.10.16. Bilingual courses in different aspects of French cooking are given. You can attend class for about $20 for one session, buy twelve tickets for about $200, or take the full course for about $650.

**Le Cordon Bleu,** 24 Rue de Champs de Mars, 75007. Tel. 45.55.22.77. Also two other locations. Four-week intensive courses at various levels start at about $880. Demonstration tickets are about $20 each.

**Maxim's Cooking Courses,** 3 Rue Royale, 75008. Tel. 42.65.27.94. Special courses are offered for English-speaking foreigners. Month-long courses, usually from late June through July, at about $2,500.

# 14/GENERAL INFORMATION
## DAYS, MONTHS, AND SEASONS

### Days of the Week

| | | |
|---|---|---|
| Monday | **lundi** | luh(n)dee |
| Tuesday | **mardi** | mahrdee |
| Wednesday | **mercredi** | mehrkruhdee |
| Thursday | **jeudi** | zhuhdee |
| Friday | **vendredi** | vah(n)druhdee |
| Saturday | **samedi** | sahmdee |
| Sunday | **dimanche** | deemah(n)sh |

### Months

| | | |
|---|---|---|
| January | **janvier** | zhah(n)vyay |
| February | **février** | fayvryay |
| March | **mars** | mahrs |
| April | **avril** | ahvreel |
| May | **mai** | meh |
| June | **juin** | zhwa(n) |
| July | **juillet** | zhweeyay |
| August | **août** | oot |
| September | **septembre** | sehptah(m)br |
| October | **octobre** | ohktohbr |
| November | **novembre** | nohvah(m)br |
| December | **décembre** | daysah(m)br |

### Seasons

| | | |
|---|---|---|
| Winter | **l'hiver** | leevehr |
| Spring | **le printemps** | luh pra(n)tah(m) |
| Summer | **l'été** | laytay |
| Fall | **l'automne** | lohtohn |
| | | |
| in Winter | **en hiver** | ah(n) neevehr |
| in Spring | **au printemps** | oh pra(n)tah(m) |
| in Summer | **en été** | ah(n) naytay |
| in Fall | **en automne** | ah(n) nohtohn |

## THE DATE

| What is today's date? | **Quelle est la date d'aujourd'hui?** | Kehl eh lah daht dohzhoordwee? |
| What day is it today? | **Quel jour est-ce aujourd'hui?** | Kehl zhoor ehs ohzhoordwee? |
| Today is Friday, April 1. | **Aujourd'hui c'est le vendredi, premier\* avril.** | Ohzhoordwee seh luh vah(n)druhdee, pruh-myehr ahvreel. |
| Today is May 18, 1989. | **Aujourd'hui c'est le dix-huit mai mil neuf cent quatre-vingt-dix-neuf.** | Ohzhoordwee seh luh deezwee may, meel nuhf sah(n) kahtruh-va(n)-deez-nuhf. |

\*Note: *Le premier* (the first) is used for the first day of each month. Otherwise, regular cardinal numbers are used for dates.

## AGE

| How old are you? | **Quel âge avez-vous?** | Kehl ahzh ahvay-voo? |
| I'm 36. | **J'ai trente-six ans.** | Zheh trah(n)t-see zah(n). |
| How old is he/she? | **Quel âge a-t-il/a-t-elle?** | Kehl ahzh ahteel/ahtehl? |
| He's (she's) 20. | **Il a (elle a) vingt ans.** | Eel ah (ehl ah) va(n) tah(n). |
| I'm younger than he is. | **Je suis plus jeune que lui.** | Zhuh swee plew zhuhn kuh lwee. |
| I was born in 1940. | **Je suis né(e) en mille neuf cents quarante.** | Zhuh swee nay ah(n) meel nuhf sah(n) kahrah(n)t. |
| His birthday is December 2, 1956. | **Son anniversaire est le deux décembre, mil neuf cent cinquante-six.** | Soh(n) nahneevehr-sayr ay luh duh day-sah(m)br, meel nuhf sah(n) sa(n)kah(n)t-sees. |

180

## EXPRESSIONS OF TIME

| | | |
|---|---|---|
| now | **maintenant** | ma(n)tuhnah(n) |
| earlier | **plus tôt** | plew toh |
| later | **plus tard** | plew tahr |
| before | **avant** | ahvah(n) |
| after/afterward | **après** | ahpreh |
| soon | **bientôt** | byeh(n)toh |
| once | **une fois** | ewn fwah |
| in the morning | **le matin** | luh mata(n) |
| at noon | **à midi** | ah meedee |
| in the afternoon | **dans l'après-midi** | dah(n) lahpreh-mee-dee |
| in the evening | **au soir** | oh swahr |
| at night | **dans la nuit** | dah(n) lah nwee |
| at midnight | **à minuit** | ah meenwee |
| tomorrow | **demain** | duhma(n) |
| yesterday | **hier** | eeyehr |
| the day after tomorrow | **après-demain** | ahpreh-duhma(n) |
| the day before yesterday | **avant-hier** | ahvah(n)-tyehr |
| this week | **cette semaine** | seht suhmehn |
| next week | **la semaine prochaine** | lah suhmehn proh-shehn |
| last week | **la semaine passée** | lah suhmehn pahsay |
| every day | **tous les jours** | too lay zhoor |
| in 3 days | **dans trois jours** | dah(n) trwah zhoor |
| 2 days ago | **il y a deux jours** | eelyah duh zhoor |
| on Saturdays | **le samedi** | luh suhmdee |
| on weekends | **le weekend** | luh weekehnd |
| on weekdays (during the week) | **pendant la semaine** | pah(n)dah(n) lah suhmehn |
| a working day | **un jour ouvrable** | uh(n) zhoor oovrahbl |
| a day off | **un jour de congé** | uh(n) zhoor duh koh(n)zhay |
| in January | **en janvier** | ah(n) zhah(n)vyay |
| last January | **janvier dernier** | zhah(n)vyay dehrnyay |
| next January | **janvier prochain** | zhah(n)vyay proh-sha(n) |

181

| each month | **chaque mois** | shahk mwah |
| every month | **tous les mois** | too lay mwah |
| since August | **depuis août** | duhpwee oot |
| this month | **ce mois-ci** | suh mwah-see |
| next month | **le mois prochain** | luh mwah prohsha(n) |
| last month | **le mois passé** | luh mwah pahsay |
| this year | **cette année** | seht ahnay |
| next year | **l'année prochaine** | lahnay prohshehn |
| last year | **l'année passée** | lahnay pahsay |
| every year | **chaque année** | shahk ahnay |
| In what year... | **En quelle année ...** | Ah(n) kehl ahnay... |
| In 1980... | **En mil neuf cents quatre-vingts ...** | Ah(n) meel nuhf sah(n) kahtruh-va(n)... |
| In the nineteenth century... | **Au dix-neuvième siècle ...** | Oh deeznuhvyehm syehkl... |
| In the forties... | **Dans les années quarante ...** | Dah(n) lay zahnay kahrah(n)t... |

## HOLIDAYS

The following are public holidays in France. Be aware that when a holiday falls on a Thursday or a Tuesday, many businesses close for a four-day weekend.

| January 1 | **Le jour de l'an** | New Year's Day |
| January 2 | (extension of the New Year's holiday) | |
| April–May | **Le Vendredi Saint** | Good Friday |
| April–May | **Pâques** | Easter |
| April–May | **Lundi de Pâques** | Easter Monday |
| May 1 | **La Fête du Travail** | May Day (Labor Day) |
| May–June | **L'Ascension** | Ascension Thursday |
| May–June | **Lundi de la Pentecôte** | Whitmonday |
| July 14 | **La Fête Nationale** | Bastille Day |
| August 15 | **L'Assomption** | Assumption Day |

| | | |
|---|---|---|
| November 1 | **La Toussaint** | All Saints' Day |
| November 11 | **L'Armistice** | Armistice Day |
| December 25 | **Noël** | Christmas Day |
| December 26 | **Saint-Etienne** | Saint Stephen's Day |

| | | |
|---|---|---|
| Merry Christmas! | **Joyeux Noël!** | Zhwahyuh noh-ehl! |
| Happy New Year! | **Bonne Année!** | Bohn ahnay! |
| Happy Easter! | **Joyeuses Pâques!** | Zhwahyuhz pahk! |
| Happy holidays! | **Passez de bonnes fêtes!** | Pahsay duh bohn feht! |
| Happy name's day! | **Bonne fête!** | Bohn feht! |

## WEATHER

| | | |
|---|---|---|
| What's the weather today? | **Quel temps fait-il aujourd'hui?** | Kehl tah(m) fayteel ohzhoordwee? |
| It's raining/snowing. | **Il pleut/neige.** | Eeh pluh/nehzh. |
| It's . . . | **Il fait . . .** | Eel feh . . . |
| • cold. | • **froid.** | • frwah. |
| • cool. | • **frais.** | • freh. |
| • cloudy. | • **un temps couvert.** | • uh(n) tah(m) koovehr. |
| • foggy. | • **du brouillard.** | • dew brooyahr. |
| • warm. | • **chaud.** | • shoh. |
| • hot. | • **très chaud.** | • tray shoh. |
| • nice. | • **beau.** | • boh. |
| • sunny. | • **du soleil.** | • dew sohlehy. |
| • windy. | • **du vent.** | • dew vah(n). |
| What's the forecast for tomorrow? | **Quel est la météo pour demain?** | Kehl eh lah maytayoh poor duhma(n)? |
| It's going to rain. | **Il va pleuvoir.** | Eel vah pluhvwahr. |
| What is the average temperature at this time of year? | **Quel est la tempé-rature normale en cette saison?** | Kehl eh lah tah(m)pay-rahtewr nohrmahl ah(n) seht sayzoh(n)? |

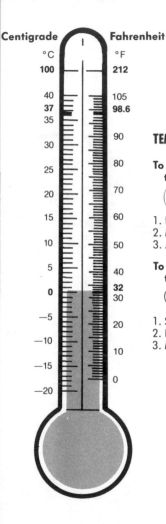

Centigrade | Fahrenheit
°C | °F
100 | 212
40 | 105
37 | 98.6
35 |
30 | 90
25 | 80
20 | 70
15 | 60
10 | 50
5 | 40
0 | 32 / 30
−5 | 20
−10 | 10
−15 | 0
−20 |

## TEMPERATURE CONVERSION

### To Convert Centigrade to Fahrenheit

$$\left(\frac{9}{5}\right)C° + 32 = F°$$

1. Divide by 5.
2. Multiply by 9.
3. Add 32.

### To Convert Fahrenheit to Centigrade

$$(F° - 32)\frac{5}{9} = C°$$

1. Subtract 32.
2. Divide by 9.
3. Multiply by 5.

## NATIONAL ORIGINS

| Where do you come from? | **D'où venez-vous?** | Doo vuhnay-voo? |
|---|---|---|
| I come from Belgium. | **Je viens de la Belgique.** | Zhuh vya(n) duh lah Behlzheek. |

Note: To express the idea of *from* ___, use *de la* before a feminine country, *du* before a masculine country, *de l'* before a country or continent beginning with a vowel, and *des* with a country that is plural (like the United States).

| I come... | **Je viens...** | Zhuh vya(n)... |
|---|---|---|
| • from France. | • **de la France.** | • duh lah Frah(n)s. |
| • from Portugal. | • **du Portugal.** | • dew Pohrtewgahl. |
| • from Ireland. | • **de l'Irlande.** | • duh leerlah(n)d. |
| • from the United States. | • **des Etats-Unis.** | • day zaytah-zewnee. |

Note: For *in* or *to,* use *en* before a feminine country, continents, and masculine countries beginning with a vowel. For other masculine countries, *to* or *in* is rendered by *au*. Plural countries take *aux*.

| I'm going... | **Je vais...** | Zhuh veh... |
|---|---|---|
| • to France. | • **en France.** | • ah(n) Frah(n)s. |
| • to Portugal. | • **au Portugal.** | • oh Pohrtewgahl. |
| • to Israel. | • **en Israël.** | • ah(n) neezra-ehl. |
| • to the United States. | • **aux Etats-Unis.** | • oh zaytah-zewnee. |

Also note that for cities, use *de* alone to express *from—je viens de Paris* [zhuh vyeh(n) duh Pahree]—and use *a* alone to express *to—je vais à Paris* [zhuh vay zah Pahree].

## CONTINENTS

| Africa | **l'Afrique** | lahfreek |
|---|---|---|
| Asia | **l'Asie** | lahzee |
| Australia | **l'Australie** | lohstrahlee |
| Europe | **l'Europe** | luhrohp |

| North America | l'Amérique du Nord | lahmayreek dew nohr |
| South America | l'Amérique du Sud | lahmayreek dew sewd |

## COUNTRIES AND NATIONALITIES

| Algeria | l'Algérie ( f ) | lahlzhayree |
| Algerian | algérien(ne) | ahlzhayrya(n)/yehn |
| Argentina | l'Argentine ( f ) | lahrzhah(n)teen |
| Argentinian | argentin(e) | ahrzhah(n)ta(n)/teen |
| Austria | l'Autriche ( f ) | lohtreesh |
| Austrian | autrichien(ne) | ohtreeshya(n)/yehn |
| Belgium | la Belgique | lah Behlzheek |
| Belgian | belge | behlzh |
| Brazil | le Brésil | luh Brayzeel |
| Brazilian | brésilien(ne) | brayzeelya(n)/yehn |
| Canada | le Canada | luh Kahnahdah |
| Canadian | canadien(ne) | kahnahdya(n)/yehn |
| China | la Chine | lah Sheen |
| Chinese | chinois(e) | sheenwah/wahz |
| Denmark | le Danemark | luh dahnmahrk |
| Danish | danois(e) | dahnwah/wahz |
| East Germany | l'Allemagne de l'Est ( f ) | lahlmahnyuh duh lehst |
| East German | allemand(e) de l'Est | ahlmah(n)/mah(n)d duh lehst |
| England | l'Angleterre ( f ) | lah(n)gluhtehr |
| English | anglais(e) | ah(n)glay/glehz |
| Finland | la Finlande | lah Fa(n)lah(n)d |
| Finnish | finlandais(e) | fa(n)lah(n)day/dehz |
| France | la France | lah Frah(n)s |
| French | français(e) | frah(n)say/sehz |
| Great Britain | la Grande Bretagne | lah Grah(n)d Bruhtah-nyuh |
| British | britannique | breetahneek |
| Greece | la Grèce | lah Grehs |
| Greek | grec(que) | grehk |
| India | l'Inde ( f ) | la(n)d |
| Indian | indien(ne) | a(n)dya(n)/yehn |

| | | |
|---|---|---|
| Ireland | l'Irlande (f) | leerlah(n)d |
| Irish | irlandais(e) | eerlah(n)day/dehz |
| Israel | l'Israël (m) | leezrah-ehl |
| Israeli | israélien(ne) | eezrahaylya(n)/yehn |
| Italy | l'Italie (f) | leetahlee |
| Italian | italien(ne) | eetalya(n)/yehn |
| Japan | le Japon | luh Zhahpoh(n) |
| Japanese | japonais(e) | zhahpohnay/nehz |
| Korea | la Corée | lah Kohray |
| Korean | coréen(ne) | kohraya(n)/yehn |
| Luxembourg | le Luxembourg | luh Lewksah(n)boor |
| Luxembourger (-ian) | luxembourgeois(e) | lewksah(n)boorzhwah/ zhwahz |
| Mexico | le Mexique | luh Mehkseek |
| Mexican | mexicain(e) | mehkseeka(n)/kehn |
| Morocco | Le Maroc | luh Mahrohk |
| Moroccan | marocain(e) | mahrohka(n)/kehn |
| Netherlands | les Pays-Bas (m) | lay Payee-Bah |
| Dutch | néerlandais(e) | nayehrlah(n)deh/dehz |
| New Zealand | la Nouvelle Zélande | lah Noovehl Zay- lah(n)d |
| New Zealander | nouvelle zéerlandais(e) | noovehl zayehr- lah(n)deh/dehz |
| Norway | la Norvège | lah Nohrvehzh |
| Norwegian | norvégien(ne) | nohrvayzhya(n)/yehn |
| Portugal | le Portugal | luh Pohrtewgahl |
| Portuguese | portugais(e) | pohrtewgeh/gehz |
| Scotland | l'Ecosse (f) | laykohs |
| Scottish | écossais(e) | aykohseh/sehz |
| Soviet Union | l'Union Soviétique (f) | lewnyoh(n) Sohvyay- teek |
| Soviet | soviétique | sohvyayteek |
| Spain | l'Espagne (f) | lehspahnyuh |
| Spanish | espagnol(e) | ehspahnyohl |
| Sweden | la Suède | lah Swehd |
| Swedish | suédois(e) | swaydwah/dwahz |
| Switzerland | la Suisse | lah Swees |
| Swiss | suisse | swees |
| Thailand | la Thäilande | lah Tah-eelah(n)d |
| Thai | thäilandais(e) | tah-eelah(n)deh/dehz |
| Turkey | la Turquie | lah Tewrkee |

| | | |
|---|---|---|
| Turkish | **turc(que)** | tewrk |
| United States | **les Etats-Unis (m)** | lay zaytah-zewnee |
| American | **américain(e)** | ahmayreeka(n)/kehn |
| West Germany | **l'Allemagne de l'Ouest (f)** | lahlmah(n)nyuh duh lwehst |
| West German | **allemand(e) de l'Ouest** | ahlmah(n)/mah(n)d duh lwehst |

## LANGUAGES

| | | |
|---|---|---|
| Arabic | **l'arabe** | lahrahb |
| Chinese | **le chinois** | luh sheenwah |
| English | **l'anglais** | lah(n)gleh |
| French | **le français** | luh frah(n)seh |
| German | **l'allemand** | lahlmah(n) |
| Japanese | **le japonais** | luh zhahpohneh |
| Portuguese | **le portugais** | luh pohrtewgeh |
| Russian | **le russe** | luh rews |
| Spanish | **l'espagnol** | lehspahnyohl |
| I speak French. | **Je parle français** | Zhuh pahrl frah(n)seh. |
| I like French. | **J'aime le français.** | Zhehm luh frah(n)seh. |

Note: The definite article is used with names of languages but commonly omitted after the verb *parler* (to speak).

## OCCUPATIONS

| | | |
|---|---|---|
| accountant | **comptable** | koh(m)tahbl |
| architect | **architecte** | ahrsheetehkt |
| artist | **artiste** | ahrteest |
| baker | **boulanger** | boolah(n)zhay |
| blacksmith | **forgeron(ne)** | fohrzhroh(n) |
| butcher | **boucher** | booshay |
| cardiologist | **cardiologue** | kahrdeeohlohg |
| carpenter | **charpentier** | shahrpah(n)tyay |
| chef | **chef** | shehf |
| clerk | **clerc** | klehr |
| cook | **cuisinièr(e)** | kweezeenyay(-yehr) |
| dentist | **dentiste** | dah(n)teest |
| doctor | **médecin** | maydsa(n) |

| electrician | **électricien** | aylehktreesyeh(n) |
| engineer | **ingénieur** | a(n)zhaynyuhr |
| lawyer | **avocat** | ahvohkah |
| locksmith | **serrurier** | sehrewryay |
| maid | **domestique** | dohmehsteek |
| neurologist | **neurologue** | nuhrohlohg |
| nurse | **infirmièr(-e)** | a(n)fehrmyay(-yehr) |
| ophthalmologist | **ophtamologue** | ohftahmohlohg |
| optometrist | **optométriste** | ohptohmaytreest |
| painter | **peintre** | pa(n)tr |
| plumber | **plombier(-e)** | plohmbyay(-yehr) |
| salesperson | **vendeur(-euse)** | vah(n)duhr(-duhz) |
| sculptor | **sculpteur** | skewltuhr |
| shoemaker | **bottier(-e)** | bohtyay(-yehr) |
| shopkeeper | **commerçant(-e)** | kohmehrsah(n) (-sah(n)t) |
| | | |
| waiter | **serveur** | sehrvuhr |
| waitress | **serveuse** | sehrvuhz |
| writer | **écrivain** | aykreeva(n) |

## EMERGENCY EXPRESSIONS

| Fire! | **Au feu!** | Oh fuh! |
| Hurry! | **Vite!** | Veet! |
| Call the police! | **Appelez la police!** | Ahplay lah pohlees! |
| Call the fire department! | **Appelez les pompiers!** | Ahplay lay poh(m)-pyay! |
| Help! | **Au secours!** | Oh skoor! |
| I'm sick. | **Je suis malade.** | Zhuh swee mahlahd. |
| Call a doctor. | **Appelez un médecin.** | Ahplay uh(n) mayd-sa(n). |
| I'm lost. | **Je suis perdu(e).** | Zhuh swee pehrdew. |
| Can you help me, please? | **Pourriez-vous m'aider, s'il vous plaît?** | Pooryay-voo mehday, seel voo pleh? |
| Stop, thief! | **Au voleur!** | Oh vohluhr! |

| Someone/they stole . . . | **On m'a volé . . .** | Oh(n) mah vohlay. . . |
|---|---|---|
| • my camera! | • **mon appareil!** | • moh(n) nahpahrehy! |
| • my car! | • **ma voiture!** | • mah vwahtewr! |
| • my handbag! | • **mon sac à main!** | • moh(n) sahk ah ma(n)! |
| • my money! | • **mon argent!** | • moh(n) nahrzhah(n)! |
| • my passport! | • **mon passeport!** | • moh(n) pahspohr! |
| • my suitcase! | • **ma valise!** | • mah vahleez! |
| • my wallet! | • **mon portefeuille!** | • moh(n) pohrtuhfuhy! |
| • my watch! | • **ma montre!** | mah moh(n)tr! |
| He's the thief. | **C'est lui, le voleur.** | Seh lwee, luh vohluhr. |
| Stop him/her! | **Arrêtez-le/la!** | Ahrehtay-luh/-lah! |
| Leave me alone! | **Laissez-moi!** | Lehsay-mwah! |
| I'm going to call the police. | **Je vais appeler la police.** | Zhuh vay zahplay lah pohlees. |
| Where's the police station? | **Où est le poste de police?** | Oo eh luh pohst duh pohlees? |
| I want a lawyer. | **Je veux un avocat.** | Zhuh vuh zuh(n) nahvohkah. |
| I want an interpreter. | **Je veux un interprète.** | Zhuh vuh zuh(n) na(n)tehrpreht. |
| Is there someone here who speaks English? | **Y a-t-il quelqu'un ici qui parle anglais?** | Yahteel kehlkuh(n) nee-see kee pahrl ah(n)glay? |
| I want to go to the American consulate. | **Je veux aller au consulat américain.** | Zhuh vuh zahlay oh koh(n)sewlah ahmayreeka(n). |

## SPECIAL ABBREVIATIONS

| A.C.F. | **Automobile Club de France** | Automobile Club of France |
|---|---|---|
| apr. J.-C. | **après Jésus-Christ** | A.D. |

190

| | | |
|---|---|---|
| av. J.-C. | avant Jésus-Christ | B.C. |
| arr. | arrondissement | district (in Paris) |
| bd./boul. | boulevard | boulevard |
| c.-à-d. | c'est-à-dire | that is to say |
| C.C.P. | compte de chèques postaux | postal accounts |
| C.E.E. | Communanté économique euro-péenne | European Economic Community (Common Market) |
| Cie | Compagnie | Company |
| C.R.S. | Compagnies Républi-caines de Sécurité | French Riot Police |
| cv | chevaux-vapeur | horsepower |
| E.U. | Etats-Unis | United States |
| exp. | expéditeur | sender |
| F.B. | franc belge | Belgian franc |
| F.F. | franc français | French franc |
| F.S. | franc suisse | Swiss franc |
| M. | Monsieur | Mr. |
| Mlle | Mademoiselle | Miss |
| MM. | Messieurs | Gentlemen |
| Mme | Madame | Mrs. |
| P.D.G. | Président et Directeur Général | Chief Executive Officer |
| p.ex. | par exemple | for example |
| p.p. | port payé | postage paid |
| P.T.T. | Postes et Télécommu-nications | Post Office & Telecommu-nications |
| R.A.T.P. | Régie Autonome des Transports Parisiens | Paris Transport Authority |

| R.D. | **Route Départementale** | local road |
| R.F. | **République Française** | French Republic |
| R.N. | **Route Nationale** | national road |
| S.A. | **Société anonyme** | Inc. |
| S.I. | **Syndicat d'Initiative** | Tourist Office |
| S.N.C.F. | **Société Nationale des Chemins de Fer Français** | French National Railway |
| s.v.p. | **s'il vous plaît** | please |
| TTC | **toutes taxes comprises** | all taxes included |
| TVA | **taxe à la valeur ajoutée** | sales tax |

# 15/GRAMMAR IN BRIEF

With *Traveltalk*, you can find and use phrases you need without formal grammar study. However, by learning some of the basic grammatical patterns of the language, you will be able to construct an unlimited number of your own sentences and greatly increase your range of expression.

## NOUNS AND ARTICLES

### Definite Article—*the*

All nouns are either masculine or feminine. As there is not one systematic way to tell the gender of most nouns from their spelling or meaning, it is best to learn the definite article with the noun.

**Masculine Singular—*le***

| the pen | **le stylo** | luh steeloh |
| the menu | **le menu** | luh muhnew |
| the man | **l'homme** | lohm |

Remember, the vowel in the definite article is dropped when the next word begins with a vowel and with some words beginning with *h*—this is referred to as elision (see page 10).

**Feminine Singular—*la***

| the lady | **la dame** | lah dahm |
| the page | **la page** | lah pazh |
| the orange | **l'orange** | lohrahnzh |

**Plural—*les***

*Les* is the definite article for all plural nouns, whether masculine or feminine.

**masculine plural:**

| the pens | **les stylos** | lay steeloh |

**feminine plural:**

| the pages | **les pages** | lay pahzh |
| the oranges | **les oranges** | lay zohrah(n)zh |

You will note from the examples above that to make a noun plural, we simply add an *s* to the spelling. The *s*, however, is silent (but note the liaison with the plural article when the following noun begins with a vowel). In speaking, therefore, we can tell if a noun is plural only from the preceding article.

| the boy | **le garçon** | luh gahrsoh(n) |
| the boys | **les garçons** | lay gahrsoh(n) |

## Indefinite Articles—*a, some*

### Masculine Singular—*un*

| a pen | **un stylo** | uh(n) steeloh |
| a menu | **un menu** | uh(n) muhnew |
| a friend | **un ami** | uh(n) nahmee |

Note: The *n* of *un* is not pronounced before a consonant but *is* pronounced in *liaison* when the next word begins with a vowel.

### Feminine Singular—*une*

| a lady | **une dame** | ewn dahm |
| a page | **une page** | ewn pahzh |
| an orange | **une orange** | ewn ohrah(n)zh |

### Plural—*des*

*Des* is the indefinite article for all nouns, whether masculine or feminine.

| some pens | **des stylos** | day steeloh |
| some pages | **des pages** | day pahzh |
| some oranges | **des oranges** | day zohrah(n)zh (note the liaison here) |

## Article System

|  | Singular | Plural |
|---|---|---|
| **Definite** | m. le<br>f. la | les |
| **Indefinite** | m. un<br>f. une | des |

## PRONOUNS

Pronouns stand for or replace nouns and perform several distinct functions.

**Subject Pronouns** are the subjects of sentences or clauses and are usually found in sentence-initial position

| | |
|---|---|
| *I* am going to the restaurant. | **Je vais au restaurant.** |
| *You* speak English. | **Vous parlez anglais.** |

**Direct Object Pronouns** represent the persons or objects acted upon by the verb. They agree in number and gender with the nouns they replace. Note: They are identical with the forms of the definite article *the*—le, la, les.

| | |
|---|---|
| Do you understand French? | **Est-ce que vous comprenez le français?** |
| Yes, I understand *it*. | **Oui, je *le* comprends.** |
| Do you like the desserts here? | **Vous aimez les desserts ici?** |
| Yes, I like *them*. | **Oui, je *les* aime.** |

As seen from the above examples, direct object pronouns generally come between the subject and the verb. However, they *follow* an imperative:

| | |
|---|---|
| Take *it*! | **Prenez-*la*!** |

**Indirect Object Pronouns** receive the action of the verb indirectly and are usually represented in English as "to him, to her, to me," etc.

195

| I am speaking *to him* (or her). | **Je *lui* parle.** |
| He's giving his map *to me*. | **Il *me* donne sa carte.** |

Indirect object pronoun placement is the same as for direct object pronouns: between subject and verb, except for commands.

| Write to him! | **Ecrivez-*lui*!** |

**Pronouns as Objects of Prepositions** always follow the preposition.

| I'm going *with him*. | **Je vais *avec lui*.** |

The following chart shows the forms of all the sets of pronouns discussed above.

| Subject | | Direct Object | | Indirect Object | | After a Preposition | |
|---|---|---|---|---|---|---|---|
| I | **je** | me | **me** | to me | **me** | me | **moi** |
| you | **tu*** | you | **te** | to you | **te** | you | **toi** |
| he | **il** | him | **le** | to him | **lui** | him | **lui** |
| she | **elle** | her | **la** | to her | **lui** | her | **elle** |
| we | **nous†** | us | **nous** | to us | **nous** | us | **nous** |
| you | **vous*** | you | **vous** | to you | **vous** | you | **vous** |
| they (masculine/mixed) | **ils** | them | **les** | to them | **leur** | them | **eux** |
| they (feminine) | **elles** | them | **les** | to them | **leur** | them | **elles** |

*Tu, Vous*—French, like many other languages, has preserved a distinction between familiar and formal *you* (the *thou* and *you* distinction that has disappeared from English). *Tu* is used for children, close friends, and relatives. *Vous* is used when addressing anyone else and is also used exclusively in the plural. As a traveler, you most probably will give and receive only *vous*. Children under twelve or thirteen should be prepared to hear *tu* but would address only other children as *tu,* addressing adults as *vous.* Note the verbs tutoyer (to say *tu* to someone) and vouvoyer (to say *vous* to someone).

†*On* (one) is often used in place of *nous* (we) in the spoken language.

| We speak French here (idiomatic). | **On parle français ici.** |
| One speaks French here (literal). | |

Note: Before a verb beginning with a vowel, a pronoun that ends in *e* or *a* drops that letter. This is an example of elision.

| | |
|---|---|
| I like/love . . . | J~~é~~ aime . . . → J'aime . . . |
| He's listening to me. | Il m~~e~~ écoute. → Il m'écoute. |
| We have it. | Nous l~~a~~ avons. → Nous l'avons. |

## ADJECTIVES

### Placement

Most adjectives are placed *after* the noun.

| | |
|---|---|
| an amusing book | **un livre amusant** |
| a French friend | **un ami français** |

A few common, short adjectives occur *before* the noun. Most of these can be grouped in pairs for easy learning.

| | |
|---|---|
| small | **petit** |
| big, great | **grand** |
| young | **jeune** |
| old | **vieux** |
| good | **bon** |
| bad | **mauvais** |
| pretty | **joli** |
| good weather | **le beau temps** |
| bad weather | **le mauvais temps** |
| a young man | **un jeune homme** |

### Gender

Adjectives agree in gender with the nouns they modify. Adjectives which end in a silent final consonant in the masculine, add an *e* and sound the preceding consonant in the feminine.

| | | |
|---|---|---|
| an amusing book | **un livre amusant** | uh(n) leevr ahmew-zah(n) |

197

| an amusing play | **une pièce** **amusante** | ewn pyehs ahmew-zah(n)t |

Adjectives that end in a vowel in the masculine, add *e* to form the feminine but don't change their pronunciation. Adjectives ending in *e* with no accent mark remain the same.

| pretty (*m*) | **joli** | zhohlee |
| (*f*) | **jolie** | zhohlee |

| sincere (*m*) | **sincère** | sa(n)sehr |
| (*f*) | **sincère** | sa(n)sehr |

| pleased (*m*) | **enchanté** | ah(n)shah(n)tay |
| (*f*) | **enchantée** | ah(n)shah(n)tay |

Adjectives ending in *-ier* add *e* to form the feminine and add an accent grave as in the following. Note the pronunciation change.

| entire (*m*) | **entier** | ah(n)tyay |
| (*f*) | **entière** | ah(n)tyehr |

Adjectives that end in a vowel + *n* in the masculine double the *n* and add *e* in the feminine.

| good (*m*) | **bon** | boh(n) |
| (*f*) | **bonne** | bohn |

| Italian (*m*) | **italien** | eetahlya(n) |
| (*f*) | **italienne** | eetahlyehn |

## Number

Like the nouns they describe, adjectives add *s* to the singular form to indicate the plural, masculine or feminine as required. The *s* is not pronounced.

| some amusing friends | **des amis** **amusants** | day zahmee zahmew-zah(n) |

| some amusing women | **des femmes** **amusantes** | day fahm zahmew-zah(n)t |

If the singular adjective ends in *s*, there is no change for the plural.

a French book **un livre français**
some French books **des livres français**

## Possessive Adjectives

Possessive adjectives denote ownership: *my* hat, *your* coat, *his* tickets, etc. In French, possessive adjectives agree in number and gender with the *thing possessed*.

|  | **Singular** | | **Plural** |
|  | masculine | feminine | (same for m/f) |
|---|---|---|---|
| my | **mon** | **ma** | **mes** |
| your | **ton***  | **ta*** | **tes*** |
| his/her | **son** | **sa** | **ses** |
| our | **notre** | **notre** | **nos** |
| your | **votre** | **votre** | **vos** |
| their | **leur** | **leur** | **leurs** |

*The distinction between *tu* and *vous*, described under *Pronouns*, is also found in the possessive adjectives.

Here are some examples of the use of possessive adjectives.

| my wife | **ma femme** | his aunt | **sa tante** |
| my book | **mon livre** | his ideas | **ses idées** |
| my friends | **mes amis** | our house | **notre maison** |
| your suitcase | **ta valise** | your child | **votre enfant** |
| your friend | **ton ami** | their book | **leur livre** |
| his pencil | **son crayon** | | |

Note: We have seen how liaison and elision help preserve the pleasing alternation of vowel and consonant. For the same reason, we do not use *ma, ta,* or *sa* before a feminine noun beginning with a vowel. Instead, we use the masculine variants *mon, ton,* and *son.*

| my friend (f.) | **mon amie** | moh(n) nahmee |
| his (or her) omelette (f.) | **son omelette** | soh(n) nohmleht |

199

## Demonstrative Adjectives

|  | Singular<br>This/That | Plural<br>These/Those |
|---|---|---|
| Masculine | ce | ces |
| Masculine before<br>vowel or "h" | cet | ces |
| Feminine | cette | ces |

Here are some examples of demonstrative adjectives.

| this/that boy | ce garçon |
|---|---|
| this/that man | cet homme |
| this/that woman | cette femme |
| these/those boys | ces garçons |
| these/those men | ces hommes |
| these/those women | ces femmes |

## Comparative and Superlative Adjectives

| Positive | Comparative | Superlative |
|---|---|---|
| big | bigger | biggest |
| **grand(e)** | **plus grand(e)** | **le/la/les plus grand(e)(s)** |
| interesting | more interesting | most interesting |
| **intéressant(e)** | **plus intéressant(e)** | **le/la/les plus intéressant(e)(s)** |

Here are some examples of comparative and superlative adjectives.

This hat is big.
**Ce chapeau est grand.**

This hat is bigger than the other.
**Ce chapeau est plus grand que l'autre.**

This hat is the biggest in the store.
**Ce chapeau est le plus grand du magasin.**

These hats are the biggest.
**Ces chapeaux sont les plus grands.**

**Comparatives of the Lesser Degree** To say that something is less ___ or the least ___, we use the same pattern as above, simply substituting the word *moins* for *plus*.

This hat is less interesting than the other.
**Ce chapeau est moins intéressant que l'autre.**

This hat is the least interesting.
**Ce chapeau est le moins intéressant.**

Note the following irregular comparisons and superlatives.

| Positive | Comparative | Superlative |
| --- | --- | --- |
| good **bon(ne)** | better **meilleur(e)** | best **le/la/les meilleur(e)(s)** |
| bad **mauvais(e)** | worse **pire** | worst **le/la/les pire(s)** |

Here are some examples using these irregular comparisons/superlatives.

It's the best ice cream in the world!
**C'est la meilleure glace du monde!**

This hotel is worse than the other.
**Cet hôtel est pire que l'autre.**

## ADVERBS

In general, adverbs are formed by adding *-ment* to the feminine form of the corresponding adjective.

| | |
| --- | --- |
| rapid **rapide** | rapidly **rapidement** |
| serious **sérieux(euse)** | seriously **sérieusement** |

201

Note the following common adverbs that are irregular.

| fast | **vite** | veet |
| well | **bien** | byeh(n) |
| badly | **mal** | mahl |
| better | **mieux** | myuh |
| worse | **pire** | peer |

## PREPOSITIONS

| about | **de** | duh |
| according to | **selon** | suhloh(n) |
| across | **à travers** | ah trahvehr |
| after | **après** | ahpreh |
| among | **parmi** | pahrmee |
| around | **autour de** | ohtoor duh |
| at | **à** | ah |
| at ( + name of person or profession) | **chez** | shay |
| before | **avant** | ahvah(n) |
| behind | **derrière** | dehryehr |
| between | **entre** | ah(n)tr |
| by | **par** | pahr |
| during | **pendant** | pah(n)dah(n) |
| except | **sauf** | sohf |
| for | **pour** | poor |
| from | **de** | duh |
| in | **dans, en** | dah(n), ah(n) |
| in front of | **devant** | duhvah(n) |
| on | **sur** | sewr |
| opposite | **en face de** | ah(n) fahs duh |
| through | **à travers** | ah trahvehr |
| to | **à** | ah |
| toward | **vers** | vehr |
| under | **sous** | soo |

- until
- with
- without

- **jusqu'a**
- **avec**
- **sans**

- zhewskah
- ahvehk
- sah(n)

## CONTRACTIONS

The common prepositions *à* (to, at) and *de* (of, from) have special contracted forms when combined with certain forms of the definite article:

à + le = au
à + les = aux

de + le = du
de + les = des

(There are no contractions with *à la, à l', de la,* or *de l'.*)

I'm going to the movies.
**Je vais au cinéma.**

I'm coming from the movies.
**Je viens du cinéma.**

Peter is going to go to the museums.
**Pierre va aller aux musées.**

## NEGATIVE SENTENCES

Negative sentences require two negative elements, one preceding and one following the verb.

not (simple negation)
**ne (verb) pas**

never
**ne (verb) jamais**

nothing
**ne (verb) rien**

no longer
**ne (verb) plus**

no one
**ne (verb) personne**

Here are some examples of negative forms.

I know.
**Je sais\*.**

I don't know his name.
**Je ne sais pas son nom.**

I know nothing.
**Je ne sais rien.**

I no longer know.
**Je ne sais plus.**

I know nobody.
**Je ne connais\* personne.**

\*Note: Both *savoir* and *connaître* mean *to know*. Savoir is used when referring to facts. Connaître is used when referring to people and places.

## QUESTIONS

The easiest way to ask a question that can be answered by *yes* or *no* is simply to say a declarative sentence using rising intonation, i.e., raise your voice at the end as you would with a question in English.

| | |
|---|---|
| We're going to the restaurant. | **On va au restaurant.** |
| Shall we go to the restaurant? | **On va au restaurant?** |
| You're French. | **Vous êtes français.** |
| Are you French? | **Vous êtes français?** |

Another common way to ask a yes/no question is to place the phrase *Est-ce que* [ehskuh] before a declarative sentence:

| | |
|---|---|
| Are you French? | **Est-ce que vous êtes français?** |

**WH- questions** are another major category. These are the questions which in English begin with *wh*.

| who | **qui** | kee |
|---|---|---|
| what | **que** | kuh |
| where | **où** | oo |
| when | **quand** | kah(n) |
| why | **pourquoi** | poorkwah |
| how | **comment** | kohmah(n) |

In French, WH questions are formed as follows.

WH-word + est-ce que + declarative

| | |
|---|---|
| When does the train leave? | **Quand est-ce que le train part?** |
| Where can I change my money? | **Où est-ce que je peux changer mon argent?** |

You may also hear *pronoun-verb inversion questions:*

| | |
|---|---|
| Do you speak French? | **Parlez-vous français?** |
| Do you like ice cream? | **Aimez-vous la glace?** |

Note: Pronoun inversion may be used to form a question with any pronoun except, in most cases, *je* (I). Here you generally use the *est-ce que* structure.

| | |
|---|---|
| Are we on time? | **Sommes-nous à l'heure?** |
| Am I on time? | **Est-ce que je suis à l'heure?** |

To change the expression *Il y a* (There is) to a question, a *t* is added for easier pronunciation—*y'a-t-il?* (Is there?), pronounced *yahteel.*

## VERBS

There are three principal types of verb conjugations in French, each signaled by a distinctive verb ending or infinitive.

### -*er* Verbs

Verbs ending in *-er*, such as *parler* (to speak), are by far the most common verb category.

| | | |
|---|---|---|
| I speak | **je parle** | zhuh parl |
| you speak | **tu parles** | tew parl |
| he/she/one speaks | **il/elle/on parle** | eel/ehl/oh(n) parl |
| we speak | **nous parlons** | noo parloh(n) |
| you speak | **vous parlez** | voo parlay |
| they speak | **ils/elles parlent** | eel/ehl parl |
| Speak! | **Parlez !** | Parlay! |

The following is a list of some of the more common *-er* verbs that are conjugated according to the regular pattern above.

| | | | |
|---|---|---|---|
| to like, love | **aimer** | to close | **fermer** |
| to change | **changer** | to eat | **manger** |
| to look for | **chercher** | to speak | **parler** |
| to cost | **coûter** | to look at | **regarder** |
| to eat dinner | **dîner** | to work | **travailler** |
| to give | **donner** | to find | **trouver** |
| to listen to | **écouter** | to travel | **voyager** |

GRAMMAR

### -*ir* Verbs

The second type of verb ends in -*ir*, such as *finir* (to finish).

| I finish | **je finis** | zhuh feenee |
| you finish | **tu finis** | tew feenee |
| he/she/one finishes | **il/elle/on finit** | eel/ehl/oh(n) feenee |
| we finish | **nous finissons** | noo feeneesoh(n) |
| you finish | **vous finissez** | voo feeneesay |
| they finish | **ils/elles finissent** | eel/ehl feenees |
| Finish! | **Finissez!** | Feeneesay! |

### -*re* Verbs

The third category of verb ends in -*re*, such as *rendre* (to give back).

| I give back | **je rends** | zhuh rah(n) |
| you give back | **tu rends** | tew rah(n) |
| he/she/one gives back | **il/elle/on rend** | eel/ehl/oh(n) rah(n) |
| we give back | **nous rendons** | noo rah(n)doh(n) |
| you give back | **vous rendez** | voo rah(n)day |
| they give back | **ils/elles rendent** | eel/ehl rah(n)d |
| Give it back! | **Rendez -le/la!** | Rah(n)day-luh/lah! |

The following is a list of several common -*re* verbs that are conjugated according to the regular pattern above.

| to wait | **attendre** |
| to descend, get off | **descendre** |
| to listen | **entendre** |
| to give back | **rendre** |
| to answer | **répondre (à)** |

## Most Common Irregular Verbs

As in most languages, the French verbs used most frequently are those that show the greatest irregularities. Here are conjugations of a few of the most common irregular verbs.

| Infinitive: | Être (Are) | Avoir (Have) | Aller (Go) | Faire (Make/Do) |
|---|---|---|---|---|
| je | suis | ai | vais | fais |
| tu | es | as | vas | fais |
| il/elle/on | est | a | va | fait |
| nous | sommes | avons | allons | faisons |
| vous | êtes | avez | allez | faîtes |
| ils/elles | sont | ont | vont | font |
| imperative | soyez | ayez | allez | faîtes |

| Infinitive: | Venir (Come) | Pouvoir (Be able) | Vouloir (Want) |
|---|---|---|---|
| je | viens | peux | veux |
| tu | viens | peux | veux |
| il/elle/on | vient | peut | veut |
| nous | venons | pouvons | voulons |
| vous | venez | pouvez | voulez |
| ils/elles | viennent | peuvent | veulent |
| imperative | venez | — | — |

## Future Action

As in English, you may express upcoming action in French by using the conjugated form of the helping verb *to go—aller—*plus the infinitive of the main verb.

| | |
|---|---|
| I'm going to leave tomorrow. | **Je vais partir demain.** |
| We're going to visit Paris tomorrow. | **Nous allons visiter Paris demain.** |

## Past Tense

To express an action in the past, French uses the following structure: Subject + proper form of helping verb *avoir* + past participle.

Pierre sang.                    **Pierre a chanté.**
We ate.                      **Nous avons mangé.**

The past participle of regular verbs is predictable from the type of infinitive ending.

- Type of Infinitive    -er    -ir    -re
- Past Participle         -é     -i    -u

| Verb | | Infinitive | Past Participle |
|------|------|------------|-----------------|
| **-er** | to speak | **parler** | **parlé** |
| | to sing | **chanter** | **chanté** |
| | to love | **aimer** | **aimé** |
| **-ir** | to finish | **finir** | **fini** |
| | to choose | **choisir** | **choisi** |
| | to lose weight | **maigrir** | **maigri** |
| **-re** | to give back | **rendre** | **rendu** |
| | to sell | **vendre** | **vendu** |
| | to wait | **attendre** | **attendu** |

I sold my ticket.           **J'ai vendu mon billet.**
They chose a hotel.         **Ils ont choisi un hôtel.**
We sang a French song.     **Nous avons chanté une chanson française.**

Note: a number of common verbs are conjugated with *être* as the helping verb instead of *avoir* to form the past tense. In this case, the past participle must agree with the subject (masculine or feminine) of the sentence. These verbs, with their corresponding past participles, are shown on the following page.

| Verb | Infinitive | Past Participle |
|------|-----------|-----------------|
| to arrive | **arriver** | arrivé(e) |
| to return | **retourner** | retourné(e) |
| to go up | **monter** | monté(e) |
| to go down | **descendre** | descendu(e) |
| to enter | **entrer** | entré(e) |
| to return | **rentrer** | rentré(e) |
| to leave | **sortir** | sorti(e) |
| to leave | **partir** | parti(e) |
| to go | **aller** | allé(e) |
| to die | **mourir** | mort(e) |
| to be born | **naitre** | né(e) |

| | |
|---|---|
| Pierre left at two o'clock. | **Pierre est sorti à deux heures.** |
| Marie left at three o'clock. | **Marie est sortie à trois heures.** |
| Nicole was born in 1952. | **Nicole est née en 1952.** |
| We went to the concert yesterday. | **Nous sommes allés au concert hier.** |

**Irregular Past Participles:** Some of the most commonly used French verbs have irregular past participles. A number of these are listed below.

| Verb | Infinitive | Past Participle |
|------|-----------|-----------------|
| to have | **avoir** | eu |
| to be | **être** | été |
| to be able | **pouvoir** | pu |
| to make/do | **faire** | fait |
| to see | **voir** | vu |
| to want | **vouloir** | voulu |
| to drink | **boire** | bu |
| to open | **ouvrir** | ouvert |
| to write | **écrire** | écrit |
| to take | **prendre** | pris |

| I had (literally: took) my breakfast at 7 a.m. | **J'ai pris mon petit déjeuner à 7 heures.** |
| They saw the Eiffel Tower yesterday. | **Ils ont vu la Tour Eiffel hier.** |

## Reflexive Verbs

Reflexive verbs are those for which the subject and the object of the action are one and the same, i.e., the subject performs the action on himself or herself. The following sentence pattern is used with reflexive verb forms: Subject + reflexive pronoun + verb.

| I am washing myself. | **Je me lave.** | zhuh muh lahv. |
| Pierre is shaving himself. | **Pierre se rase.** | Pyehr suh rahz. |
| We are hurrying. | **Nous nous dépêchons.** | Noo noo daypehshoh(n). |

The *reflexive pronoun* must agree with the subject of the sentence.

| Subject | Reflexive Pronoun |
| --- | --- |
| je | me |
| tu | te |
| il, elle, on | se |
| nous | nous |
| vous | vous |
| ils, elles | se |

A number of verbs which are not reflexive in English are reflexive in French. The most common ones include:

| to be called | **s'appeler** |
| to sit down | **s'asseoir** |
| to change clothes | **se changer** |

| | |
|---|---|
| to go to bed | **se coucher** |
| to hurry | **se dépêcher** |
| to get undressed | **se déshabiller** |
| to get dressed | **s'habiller** |
| to get up | **se lever** |
| to take a walk | **se promener** |
| to wake up | **se réveiller** |
| to make a mistake | **se tromper** |

# ENGLISH-FRENCH DICTIONARY

The gender of nouns is indicated by *m.* (masculine) or *f.* (feminine). Nouns commonly used in the plural are shown in the plural form and are followed by the notation *pl.*

Adjectives are listed in the masculine singular form. The formation of feminine and plural adjectives is described in the chapter on grammar. Irregular feminine and plural adjective forms are listed in the dictionary.

## A

**a, an**  un, *m.* *[uh(n)]*
  une, *f.* *[ewn]*
**to be able to**  pouvoir *[poovwahr]*
**above**  dessus *[duhsew]*
**abroad**  à l'étranger *[ah laytrah(n)zhay]*
**to accept**  accepter *[ahksehp-tay]*
**accident (auto)**  panne, *f.* *[pahn]*
**to accompany**  accompagner *[ahkoh(m)pahnyay]*
**accompanying vegetables**  garniture, *f.* *[gahrneetewr]*
**according to**  selon *[suhloh(n)]*
**acquaintance**  connaissance, *f.* *[koynehsah(n)s]*
**address**  adresse, *f.* *[ahdrehs]*
**to adore**  adorer *[ahdohray]*
**adult**  adulte, *m.* *[ahdewlt]*
**to be afraid of**  avoir peur de *[ahvwahr puhr duh]*
**after**  après *[ahpreh]*
**afternoon**  après-midi, *m.* *[ahpreh-meedee]*

**afterwards**  ensuite *[ah(n)sweet]*
**again**  encore *[ah(n)kohr]*
**against**  contre *[koh(n)tr]*
**age**  âge, *m.* *[ahzh]*
**agency**  agence, *f.* *[ahzhah(n)s]*
**ago**  il y a *[eel yah]*
**agreed**  entendu *[ah(n)tah(n)-dew]*, d'accord *[dahkohr]*
**air-conditioned**  climatisé *[kleemahteezay]*
**air-letter**  aérogramme, *m.* *[ah-ayrohgrahm]*
**airplane**  avion *m.* *[ahvyoh(n)]*
**airport**  aéroport, *m.* *[ah-ayrohpohr]*
**alarm clock**  réveil, *m.* *[rayvehy]*
**all**  tout *[too]*
**all directions**  toutes directions *[toot deerehksyoh(n)]*
**almonds**  amandes, *f.pl.* *[ahmah(n)d]*
**almost**  presque *[prehsk]*
**alone**  seul *[suhl]*
**also**  aussi *[ohsee]*
**America**  Amérique, *f.* *[Ahmayreek]*

**American** américain [ahmay-reeka(n)]

**among** parmi [pahrmee]

**to amuse** (s')amuser [(s)ahmewzay]

**anchovies** anchois, m.pl. [ah(n)shwah]

**and** et [ay]

**answer** réponse, f. [raypoh(n)s]

**to answer** répondre [raypoh(n)dr]

**antique dealer** antiquaire, m. [ah(n)teekehr]

**antiques** antiquités, f.pl. [ah(n)teekeetay]

**aperitif** apéritif, m. [ahpayreeteef]

**apology** pardon, m. [pahrdoh(n)]

**to apologize** s'excuser [sehkskewzay]

**appetite** appétit, m. [ahpaytee]

**appetizers** hors d'oeuvres, m.pl. [ohr duhvr]

**apple** pomme, f. [pohm]

**appointment** rendez-vous, m. [rah(n)day-voo]

**apricot** abricot, m. [ahbreekoh]

**April** avril [ahvreel]

**are there . . .** y a-t-il . . . [yahteel . . .]

**area code** indicatif, m. [a(n)deekahteef]

**arm** bras, m. [brah]

**armchair** fauteuil, m. [fohtuhy]

**to arrive** arriver [ahreevay]

**art** art, m. [ahr]

**art gallery** galerie d'art, f. [gahlree dahr]

**artichoke** artichaut, m. [ahrteeshoh]

**artichoke heart** fond d'artichaut, m. [foh(n) dahrteeshoh]

**article** article, m. [ahrteekl]

**ashtray** cendrier, m. [sah(n)dreeay]

**to ask** demander [duhman(n)day]

**asparagus** asperge, f. [ahspehrzh]

**at** à [ah]

**at the house of** chez [shay]

**to attach** attacher [ahtahshay]

**attention** attention, f. [ahtah(n)syoh(n)]

**attic** grenier, m. [gruhnyay]

**attraction** curiosité, f. [kewryohzeetay]

**August** août [oot]

**aunt** tante, f. [tah(n)t]

**automatic** automatique [ohtohmahteek]

**autumn** automne, m. [ohtohn]

**avocado** avocat, m. [ahvohkah]

## B

**babysitter** garde d'enfants, f. [gahrd dah(n)fah(n)]

**back** dos, m. [doh]

**in back of** derrière [dehryehr]

**bacon** lard, m. [lahr]

**bad** mauvais [mohvay]

214

**badly** mal *[mahl]*

**bag** sac, m. *[sahk]*

**baggage locker** consigne automatique, f. *[koh(n)seen yohtohmahteek]*

**bake shop** boulangerie, f. *[boolah(n)zhree]*

**balcony** balcon, m. *[bahlkoh(n)]*

**banana** banane, f. *[bahnahn]*

**bank** banque, f. *[bah(n)k]*

**bar** bar, m. *[bahr]*

**barber** coiffeur, m. *[kwahfuhr]*

**basement** cave, f. *[kahv]*

**basket** panier, m. *[pahnyay]*

**basketball** basket, m. *[bahskeht]*

**bath** bain, m. *[ba(n)]*

**to bathe** (se) baigner *[(suh) behnyay]*

**bathing suit** maillot de bain, m. *[mahyoh duh ba(n)]*

**bathrobe** robe de chambre, f. *[rohb duh shah(m)br]*

**bathroom** salle de bain, f. *[sahl duh ba(n)]*

**battery** pile, f. *[peel]*

**to be** être *[ehtr]*

**beach** plage, f. *[plahzh]*

**bean** haricot, m. *[ahreekoh]*

**beard** barbe, f. *[bahrb]*

**beautiful** beau, m. *[boh]* belle, f. *[behl]*

**beauty parlor** salon de beauté, m. *[sahlon(n) duh bohtay]*

**because** parce que *[pahrs kuh]*

**to become** devenir *[duhvuh-neer]*

**bed** lit, m. *[lee]*

**bed and breakfast** chambre d'hôte, f. *[shah(m)br doht]*

**bedroom** chambre, f. *[shah(m)br]*

**beef** boeuf, m. *[buhf]*

**beer** bière, f. *[byehr]*

**beet** betterave, f. *[behtrahv]*

**before** avant *[ahvah(n)]*

**to begin** commencer *[kohmah(n)say]*

**beginner** débutant, m. *[daybewtah(n)]*

**behind** derrière *[dehryehr]*

**Belgian** belge *[behlzh]*

**Belgium** Belgique, f. *[Behlzheek]*

**to believe** croire *[krwahr]*

**bellboy** chasseur, m. *[shahsuhr]*

**below** en bas *[ah(n) bah]*

**belt** ceinture, f. *[sa(n)tewr]*

**beneath** dessous *[duhsoo]*

**beside** à côté de *[ah kohtay duh]*

**better (adj.)** meilleur *[mehyuhr]*

**better (adv.)** mieux *[myuh]*

**between** entre *[ah(n)tr]*

**beyond** au delà de *[oh duhlah duh]*

**big** grand *[grah(n)]*

**bill** addition, f. *[ahdeesyoh(n)]* note, f. *[noht]*

**birthday** anniversaire, m. *[ahneevehrsehr]*

**bitter** amer *[ahmehr]*

**black** noir *[nwahr]*

**blanket** couverture, f. *[koovehrtewr]*

**blinker** clignotant, *m.*
*[kleenyohtah(n)]*
**blond** blond *[bloh(n)]*
**blood** sang, *m.* *[sah(n)]*
**blouse** blouse, *f.* *[blooz]*
**blue** bleu *[bluh]*
**blue zone (parking area)**
zone bleue, *f.* *[zohn bluh]*
**boarding pass** carte d'accès
à bord, *f.* *[kahrt dahksay ah
bohr]*
**boat** barque, *f.* *[bahrk]*
bâteau, *m.* *[bahtoh]*
**body** corps, *m.* *[kohr]*
**boiled** bouilli *[booyee]*
**bone** os, *m.* *[ohs]*
**book** livre, *m.* *[leevr]*
**book (of tickets)** carnet, *m.*
*[kahrnay]*
**bookstore** librairie, *f.* *[lee-
brehree]*
**boot** botte, *f.* *[boht]*
**booth** cabine, *f.* *[kahbeen]*
**border** frontière, *f.* *[froh(n)-
tyehr]*
**born** né *[nay]*
**to borrow** emprunter
*[ah(m)pruh(n)tay]*
**boss** chef, *m.* *[shehf]*
**to bother** gêner *[zhehnay]*
**bottle** bouteille, *f.* *[bootehy]*
**box** boîte, *f.* *[bwaht]*
**boy** garçon, *m.* *[gahrsoh(n)]*
**bracelet** bracelet, *m.*
*[brahslay]*
**brain** cervelle, *f.* *[sehrvehl]*
**brakes** freins, *m.pl.* *[fra(n)]*
**bread** pain, *m.* *[pa(n)]*
**to break** briser *[breezay]*
**breakdown (car)** panne, *f.*
*[pahn]*

**breakfast** petit déjeuner, *m.*
*[puhtee dayzhuhnay]*
**bridge** pont, *m.* *[poh(n)]*
**briefcase** serviette, *f.* *[sehr-
vyeht]*
**to bring** amener *[ahmnay]*
apporter *[ahpohrtay]*
**broken** cassé *[kahsay]*
**brother** frère, *m.* *[frehr]*
**brother-in-law** beau-frère,
*m.* *[boh-frehr]*
**brown** brun *[bruh(n)]*
**brush** brosse, *f.* *[brohs]*
**Brussels** Bruxelles *[Brewsehl]*
**Brussels sprouts** chou de
Bruxelles, *m.* *[shoo duh
Brewsehl]*
**to buckle** attacher *[ahtah-
shay]*
**bulb** ampoule, *f.* *[ah(m)pool]*
**to burn** brûler *[brewlay]*
**bus** autobus, *m.* *[ohtohbews]*
car, *m.* *[kahr]*
**bus stop** arrêt d'autobus,
*m.* *[ahreh dohtohbews]*
**business** affaires, *f.pl.*
*[ahfehr]*
**busy** occupé *[ohkewpay]*
**but** mais *[meh]*
**butcher shop** boucherie, *f.*
*[booshree]*
**butter** beurre, *m.* *[buhr]*
**button** bouton, *m.* *[bootoh(n)]*
**buy** acheter *[ahshtay]*
**by** par *[pahr]*

## C

**cabaret** cabaret, *m.*
*[kahbahray]*

**cabbage** chou, m. *[shoo]*

**café** café, m. *[kahfay]*

**cake** gâteau, m. *[gahtoh]*

**calico** toile de coton, f. *[twahl duh kohtoh(n)]*

**to call (by name)** (s')appeler *[(s)ahplay]*

**to call back** rappeler *[rahplay]*

**calm** tranquil *[trah(n)keel]*

**camera** appareil de photo, m. *[ahpahrehy duh fohtoh]*

**camomile** camomille, m. *[kahmohmeel]*

**to camp** camper *[kah(m)pay]*

**can I...** puis-je... *[pweezh]*

**Canada** Canada, m. *[Kahnahdah]*

**Canadian** canadien *[kahnahdya(n)]*

**to cancel** annuler *[ahnewlay]*

**candle** bougie, f. *[boozhee]*

**car** auto, f. *[ohtoh]* voiture, f. *[vwahtewr]*

**car breakdown** panne, f. *[pahn]*

**car rental agency** agence de location de voiture, f. *[ahzhah(n)s duh lohkahsyoh(n) duh vewahtewr]*

**carafe** carafe, f. *[kahrahf]*

**carbonated** gazeux *[gahzuh]*

**carburetor** carburateur, m. *[kahrbewrahtuhr]*

**card** fiche, f. *[feesh]*

**carefully** avec soin *[ahvehk swa(n)]*

**carrot** carotte, f. *[kahroht]*

**to carry** porter *[pohrtay]*

**cart** chariot, m. *[shahryoh]*

**to cash (a check)** toucher *[tooshay]*

**cash register** caisse, f. *[kehs]*

**cashier** caissier, m. *[kehsyay]*

**cassette recorder** magnétophone à cassette, m. *[mahnyaytohfohn ah kahseht]*

**castle** château, m. *[shahtoh]*

**cat** chat, m. *[shah]*

**to catch** attraper *[ahtrahpay]*

**cathedral** cathédrale, f. *[kahtaydrahl]*

**cauliflower** chou-fleur, m. *[shoo-fluhr]*

**cave** grotte, f. *[groht]*

**ceiling** plafond, m. *[plahfoh(n)]*

**celery** céleri, m. *[saylree]*

**cell** cellule, f. *[sehlewl]*

**cemetery** cimetière, m. *[seemtyehr]*

**center** centre, m. *[sah(n)tr]*

**centime (1/100 franc)** centime, m. *[sah(n)teem]*

**certainly** certainement *[sehrtehnmah(n)]*

**chain** chaînette, f. *[shehnneht]*

**chair** chaise, f. *[shehz]*

**change** monnaie, f. *[mohneh]*

**to change** changer *[shah(n)zhay]*

**change of train/bus** correspondance, f. *[kohrehspoh(n)dah(n)s]*

**chapel** chapelle, f. *[shahpehl]*

**cheap** bon marché *[boh(n) mahrshay]*

**check** chèque, m. *[shehk]*

**to check** enregistrer *[ah(n)rehzheestray]*

217

**cheese** fromage, m. *[frohmahzh]*

**cherry** cerise, f. *[suhreez]*

**chest** poitrine, f. *[pwahtreen]*

**chicken** poulet, m. *[poolay]*

**child** enfant, m. or f. *[ah(n)fah(n)]*

**chin** menton, m. *[mah(n)toh(n)]*

**choice** choix, m. *[shwah]*

**to choose** choisir *[shwahzeer]*

**church** église, f. *[aygleez]*

**cider** cidre, m. *[seedr]*

**cigar** cigare, f. *[seegahr]*

**cigarette** cigarette, f. *[seegahreht]*

**cigarette case** étui, m. *[aytwee]*

**cinnamon** cannelle, f. *[kahnehl]*

**city** ville, f. *[veel]*

**classic** classique *[klahseek]*

**clean** propre *[prohpr]*

**to clean** nettoyer *[nehtwahyay]*

**clear** clair *[klehr]*

**cliff** falaise, f. *[fahlehz]*

**clock** pendule, f. *[pah(n)dewl]*

**to close** fermer *[fehrmay]*

**closet** armoire, f. *[ahrmwahr]*

**clothes** vêtements, m.pl. *[vehtmah(n)]*

**cloudy** couvert *[koovehr]*

**coast** côte, f. *[koht]*

**coat** manteau, m. *[mah(n)toh]*

**cod** morue, f. *[mohrew]*

**coffee** café, m. *[kahfay]*

**coffee with milk** café au lait, m. *[kahfay oh leh]*

**cognac** cognac, m. *[koh-nyahk]*

**cold** froid *[frwah]*

**cold (virus)** rhûme, f. *[rewm]*

**cold (weather)** froid, m. *[frwah]*

**cold cuts** charcuterie, f. *[shahrkewtree]*

**collar** col, m. *[kohl]*

**colleague** collègue, m. or f. *[kohlehg]*

**collect (call)** en P.C.V. *[ah(n) pay say vay]*

**color** couleur, f. *[kooluhr]*

**comb** peigne, m. *[pehnyuh]*

**to come** venir *[vuhneer]*

**to come back** revenir *[ruhvuhneer]*

**company** compagnie, f. *[koh(m)pahnyee]*

**compartment** compartiment, m. *[koh(m)pahrteemah(n)]*

**complaint** plainte, f. *[pla(n)t]*

**concert** concert, m. *[koh(n)sehr]*

**to confirm** confirmer *[koh(n)feermay]*

**congratulations!** félicitations! *[fayleeseetahsyoh(n)!]*

**contact lens** verre de contact, m. *[vehr duh koh(n)tahkt]*

**contents** contenu, m. *[koh(n)tuhnew]*

**continental breakfast** café complet, m. *[kahfay koh(m)play]*

**to continue** continuer *[koh(n)teenway]*

218

**cook** cuisinier, m. [kwee-zeenyay]
**to cook** faire cuire [fehr kweer]
**cooked** cuit [kwee]
**cookies** biscuits [beeskwee]
**cooking** cuisine, f. [kweezeen]
**cool** frais [freh]
**corduroy** velour côtelé, m. [vuhloor kohtuhlay]
**corkscrew** tire-bouchon, m. [teer-booshoh(n)]
**corn** maïs, m. [mah-ees]
**corner** coin, m. [kwa(n)]
**correspondence** correspon-dance, f. [kohrehspoh(n)dah(n)s]
**to cost** coûter [kootay]
**cotton** coton, m. [kohtoh(n)]
**cough** toux, f. [too]
**to cough** tousser [toosay]
**to count** compter [koh(m)tay]
**country (landscape)** campagne, f. [kah(m)pahnyuh]
**country (nation)** pays, m. [payee]
**course** cours, m. [koor]
**courthouse** palais de justice, m. [pahleh duh zhewstees]
**cousin** cousin, m. [kooza(n)] cousine, f. [koozeen]
**to cover** couvrir [koovreer]
**cover charge** couvert, m. [koovehr]
**covered** couvert [koovehr]
**crab** crabe, m. [krahb]
**cream** crème, f. [krehm]
**credit card** carte de crédit, f. [kahrt duh kraydee]
**creole** créole [krayohl]

**creperie** crêperie, f. [krehpree]
**to cross (go across)** tra-verser [trahvehrsay]
**crosswalk** passage clouté, m. [pahsahzh klootay]
**crust** croûte, f. [kroot]
**to cry** pleurer [pluhray]
**cucumber** concombre, m. [koh(n)koh(m)br]
**cup** tasse, f. [tahs]
**curl** boucle, f. [bookl]
**curlers** bigoudis, m.pl. [beegoodee]
**currency** change, m. [shah(n)zh]
**currency exchange office** bureau de change, m. [bewroh duh shah(n)zh]
**custard** flan, m. [flah(n)]
**customer** client, m. [kleeah(n)]
**customs** douane, f. [dwahn]
**cut** coupe, f. [koop]
**to cut, cut off** couper [koopay]
**cutlet** côtelette, f. [kohtleht]
**cycling** cyclisme, m. [seek-leezm]

# D

**daily** quotidien [kohteedya(n)]
**dance** danse, f. [dah(n)s]
**to dance** danser [dah(n)say]
**dangerous** dangereux [dah(n)zhuhruh]
**dark** foncé [foh(n)say]
**date (fruit)** datte, f. [daht]
**daughter** fille, f. [feey]

**day** jour, m. *[zhoor]*
**by the day** à la journée *[ah lah zhoornay]*
**the day after tomorrow** après-demain *[ahpreh-duhma(n)]*
**dead end** voie sans issue, f. *[vwah sah(n) zeesew]*
**dear** cher *[shehr]*
**decaffeinated** décaféiné *[daykahfayeenay]*
**December** décembre *[daysah(m)br]*
**to decide** décider *[dayseeday]*
**to declare** déclarer *[dayklahray]*
**deep-sea diving** plongée sous-marine, f. *[ploh(n)zhay soo-mahreen]*
**delay** retard, m. *[ruhtahr]*
**delicatessen** charcuterie, f. *[shahrkewtree]*
**delighted** enchanté *[ah(n)-shah(n)tay]*
**department store** grand magasin, m. *[grah(n) mahgahza(n)]*
**desire** envie, f. *[ah(n)vee]*
**desk** bureau, m. *[bewroh]*
**detour** déviation, f. *[dayvyah-syoh(n)]*
**diabetic** diabétique *[dyah-bayteek]*
**to dial** composer *[koh(m)pohzay]*
**diamond** diamant, m. *[dyahmah(n)]*
**diaper** couche, f. *[koosh]*
**dictionary** dictionnaire, f. *[deeksyohnehr]*

**diesel fuel** gas oil, m. *[gahzwahl]*
**diet** régime, m. *[rayzheem]*
**different** différent *[deefayrah(n)]*
**difficult** difficile *[deefeeseel]*
**to diminish** diminuer *[deemeeneway]*
**to dine** dîner *[deenay]*
**dining room** salle à manger, f. *[sahl ah mah(n)zhay]*
**dinner** dîner, m. *[deenay]*
**direct flight** vol direct, m. *[vohl deerehkt]*
**direction** direction, f. *[deerehksyoh(n)]*
sens, m. *[sah(n)s]*
**directory (telephone)** annuaire, m. *[ahnwehr]*
**dirty** sale *[sahl]*
**disappointed** déçu *[daysew]*
**dish** plat, m. *[plah]*
**distance** distance, f. *[deestah(n)s]*
**to disturb** déranger *[dayrah(n)zhay]*
**divorced** divorcé *[deevohrsay]*
**do . . . ?** est-ce que . . . ? *[ehskuh . . . ?]*
**to do** faire *[fehr]*
**doctor** médecin, m. *[maydsa(n)]*
**dog** chien, m. *[shyeh(n)]*
**donut** beignet, m. *[behnyay]*
**door** porte, f. *[pohrt]*
**downstairs** en bas *[ah(n) bah]*
**downtown** centre ville, m. *[sah(n)truh veel]*

**dozen** douzaine, f. *[doozehn]*
**drama** drame, m. *[drahm]*
**dress** robe, f. *[rohb]*
**to dress** s'habiller *[sahbeeyay]*
**dried fruit** fruits secs m.pl.
*[frwee sehk]*
**drink** boisson, f. *[bwahsoh(n)]*
**to drink** boire *[bwahr]*
**to drive (a car)** conduire
*[koh(n)dweer]*
**to drop off** déposer *[daypoh-zay]*
**drunk** ivre *[eevr]*
**dry** sec *[sehk]*
**to dry clean** nettoyer à sec
*[nehtwahyay ah sehk]*
**dry cleaners** teinturerie, f.
*[ta(n)tewruhree]*
**dry wine** vin brut, m. *[va(n) brewt]*
**dubbed** doublé *[dooblay]*
**duck** canard, m. *[kahnahr]*
**duckling** caneton, m.
*[kahntoh(n)]*
**during** pendant *[pah(n)-dah(n)]*
**duty-free shop** magasin
hors-taxe, m. *[mahgahza(n) ohr-tahks]*

## E

**each** chaque *[shahk]*
**each one** chacun *[shahkuh(n)]*
**ear** oreille, f. *[ohrehy]*
**early** tôt *[toh]*
**to earn** gagner *[gahnyay]*
**earring** boucle d'oreille, f.
*[bookl dohrehy]*
**east** est, m. *[ehst]*

**easy** facile *[fahseel]*
**to eat** manger *[mah(n)zhay]*
**éclair (type of pastry)**
éclair, m. *[ayklehr]*
**eel** anguille, f. *[ah(n)geey]*
**egg** oeuf, m. *[uhf]*
**eggplant** aubergine, f.
*[ohbehrzheen]*
**eight** huit *[weet]*
**eighteen** dix-huit *[dee-zweet]*
**eighty** quatre-vingts *[kahtr-va(n)]*
**eldest** aîné *[ehnay]*
**electricity** électricité, f.
*[aylehktreeseetay]*
**elevator** ascenseur, m.
*[ahsah(n)suhr]*
**eleven** onze *[oh(n)z]*
**elsewhere** ailleurs *[ahyuhr]*
**emergency** urgence, f.
*[ewrzhah(n)s]*
**emergency road service**
dépannage, m. *[day-pahnahzh]*
**empty** vide *[veed]*
**end** fin, f. *[fa(n)]*
**to end** terminer *[tehrmeenay]*
**England** Angleterre, f.
*[Ah(n)gluhtehr]*
**English** anglais *[ah(n)gleh]*
**enlargement**
agrandissement, m. *[ah-grah(n)deesmah(n)]*
**enough** assez *[ahsay]*
**entire** entier *[ah(n)tyay]*
**entrance** entrée, f. *[ah(n)tray]*
**entry prohibited** défense
d'entrée *[dayfah(n)s dah(n)tray]*
**environment** milieu, m.
*[meelyuh]*

**error** erreur, f. [ehruhr]

**evening** soir, m. [swahr]

**evening party** soirée, f. [swahray]

**every** chaque [shahk]

**everybody** tout le monde [too luh moh(n)d]

**everything** tout [too]

**everywhere** partout [pahrtoo]

**example** exemple, m. [ehgzah(m)pl]

**excellent** excellent [eksehlah(n)]

**exchange** change, m. [shah(n)zh]

**to exchange** échanger [ayshah(n)zhay]

**exchange office** bureau de change, m. [bewroh duh shah(n)zh]

**excursion** excursion, f. [ehkskewrsyoh(n)]

**excuse** pardon, m. [pahrdoh(n)]

**to excuse** pardonner [pahrdohnay]

**exhausted** épuisé [aypweezay]

**exit** sortie, f. [sohrtee]

**expensive** cher [shehr]

**extra** supplément, m. [sewplaymah(n)]

**eye** oeil, m. [uhy]

**eyeglasses** lunettes, f.pl. [lewneht]

**eyelash** cil, m. [seel]

# F

**face** visage, m. [veezahzh]

**factory** usine, f. [ewzeen]

**fall (season)** automne, m. [ohtohn]

**to fall** tomber [toh(m)bay]

**false** faux [foh]

**to be familiar with** connaître [kohnehtr]

**family** famille, f. [fahmeey]

**far** loin [lwa(n)]

**farm** ferme, f. [fehrm]

**fast** rapide [rahpeed]

**fat** gros [groh]

**father** père, m. [pehr]

**father-in-law** beau-père, m. [boh-pehr]

**faucet** robinet, m. [rohbeenay]

**fear** peur, f. [puhr]

**to fear** avoir peur de [ahvwahr puhr duh]

**February** février [fayvreeyay]

**to feel** se sentir [suh sah(n)teer]

**fever** fièvre, f. [fyehvr]

**few** peu de [puh duh]

**field** champ, m. [shah(m)]

**fifteen** quinze [ka(n)z]

**fifty** cinquante [se(n)kah(n)t]

**fig** figue, f. [feeg]

**filet** filet, m. [feelay]

**fill it up** faîtes le plein [feht luh pla(n)]

**film** cinéma, m. [seenaymah]

**film cartridge** pellicule, f. [pehleekewl]

**to find** trouver [troovay]

**fine arts** beaux arts, m.pl. [boh zahr]

**finger** doigt, m. [dwah]
**to finish** finir [feeneer]
**fire** feu, m. [fuh]
**first** premier [pruhmyay]
**fish** poisson, m. [pwahsoh(n)]
**fish soup** bouillabaisse, f. [booyahbehs]
**five** cinq [sa(n)]
**fixed** fixe [feeks]
**fixed price menu** menu à prix fixe, m. [muhnew ah pree feeks]
**flashlight** lampe de poche, f. [lah(m)p duh pohsh]
**flat** plat [plah]
**flavor** parfum, m. [pahr-fuh(m)]
**flea market** marché aux puces, m. [mahrshay oh pews]
**flight** vol, m. [vohl]
**floor** plancher, m. [plah(n)-shay]
**flour** farine, f. [fahreen]
**flower** fleur, f. [fluhr]
**flute** flûte, f. [flewt]
**to fly** voler [vohlay]
**fog** brouillard, m. [brooyahr]
**folkloric** folklorique [fohlklohreek]
**to follow** suivre [sweevr]
**food** nourriture, f. [nooreetewr]
**foot** pied, m. [pyay]
**on foot** à pied [ah pyay]
**for** pour [poor]
**forbidden** interdit [a(n)tehr-dee]
**foreign** étranger [aytrah(n)zhay]
**foreigner** étranger, m. [aytrah(n)zhay]

**forest** forêt, f. [fohreh]
**to forget** oublier [oobleeyay]
**fork** fourchette, f. [foorsheht]
**form** formulaire, m, [fohr-mewlehr]
**format** format, m. [fohrmah]
**fortress** forteresse, f. [fohr-tuhrehs]
**forty** quarante [kahrah(n)t]
**forward** en avant [ah(n) nahvah(n)]
**fountain** fountaine, f. [foh(n)-tehn]
**four** quatre [kahtr]
**fourteen** quatorze [kahtohrz]
**fowl** volaille, f. [vohlahy]
**franc** franc, m. [frah(n)]
**France** France, f. [Frah(n)s]
**free** libre [leebr]
**French** français [frah(n)say]
**French bread** baguette, f. [bahgeht]
**fresh** frais [freh]
**Friday** vendredi [vah(n)druh-dee]
**fried** frit [free]
**friend** ami, m. [ahmee] amie, f. [ahmee]
**friendship** amitié, f. [ah-meetyay]
**frog** grenouille, f. [gruhnooy]
**from** de [duh]
**in front of** devant [duhvah(n)]
**frost** verglas, m. [vehrglah]
**frozen** glacé [glahsay]
**fruit** fruit, m. [frwee]
**to have fun** s'amuser [sahmewzay]
**furnished** meublé [muhblay]

223

**furniture** meubles, *m.pl.*
*[muhbl]*

## G

**to gain weight** grossir
*[grohseer]*

**game (child's play)** jeu,
*m. [zhuh]*

**game (wild)** gibier, *m.*
*[zheebyay]*

**garage** garage, *m.*
*[gahrahzh]*

**garden** jardin, *m. [zhahr-da(n)]*

**garlic** ail, *m. [ahy]*

**gasoline** essence, *f.*
*[ehsah(n)s]*

**gasoline emergency**
panne d'essence, *f. [pahn dehsah(n)s]*

**gastronomical** gastronomique *[gahstrohnohmeek]*

**general delivery** poste res-
tante, *f. [pohst rehstah(n)t]*

**German** allemand
*[ahlmah(n)]*

**Germany** Allemagne, *f.*
*[Ahlmahnyuh]*

**to get off** descendre *[deh-sah(n)dr]*

**to get up** se lever *[suh luhvay]*

**gift** cadeau, *m. [kahdoh]*

**ginger** gingembre, *m.*
*[zha(n)zhah(m)br]*

**girl** fille, *f. [feey]*

**to give** donner *[dohnay]*

**glass** verre, *m. [vehr]*

**glove** gant, *m. [gah(n)]*

**to go** aller *[ahlay]*

**to go down** descendre *[deh-sah(n)dr]*

**to go up** monter *[moh(n)tay]*

**gold** or, *m. [ohr]*

**golf course** terrain de golf,
*m. [tehra(n) duh gohlf]*

**good** bon *[boh(n)]*

**good-bye** au revoir *[oh rvwahr]*

**goodness!** tiens! *[tyeh(n)]*

**goose** oie, *f. [wah]*

**gourmet cooking** haute
cuisine, *f. [oht kweezeen]*

**gourmet menu** menu
gastronomique, *m. [muhnew gahstrohnohmeek]*

**granddaughter** petite fille,
*f. [puhteet feey]*

**grandfather** grand-père,
*m. [grah(n)-pehr]*

**grandmother** grand-mère,
*f. [grah(n)-mehr]*

**grandson** petit fils, *m.*
*[puhtee fees]*

**grape** raisin, *m. [rayza(n)]*

**grapefruit** pamplemousse,
*m. [pah(m)pluhmoos]*

**grass** herbe, *f. [ehrb]*

**grave** tombe, *f. [toh(m)b]*

**gray** gris *[gree]*

**great** super *[sewpehr]*

**green** vert *[vehr]*

**green beans** haricots verts,
*m.pl. [ahreekoh vehr]*

**grilled** grillé *[greeyay]*

**grocery** épicerie, *f.*
*[aypeesree]*

**ground** sol, *m. [sohl]*

**ground floor** rez-de-chaussée, m. [ray-duh-shohsay]
**guide** guide, m. or f. [geed]
**guided** guidé [geeday]

## H

**hair** cheveux, m.pl. [shuhvuh]
**hair dryer** sèche-cheveux, m. [sehsh-shuhvuh]
**haircut** coupe de cheveux, f. [koop duh shuhvuh]
**hairdresser** coiffeur, m. [kwahfuhr]
**hairdresser's shop** salon de beauté, m. [sahloh(n) duh bohtay]
**hairpin** épingle à cheveux, f. [aypa(n)gl ah shuhvuh]
**half** demi [duhmee]
**half-bottle** demi-bouteille, f. [duhmee-bootehy]
**hall porter** concierge, m. or f. [koh(n)syehrzh]
**ham** jambon, m. [zhah(m)-boh(n)]
**hand** main, f. [ma(n)]
**handbag** sac, m. [sahk]
**handicapped** invalide [a(n)-vahleed]
**handkerchief** mouchoir, m. [mooshwahr]
**handmade** fait à la main [feh tah lah ma(n)]
**handsome** beau [boh]
**hanger** cintre, m. [sa(n)tr]
**happy** heureux [uhruh]
**harbor** port, m. [pohr]
**hardware store** quincaille-rie, f. [ka(n)kahyree]

**to have** avoir [ahvwahr]
**to have fun** s'amuser [sahmewzay]
**he** il [eel]
**head** tête, f. [teht]
**headlights** phares, f.pl. [fahr]
**health** santé, f. [sah(n)tay]
**to hear** entendre [ah(n)-tah(n)dr]
**heart** coeur, m. [kuhr]
**hearty appetite** bon appétit [boh(n) nahpaytee]
**heat** chauffage, m. [shohfahzh]
**heavy** lourd [loor]
**heel** talon, m. [tahloh(n)]
**height** hauteur, f. [ohtuhr]
**hello** bonjour [boh(n)zhoor]
**help** secours, m. [suhkoor]
**to help** aider [ehday]
**hen** poule, f. [pool]
**her (possessive)** sa/son/ses [sah/soh(n)/say]
**her (herself)** se/lui/la [suh/lwee/lah]
**herb** herbe, f. [ehrb]
**here** ici [eesee]
**here is . . .** voici . . . [vwahsee . . .]
**high** haut [oh]
**high school** lycée, m. [leesay]
**high tide** marée haute, f. [mahray oht]
**higher** supérieur [sewpay-ryuhr]
**highway** autoroute, f. [ohtohroot]
**highway ends** fin d'auto-route [fa(n) dohtohroot]

225

**hill**  colline, f. [kohleen]
  côte, f. [koht]
**him**  se/lui/le [suh/lwee/luh]
**to hire**  louer [looay]
**his**  sa/son/ses [sah/soh(n)/say]
**history**  histoire, f. [eestwahr]
**to hit**  frapper [frahpay]
**hole**  trou, m. [troo]
**holiday**  fête, f. [feht]
**to hope**  espérer [ehspayray]
**horse**  cheval, m. [shuhvahl]
**hospital**  hôpital, m. [oh-peetahl]
**host (restaurant)**  maître d'hôtel, m. [mehtr dohtehl]
**hot**  chaud [shoh]
**hotel**  hôtel, m. [ohtehl]
**hour**  heure, f. [uhr]
**house**  maison, f. [mehzoh(n)]
**at the house of**  chez [shay]
**household appliances**  appareils ménagers, m.pl. [ahpahrehy maynahzhay]
**how**  comment [kohmah(n)]
**how do you say. . .**  comment dit-on . . . [kohmah(n) deetoh(n) . . .]
**how many, how much**  combien [koh(m)byeh(n)]
**hundred**  cent [sah(n)]
**hunger**  faim, f. [fa(m)]
**to hurry**  se dépêcher [suh daypehshay]
**husband**  mari, m. [mahree]

**I**

**I**  je [zhuh]
**ice**  glace, f. [glahs]

**ice cream**  glace, f. [glahs]
**ice-cream cone**  cornet de glace, m. [kohrnay duh glahs]
**ice cube**  glaçon, m. [glahsoh(n)]
**iced**  glacé [glahsay]
**if**  si [see]
**ill**  malade [mahlahd]
**illness**  maladie, f. [mahlah-dee]
**important**  important [a(m)-pohrtah(n)]
**impossible**  impossible [a(m)-pohseebl]
**in**  dans [dah(n)]
  en [ah(n)]
**in back of**  derrière [dehryehr]
**in front of**  devant [duhvah(n)]
**in spite of**  malgré [mahlgray]
**included**  compris [koh(m)pree]
**to indicate**  indiquer [a(n)-deekay]
**to inform**  renseigner [rah(n)-sehnyay]
**information**  renseigne-ments, m.pl. [rah(n)-sehnyuhmah(n)]
**infusion**  infusion, f. [a(n)few-zyoh(n)]
**in-laws**  beaux-parents, m.pl. [boh-pahrah(n)]
**inn**  auberge, f. [ohbehrzh]
**inside**  dedans [duhdah(n)]
**instant coffee**  café soluble, m. [kahfay sohlewbl]
**instead of**  au lieu de [oh lyuh duh]
**intelligent**  intelligent [a(n)-tehleezhah(n)]

**to be interested in** s'intéresser [sa(n)tayrehsay]

**interesting** intéressant [a(n)tayrehsah(n)]

**intersection** carrefour, m. [kahrfoor]

**to introduce** présenter [prayzah(n)tay]

**to invite** inviter [a(n)veetay]

**iron** fer, m. [fehr]

**to iron** repasser à la vapeur [ruhpahsay ah lah vahpuhr]

**is . . . ?** est-ce que . . . ? [ehskuh . . . ?]

**it is, this is** c'est [seh]

**island** île, f. [eel]

**ivory** ivoire, f. [eevwahr]

## J

**jack** cric, m. [kreek]

**jacket** veston, m. [vehstoh(n)]

**jam** confiture, f. [koh(n)feetewr]

**January** janvier [zhah(n)vyay]

**jar** bocal, m. [bohkahl]

**jewelry box** coffret à bijoux, m. [kohfray ah beezhoo]

**jewelry shop** bijouterie, f. [beezhootree]

**jewels** bijoux, m.pl. [beezhoo]

**job** travail, m. [trahvahy]

**jogging** footing, m. [footeeng]

**joke** plaisanterie, f. [playzah(n)tree]

**to judge** juger [zhewzhay]

**juice** jus, m. [zhew]

**July** juillet [zhweeay]

**June** juin [zhwa(n)]

## K

**to keep** garder [gahrday]

**keep right** serrez à droite [sehray ah drwaht]

**key** clé, f. [klay]

**kilometer** kilomètre, m. [keelohmehtr]

**kiosk** kiosque, m. [keeohsk]

**to kiss** embrasser [ah(m)brahsay]

**kitchen** cuisine, f. [kweezeen]

**knee** genou, m. [zhuhnoo]

**knife** couteau, m. [kootoh]

**to knock** frapper [frahpay]

**to know (be familiar with)** connaître [kohnehtr]

**to know (facts)** savoir [sahvwahr]

**kosher** kasher [kahshehr]

## L

**lace** dentelle, f. [dah(n)tehl]

**lack** manque, m. [mah(n)k]

**to lack** manquer [mah(n)kay]

**ladder** échelle, f. [ayshehl]

**lake** lac, m. [lahk]

**lamb** mouton, m. [mootoh(n)]

**land** terre, f. [tehr]

**landscape** paysage, m. [payeezahzh]

**language** langue, f. [lah(n)g]

**last** dernier [dehrnyay]

**to last** durer [dewray]

**late** tard [tahr]

**to laugh** rire [reer]

**laundromat** laverie automatique, f. *[lahvree ohtohmahteek]*
**laundry** blanchisserie, f. *[blah(n)sheesree]*
**lawyer** avocat, m. *[ahvohkah]*
**layover** escale, f. *[ehskahl]*
**to learn** apprendre *[ahprah(n)dr]*
**at least** au moins *[oh mwa(n)]*
**leather** cuir, m. *[kweer]*
**to leave (depart)** partir *[pahrteer]*
**to leave (behind)** laisser *[lehsay]*
**leek** poireau, m. *[pwahroh]*
**left** gauche, f. *[gohsh]*
**leg** jambe, f. *[zhah(m)b]*
**lemon** citron, m. *[seetroh(n)]*
**lemonade** citron pressé, m. *[seetroh(n) prehsay]*
**to lend** prêter *[prehtay]*
**lens** objectif, m. *[ohbzhehkteef]* lentille, f. *[lah(n)teey]*
**less** moins *[mwa(n)]*
**lesson** leçon, f. *[luhsoh(n)]*
**to let** laisser *[lehsay]*
**letter** lettre, f. *[lehtr]*
**lettuce** laitue, f. *[lehtew]*
**level** niveau, m. *[neevoh]*
**lever** lévier, m. *[layvyay]*
**library** bibliothèque, f. *[beebleeohtehk]*
**license** permis, m. *[pehrmee]*
**life** vie, f. *[vee]*
**life guard** maître nageur, m. *[mehtr nahzhur]*
**light (adj.)** léger *[layzhay]*
**light** lumière, f. *[lewmyehr]*
**to light** allumer *[ahlewmay]*

**light meal** repas léger, m. *[ruhpah layzhay]*
**light wine** vin léger, m. *[va(n) layzhay]*
**lighter** briquet, m. *[breekay]*
**like, as** comme *[kohm]*
**to like** aimer *[ehmay]*
**I'd like** je voudrais *[zhuh voodreh]*
**lime** citron vert, m. *[seetroh(n) vehr]*
**line** ligne, f. *[leenyuh]*
**line (of people)** queue, f. *[kuh]*
**linen** lin, m. *[la(n)]*
**lipstick** rouge à lèvre, m. *[roozh ah lehvr]*
**liquor** liqueur, f. *[leekuhr]*
**list** liste, f. *[leest]*
**to listen** écouter *[aykootay]*
**liter** litre, m. *[leetr]*
**little, few** peu *[puh]*
**to live** habiter *[ahbeetay]*
**liver** foie, m. *[fwah]*
**living room** salon, m. *[sahloh(n)]*
**lobster** homard, m. *[ohmahr]* langouste, f. *[lah(n)goost]*
**local** local *[lohkahl]*
**local wine** vin du pays, m. *[va(n) dew payee]*
**long** long *[loh(n)]*
**for a long time** longtemps *[loh(n)tah(m)]*
**to look at** regarder *[ruhgahrday]*
**to look for** chercher *[shehrshay]*
**to lose** perdre *[pehrdr]*
**to lose weight** maigrir *[mehgreer]*

228

**lost** perdu *[pehrdew]*
**lost and found** bureau d'objects trouvés, m. *[bewroh dohbzhay troovay]*
**a lot** beaucoup *[bohkoo]*
**lotion** lotion, f. *[lohsyoh(n)]*
**love** amour, m. *[ahmoor]*
**to love** adorer *[ahdohray]* aimer *[ehmay]*
**low** bas *[bah]*
**low tide** marée basse, f. *[mahray bahs]*
**luck** chance, f. *[shah(n)s]*
**good luck!** bonne chance! *[bohn shah(n)s!]*
**luggage** bagages, m.pl. *[bahgahzh]*
**lunch** déjeuner, m. *[dayzhuhnay]*
**luxury** luxe, m. *[lewks]*

## M

**machine** appareil, m. *[ahpahrehy]*
**madam** madame *[mahdahm]*
**magazine** magazine, m. *[mahgahzeen]*
**mail** courrier, m. *[kooryay]*
**to mail** poster *[pohstay]*
**mailbox** boîte aux lettres, f. *[bwaht oh lehtr]*
**maitre d'** maître d'hôtel, m. *[mehtr dohtehl]*
**to make** faire *[fehr]*
**man** homme, m. *[ohm]*
**manager** gérant, m. *[zhayrah(n)]*
**manicurist** manucure, f. *[mahnewkewr]*

**many** beaucoup *[bohkoo]*
**map** carte, f. *[kahrt]* plan, m. *[plah(n)]*
**March** mars *[mahrs]*
**marjoram** marjolaine, f. *[mahrzhohlehn]*
**market** marché, m. *[mahrshay]*
**married** marié *[mahryay]*
**marvelous** merveilleux *[mehrvehyuh]*
**mass** messe, f. *[mehs]*
**match** allumette, f. *[ahlewmeht]*
**What's the matter?** Qu'est-ce qu'il y a? *[Kehs keel yah?]*
**May** mai *[meh]*
**maybe** peut-être *[puh-tehtr]*
**mayonnaise** mayonnaise, f. *[mahyohnehz]*
**me** me/moi *[muh/mwah]*
**meal** repas, m. *[ruhpah]*
**to mean** vouloir dire *[voolwahr deer]*
**meaning** sens, m. *[sah(n)s]* signification, f. *[seenyeefeekahsyoh(n)]*
**means** moyens, m.pl. *[mwahya(n)]*
**meat** viande, f. *[vyah(n)d]*
**mechanic** mécanicien, m. *[maykahneesya(n)]*
**medicine** médecine, f. *[maydseen]*
**medieval** médiéval *[maydyayvahl]*
**to meet** rencontrer *[rah(n)koh(n)tray]*
**meeting** réunion, f. *[rayewnyoh(n)]*

**melon** melon, m. [muhloh(n)]

**menu** carte, f. [kahrt]
menu, m. [muhnew]

**merchant** marchand, m. [mahrshah(n)]

**middle** milieu, m. [meelyuh]

**in the middle of** au milieu de [oh meelyuh duh]

**midnight** minuit [meenwee]

**mileage** kilométrage, m. [keelohmehtrahzh]

**milk** lait, m. [leh]

**with milk** au lait [oh leh]

**mineral** minérale [meenay-rahl]

**mineral water** eau minérale, f. [oh meenayrahl]

**mint** menthe, f. [mah(n)t]

**minute** minute, f. [meenewt]

**mirror** miroir, m, [meerwahr]

**miss (woman)** mademoi-selle [mahdmwahzehl]

**to miss** manquer [mah(n)kay]

**mistake** faute, f. [foht]

**mister, sir** monsieur [muh-syuh]

**moment** moment, m. [mohmah(n)]

**monastery** monastère, m. [mohnahstehr]

**Monday** lundi [luh(n)dee]

**money, change** monnaie, f. [mohneh]

**money, silver** argent, m. [ahrzhah(n)]

**month** mois, m. [mwah]

**moon** lune, f. [lewn]

**more** plus [plew]

**morning** matin, m. [mahta(n)]

**mosque** mosquée, f. [mohskay]

**mother** mère, f. [mehr]

**mother-in-law** belle-mère, f. [behl-mehr]

**mountain** montagne, f. [moh(n)tahnyuh]

**mountain pass** col, m. [kohl]

**mousse** mousse, f. [moos]

**mouth** bouche, f. [boosh]

**movies, movie theater** cinéma, m. [seenaymah]

**Mr.** monsieur [muhsyuh]

**Mrs.** madame [mahdahm]

**much** beaucoup [bohkoo]

**museum** musée, m. [mewzay]

**mushroom** champignon, m. [shah(m)peenyoh(n)]

**music** musique, f. [mewzeek]

**mussels** moules, f.pl. [mool]

**mustache** moustache, f. [moostahsh]

**mustard** moutarde, f. [mootahrd]

**my** ma/mon/mes [mah/moh(n)/may]

# N

**nail** ongle, m. [oh(n)gl]

**nail cutter** coupe-ongles, m. [koop-oh(n)gl]

**nail file** lime à ongles, f. [leem ah oh(n)gl]

**nail polish** vernis à ongles, m. [vehrnee ah oh(n)gl]

**name** nom, m. [noh(m)]

**to be named** s'appeler [sahplay]

**napkin** serviette, f. [sehrvyeht]

**napoleon (type of pastry)**
mille-feuille, m. [meel-fuhy]
**narrow** étroit [aytrwah]
**nationality** nationalité, f.
[nahsyohnahleetay]
**nature** nature, f. [nahtewr]
**near** près (de) [preh (duh)]
**nearby** proche [prohsh]
**necessary** nécessaire [nay-
sehsehr]
**it is necessary** il faut [eel
foh]
**neck** cou, m. [koo]
**necklace** collier, m. [kohlyay]
**necktie** cravate, f. [krahvaht]
**nectarine** brugnon, m.
[brewnyoh(n)]
**to need** avoir besoin de
[ahvwahr buhzwa(n) duh]
**neighbor** voisin, m. [vwah-
za(n)]
**neighborhood** quartier, m.
[kahrtyay]
**net** filet, m. [feelay]
**never** jamais [zhahmay]
**new** nouveau, m. [noovoh]
nouvelle, f. [noovehl]
**new cuisine** nouvelle cuisine, f. [noovchl kweezeen]
**newspaper/s** journal/
journaux, m. [zhoornal/
zhoornoh]
**newspaper stand** kiosque,
m. [keeohsk]
**next (adj.)** prochain [proh-
sha(n)]
**next** ensuite [ah(n)sweet]
**nice** gentil [zhah(n)teey]
**night** nuit, f. [nwee]
**nightclub** boîte de nuit, f.
[bwaht duh nwee]

**nine** neuf [nuhf]
**nineteen** dix-neuf [deez-
nuhf]
**ninety** quatre-vingt-dix
[kahtruh-va(n)-dees]
**no** non [noh(n)]
**non-smoking section** salle
pour non-fumeurs, f. [sahl
poor noh(n)-fumuhr]
**noodles** nouilles, f. [nooy]
**noon** midi [meedee]
**north** nord, m. [nohr]
**nose** nez, m. [nay]
**not at all** pas du tout [pah
dew too]
**notebook** cahier, m. [kahyay]
**nothing** rien [reeya(n)]
**to notice** remarquer
[ruhmahrkay]
**novel** roman, m. [rohmah(n)]
**November** novembre
[nohvah(m)br]
**now** maintenant [ma(n)-
tuhnah(n)]
**number** chiffre, m. [sheefr]
numéro, m. [newmayroh]
**numbered** numéroté [new-
mayrohtay]
**nurse** infirmière, f. [a(n)feer-
myehr]
**nut** noix, f. [nwah]

## O

**object** objet, m. [ohbzhay]
**to be obliged to** devoir
[duhvwahr]
**to obtain** obtenir [ohbtuhneer]
**ocean** océan, m. [ohsayah(n)]

**October** octobre [ohktohbr]
**odd** impair [a(m)pehr]
**of, from** de [duh]
**of course** bien sûr [byeh(n)-sewr]
**to offer** offrir [ohfreer]
**office** bureau, m. [bewroh]
**often** souvent [soovah(n)]
**oil** huile, f. [weel]
**okay** d'accord [dahkohr]
**old** vieux, m. [vyuh]
vieille, f. [vyehy]
**omelette** omelette, f. [ohmleht]
**on** sur [sewr]
**on foot** à pied [ah pyay]
**on time** à l'heure [ah luhr]
**one** un, m. [uh(n)]
une, f. [ewn]
**one (we)** on [oh(n)]
**one way** sens unique [sah(n)s ewneek]
**one-way ticket** aller simple, m. [ahlay sa(m)pl]
**onion** oignon, m. [ohnyoh(n)]
**only** seulement [suhlmah(n)]
**open** ouvert [oovehr]
**to open** ouvrir [oovreer]
**operator** téléphoniste, m. or f. [taylayfohneest]
**opportunity** occasion, f. [ohkahzyoh(n)]
**opposite** contraire, m. [koh(n)trehr]
**opposite (across from)** en face de [ah(n) fahs duh]
**or** ou [oo]
**orange** orange, f. [ohrah(n)zh]
**orangeade** orangeade, f. [ohrah(n)zhahd]

**orchestra** orchestre, m. [ohrkehstr]
**orchestra leader** chef d'orchestre, m. [shehf dohrkehstr]
**to order** commander [kohmah(n)day]
**ordinary** ordinaire [ohrdeenehr]
**oregano** origan, m. [ohreegah(n)]
**other** autre [ohtr]
**our** notre/nos [nohtr/noh]
**outdoors** plein air [pleh nehr]
**outfit** tenue, f. [tuhnew]
**outside** en plein air [ah(n)-pleh nehr]
**oven** four, m. [foor]
**over** dessus [duhsew]
**overcoat** manteau, m. [mah(n)toh]
**overseas** à l'étranger [ah laytrah(n)zhay]
**to owe** devoir [duhvwahr]
**own** propre [prohpr]
**owner** propriétaire, m. [prohpreeaytehr]
**oyster** huître, m. [weetr]

## P

**pack** paquet, m. [pahkay]
**package** colis, m. [kohlee]
**packet** paquet, m. [pahkay]
**pain** douleur, f. [dooluhr]
**painter** peintre, f. [pa(n)tr]
**painting** peinture, f. [pa(n)-tewr]
tableau, m. [tahbloh]
**pair** paire, f. [pehr]

**pajamas** pyjama, *m.*
*[peezhahmah]*

**pancake** crêpe, *f. [krehp]*

**panorama** panorama, *m.*
*[pahnohrahmah]*

**pants** pantalon, *m. [pah(n)-tahloh(n)]*

**paper** papier, *m. [pahpyay]*

**park** parc, *m. [pahrk]*

**to park** (se) garer *[(suh) gahray]*

**parking** stationnement, *m.*
*[stahsyohnmah(n)]*

**parking area** zone bleue, *f.*
*[zohn bluh]*

**parking lot** parking, *m.*
*[pahrkeeng]*

**parking meter** parcomètre, *m. [pahrkohmehtr]*

**parking prohibited** stationnement interdit *[stahsyohnmah(n) a(n)tehrdee]*

**parking side** côté de stationnement, *m. [kohtay duh stahsyohnmah(n)]*

**parsley** persil, *m. [persee]*

**part** partie, *f. [pahrtee]*

**to pass** passer *[pahsay]*

**passage** passage, *m.*
*[pahsahzh]*

**passport** passeport, *m.*
*[pahspohr]*

**pasta** pâtes, *f.pl. [paht]*

**pastry shop** pâtisserie, *f.*
*[pahteesree]*

**to pay** payer *[payay]*

**peach** pêche, *f. [pehsh]*

**peak** sommet, *m. [sohmay]*

**pear** poire, *f. [pwahr]*

**peas** petits pois, *m.pl.*
*[puhtee pwah]*

**pedestrian** piéton, *m.*
*[pyaytoh(n)]*

**pedestrian crosswalk**
passage clouté, *m. [pahsahzh klootay]*

**pedestrians prohibited**
interdit aux piétons *[a(n)tehr-dee oh pyaytoh(n)]*

**pen** stylo, *m. [steeloh]*

**pencil** crayon, *m. [krayoh(n)]*

**people** gens, *m.pl. [zhah(n)]*

**pepper** poivre, *m. [pwahvr]*

**perfect** parfait *[pahrfeh]*

**performance**
représentation, *f. [ruhpray-zah(n)tahsyoh(n)]*

**perfume** parfum, *m. [pahr-fuh(m)]*

**perhaps** peut-être *[puh-tehtr]*

**period** période, *f. [payryohd]*

**permanent wave** mise en
pli, *f. [meez ah(n) plee]*

**to permit** permettre *[pehr-mehtr]*

**person** personne, *f. [pehr-sohn]*

**person-to-person** (avec)
préavis *[(ahvehk) prayahvee]*

**personal** personnel *[pehr-sohnehl]*

**to persuade** persuader
*[pehrswahday]*

**pharmacy** pharmacie, *f.*
*[fahrmahsee]*

**phone** téléphone, *m. [taylay-fohn]*

**phone directory** annuaire,
*m. [ahnewehr]*

233

**photograph** photo, f.
[fohtoh]
**to photograph** photographier [fohtohgrahfyay]
**pickle** cornichon, m.
[kohrneeshoh(n)]
**pie** tarte, f. [tahrt]
**pig** cochon, m. [kohshoh(n)]
**pill** pillule, f. [peelewl]
**pillow** oreiller, m. [ohrehyay]
**pin** épingle, f. [aypa(n)gl]
**pineapple** ananas, m.
[ahnahnahs]
**pink** rose [rohz]
**place** endroit, m. [ah(n)drwah]
**plan** plan, m. [plah(n)]
**planetarium** planétarium,
m. [plahnaytahryuhm]
**plate** assiette, f. [ahsyeht]
**platform** quai, m. [keh]
**play (literary)** pièce, f.
[pyehs]
**to play** jouer [zhooay]
**player** joueur, m. [zhoouhr]
**playground** terrain de jeu,
m. [tehra(n) duh zhuh]
**please** s'il vous plaît [seel voo
pleh]
**pleasure** plaisir, m. [plehzeer]
**plum** prune, f. [prewn]
**pocket** poche, f. [pohsh]
**pocketbook** sac, m. [sahk]
**police station** commissariat, m. [kohmeesahryah]
**policeman** agent de police,
m. [ahzhah(n) duh pohlees]
**pond** étang, m. [aytah(n)]
**pool** piscine, f. [peeseen]
**poor** pauvre [pohvr]
**pork** porc, m. [pohr]

**porter** porteur, m. [pohrtuhr]
**portion** portion, f. [pohr-syoh(n)]
**to possess** posséder [pohsay-day]
**post office** bureau de
poste, m. [bewroh duh pohst]
**postcard** carte postale, f.
[kahrt pohstahl]
**potato** pomme de terre, f.
[pohm duh tehr]
**pottery** poterie, f. [pohtree]
**practical** pratique [prahteek]
**precious stone** pierre
précieuse, f. [pyehr praysyuhz]
**to prefer** préférer [prayfay-ray]
**pregnant** enceinte [ah(n)-sa(n)t]
**to prepare** préparer [pray-pahray]
**prescription** ordonnance, f.
[ohrdohnah(n)s]
**present** cadeau, m. [kahdoh]
**to present** présenter [pray-zah(n)tay]
**pressure** pression, f. [prehsy-oh(n)]
**pretty** joli [zhohlee]
**price (cost)** prix, m. [pree]
**price (rate)** tarif, m. [tahreef]
**priest** prêtre, m. [prehtr]
**print** épreuve, f. [aypruhv]
**priority** priorité, f. [pree-ohreetay]
**private** privé [preevay]
**private property** propriété
privée, f. [prohpreeaytay
preevay]

**profession** profession, f. [prohfehsyoh(n)]

**to prohibit** interdire [a(n)-tehrdeer]

**to promise** promettre [proh-mehtr]

**to pronounce** prononcer [prohnoh(n)say]

**to protect** protéger [prohtay-zhay]

**prune** pruneau, m. [prew-noh]

**public** public [peubleek]

**purchase** achat, m. [ahshah]

**purple** violet [vyohlay]

**to push** pousser [poosay]

**to put, put on** mettre [mehtr]

## Q

**quality** qualité, f. [kahleetay]

**quarter** quart, m. [kahr]

**question** question, f. [kehsty-oh(n)]

**quiche** quiche, f. [keesh]

**quickly** vite [veet]

## R

**rabbi** rabbin, m. [rahba(n)]

**rabbit** lapin, m. [lahpa(n)]

**radiator** radiateur, m. [rahdyahtuhr]

**radio** poste de radio, m. [pohst duh rahdyoh] radio, f. [radyoh]

**railroad** chemin de fer, m. [shuhma(n) duh fehr]

**railroad crossing** passage à niveau, m. [pahsahzh ah neevoh]

**railroad station** gare, f. [gahr]

**rain** pluie, f. [plwee]

**it's raining** il pleut [eel pluh]

**raisins** raisins secs, m.pl. [rayza(n) sehk]

**rapid** rapide [rahpeed]

**rare (meat)** saignant [seh-nyah(n)]

**raspberry** framboise, f. [frah(m)bwahz]

**rather** plutôt [plewtoh]

**raw vegetables** crudités, f.pl. [krewdeetay]

**razor** rasoir, m. [rahzwahr]

**to read** lire [leer]

**ready** prêt [preh]

**really** vraiment [vrehhmah(n)]

**reason** raison. f. [rehzoh(n)]

**reasonable** raisonnable [rehzohnahbl]

**receipt** quittance, f. [keetah(n)s]

**to receive** recevoir [ruhsuhvwahr]

**recent** récent [raysah(n)]

**to recommend** recommander [ruhkohmah(n)day]

**record** disque, m. [deesk]

**record player** tourne-disque, m. [toornuh-deesk]

**recording** enregistrement, m. [ah(n)rehzheestruhmah(n)]

**red** rouge [roozh]

**red wine** vin rouge, m. [va(n) roozh]

**reduction** rabais, m. [rahbeh]

**refreshing** rafraîchissant [rahfrehsheesah(n)]

235

**to refuse** refuser *[ruhfewzay]*

**to register, check** enregistrer *[ah(n)rehzheestray]*

**to regret** regretter *[ruhgrehtay]*

**to reimburse** rembourser *[rah(m)boorsay]*

**to remain** rester *[rehstay]*

**to remember** se rappeler *[suh rahplay]*

**rent** loyer, m. *[lwahyay]*

**to rent** louer *[looay]*

**to repair** réparer *[raypahray]*

**to repeat** répéter *[raypaytay]*

**to represent** repésenter *[ruhprayzah(n)tay]*

**to resemble** ressembler *[ruhsah(m)blay]*

**reservation** réservation, f. *[rayzehrvahsyoh(n)]*

**to reserve** réserver *[rayzehrvay]*

**reserved for buses** réservé aux autobus *[rayzehrvay oh zohtohbews]*

**responsible** responsable *[rehspoh(n)sahbl]*

**rest** repos, m. *[ruhpoh]*

**to rest** se reposer *[suh ruhpohzay]*

**restaurant** restaurant, m. *[rehstohrah(n)]*

**result** résultat, m. *[rayzewltah]*

**retirement** retraite, f. *[ruhtreht]*

**to return (something)** rendre *[rah(n)dr]*

**to return (to)** rentrer *[rah(n)tray]*

**returned** de retour *[duh ruhtoor]*

**rice** riz, m. *[ree]*

**right (direction)** droite, f. *[drwaht]*

**right (legal/moral)** droit, m. *[drwah]*

**right away** tout de suite *[tood sweet]*

**ring** bague, f. *[bahg]*

**risk** risque, m. *[reesk]*

**river** fleuve, m. *[fluhv]* rivière f. *[reevyehr]*

**road (highway)** route, f. *[root]*

**road (way)** chemin, m. *[shuhma(n)]*

**road map** carte routière, f. *[kahrt rootyehr]*

**roast** rôti, m. *[rohtee]*

**roast beef** rosbif, m. *[rohsbeef]*

**roll (bread)** petit pain, m. *[puhtee pa(n)]*

**to roll, drive** rouler *[roolay]*

**roof** toit, m. *[twah]*

**room** salle, f. *[sahl]*

**room (bedroom)** chambre, f. *[shah(m)br]*

**room service** service à l'étage, m. *[sehrvees ah laytahzh]*

**room with all meals** pension complète, f. *[pah(n)syoh(n) koh(m)pleht]*

**rooster** coq, m. *[kohk]*

**rosé wine** vin rosé, m. *[va(n) rohzay]*

**rosemary** romarin, m. *[rohmahra(n)]*

**round-trip ticket** aller-retour, m. [ahlay-ruhtoor]

**rowboat** barque à rames, f. [bahrk ah rahm]

**rug** tapis, m. [tahpee]

**ruins** ruines, f.pl. [rween]

**rule** règle, f. [rehgl]

**to run** courir [kooreer]

**running, jogging** footing, m. [footeeng]

**rye** seigle, m. [sehgl]

## S

**sad** triste [treest]

**safe** coffre-fort, m. [kohfruh-fohr]

**safety pin** épingle de sûreté, f. [aypa(n)gl duh sewrtay]

**sale** vente, f. [vah(n)t]

**salesman** vendeur, m. [vah(n)duhr]

**saleswoman** vendeuse, f. [vah(n)duhz]

**salt** sel, m. [sehl]

**salted** salé [sahlay]

**same** même [mehm]

**sand** sable, m. [sahbl]

**sandals** sandales, f.pl. [sah(n)dahl]

**sanitary napkins** serviettes hygiéniques, f.pl. [sehrvyeht eezhyayneek]

**Saturday** samedi [sahmdee]

**saucer** soucoupe, f. [sookoop]

**sausage** saucisse, f. [sohsees] saucisson, m. [sohseesoh(n)]

**to say** dire [deer]

**scenic route** circuit touristique, m. [seerkwee tooreesteek]

**schedule** horaire, m. [ohrehr]

**school** école, f. [aykohl]

**scissors** ciseaux, m.pl. [seezoh]

**screwdriver** tournevis, m. [toornuhvees]

**sculpture** sculpture, f. [skewltewr]

**sea** mer, f. [mehr]

**seafood** fruits de mer, m.pl. [frwee duh mehr]

**season** saison, f. [sehzoh(n)]

**seat** place, f. [plahs]

**second** deuxième [duhzyehm]

**section, shelf** rayon, m. [rayoh(n)]

**to see** voir [vwahr]

**to seem** sembler [sah(m)blay]

**to sell** vendre [vah(n)dr]

**to send** envoyer [ah(n)vwuh-yay]

**senior citizens** personnes âgées, f.pl. [pehrsohn zahzhay]

**sentence (grammatical)** phrase, f. [frahz]

**September** septembre [sehptah(m)br]

**serious** sérieux [sayryuh]

**to serve** servir [sehrveer]

**service station** station-service, f. [stahsyoh(n)-sehrvees]

**seven** sept [seht]

**seventeen** dix-sept [dee-seht]

**seventy** soixante-dix [swahsah(n)t-dees]

237

**several** plusieurs *[plewzyuhr]*

**shampoo** shampooing, m. *[shah(m)pwa(n)]*

**to share** partager *[pahr-tahzhay]*

**to shave** raser *[rahzay]*

**shaving cream** crème à raser, f. *[krehm ah rahzay]*

**she** elle *[ehl]*

**sheep, lamb** agneau, m. *[ahnyoh]*

**sheet (bed)** drap, m. *[drah]*

**shelf, section** rayon, m. *[rayoh(n)]*

**shell** coquillage, m. *[kohkeey-ahzh]*

**shirt** chemise, f. *[shuhmeez]*

**shoe** chaussure, f. *[shohsewr]*

**shoe size** pointure, f. *[pwa(n)tewr]*

**shop** boutique, f. *[booteek]*

**to shop** faire des achats *[fehr day zahshah]*

**shopping center** centre commercial, m. *[sah(n)tr kohmehrsyahl]*

**short** court *[koor]*

**shoulder** épaule, f. *[aypohl]*

**show** spectacle, m. *[spehktahkl]*

**to show** montrer *[moh(n)tray]*

**shower** douche, f. *[doosh]*

**shrimp** crevette, f. *[kruhveht]*

**shrunk** rétréci *[raytraysee]*

**shutter** obturateur, m. *[ohbtewrahtuhr]*

**sick** malade *[mahlahd]*

**sickness** maladie, f. *[mahlah-dee]*

**side** côté, m. *[kohtay]*

**sidewalk** trottoir, m. *[trohtwahr]*

**sign** enseigne, f. *[ah(n)seh-nyuh]*

**to sign** signer *[seenyay]*

**silk** soie, f. *[swah]*

**silver** argent, m. *[ahrzhah(n)]*

**since** depuis *[duhpwee]*

**since when?** depuis quand? *[duhpwee kah(n)]*

**to sing** chanter *[shah(n)tay]*

**single (unmarried)** célibataire *[sayleebahtehr]*

**sister** soeur, f. *[suhr]*

**sister-in-law** belle-soeur, f. *[behl-suhr]*

**to sit down** s'asseoir *[sahswahr]*

**site** site, m. *[seet]*

**six** six *[sees]*

**sixteen** seize *[sehz]*

**sixty** soixante *[swahsah(n)t]*

**size** taille, f. *[tahy]*

**skating rink** patinoire, f. *[pahteenwahr]*

**ski equipment** équipement de ski, m. *[aykeepmah(n) duh skee]*

**ski lift** téléski, m. *[taylayskee]*

**skiing** ski, m. *[skee]*

**skiing, cross-country** ski de fond, m. *[skee duh foh(n)]*

**skin** peau, f. *[poh]*

**skirt** jupe, f. *[zhewp]*

**sky** ciel, m. *[syehl]*

**to sleep** dormir *[dohrmeer]*

**sleeping berth** couchette, f. *[koosheht]*

**sleeping car** wagon-lit, m. *[vahgoh(n)-lee]*

**slice** tranche, f. *[trah(n)sh]*
**slide (photographic)** diapositive, f. *[dyahpoh-zeeteev]*
**slippers** pantoufles, f.pl. *[pah(n)toofl]*
**slippery** glissant *[gleesah(n)]*
**slow** lent *[lah(n)]*
**to slow down** ralentir *[rahlah(n)teer]*
**slowly** lentement *[lah(n)-tuhmah(n)]*
**small** petit *[puhtee]*
**smile** sourire, m. *[sooreer]*
**smoked** fumé *[fumay]*
**smokers** fumeurs, m.pl. *[foomuhr]*
**snack bar** buffet-express, m. *[bewfay-ehksprehs]* snack-bar, m. *[snahk-bahr]*
**snail** escargot, m. *[ehskahrgoh]*
**snow** neige, f. *[nehzh]*
**to snow** neiger *[nehzhay]*
**so many, so much** tant *[tah(n)]*
**so much the better** tant mieux *[tah(n) myuh]*
**so much the worse** tant pis *[tah(n) pee]*
**soap** savon, m. *[sahvoh(n)]*
**sock** chaussette, f. *[shohseht]*
**soft** doux, m. *[doo]* douce, f. *[doos]*
**solid** uni *[ewnee]*
**some** quelque(s) *[kehlkuh]*
**someone** quelqu'un *[kehlkuh(n)]*
**something** quelque chose *[kehlkuh shohz]*

**sometimes** parfois *[pahrfwah]*
**somewhere** quelque part *[kehlkuh pahr]*
**son** fils, m. *[fees]*
**song** chanson, f. *[shah(n)-soh(n)]*
**soon** bientôt *[bya(n)toh]*
**sorry** désolé *[dayzohlay]*
**sort** genre, m. *[zhah(n)r]*
**soufflé** soufflé, m. *[sooflay]*
**soup, chowder** bisque, f. *[beesk]*
**south** sud, m. *[sewd]*
**spaghetti** spaghetti, m.pl. *[spahghetee]*
**Spain** Espagne, f. *[ehspah-nyuh]*
**Spanish** espagnol *[ehspahn-yohl]*
**sparkling wine** vin mous-seux, m. *[va(n) moosuh]*
**to speak** parler *[pahrlay]*
**specialty** spécialité, f. *[spaysyahleetay]*
**speed** vitesse, f. *[veetehs]*
**to spell** épeler *[ayplay]*
**to spend** dépenser *[day-pah(n)say]*
**to spend (time)** passer *[pahsay]*
**spice** piment, m. *[peemah(n)]*
**spinach** épinards, m.pl. *[aypeenahr]*
**spoon** cuillère, f. *[kweeyehr]*
**spouse** époux, m. *[aypoo]* épouse, f. *[aypooz]*
**spring (season)** printemps, m. *[pra(n)tah(m)]*
**square (town)** place, f. *[plahs]*

239

**squash** courgette, f. [koorzheht]

**stadium** stade, m. [stahd]

**staircase** escalier, m. [ehskah-lyay]

**stamp (postage)** timbre, m. [ta(m)br]

**to start (a car)** démarrer [daymahray]

**starter (on a car)** démarreur, m. [daymahruhr]

**state** état, m. [aytah]

**station** station, f. [stahsyoh(n)]

**stationery** papier à lettres, m. [pahpyay ah lehtr]

**stationery store** papeterie, f. [pahpehtree]

**statue** statue, f. [stahtew]

**stay** séjour, m. [sayzhoor]

**to stay (lodge)** loger [lohzhay]

**to stay (remain)** rester [rehs-tay]

**steak** biftek, m. [beeftehk] steak, m. [stehk]

**to steal** voler [vohlay]

**stew** cassoulet, m. [kahsoolay]

**stewardess** hôtesse de l'air, f. [ohtehs duh lehr]

**stick, pole** bâton, m. [bahtoh(n)]

**still, again** encore [ah(n)kohr]

**stock exchange** bourse, f. [boors]

**stockings** bas, m.pl. [bah]

**stomach** estomac, m. [ehs-tohmah]

**stone** pierre, f. [pyehr]

**stop (along the way)** escale, f. [ehskahl]

**to stop** arrêter [ahrehtay]

**store** magasin, m. [mahgahza(n)]

**store window** vitrine, f. [veetreen]

**storm** tempête, f. [tah(m)-peht]

**story (of a building)** étage, m. [aytahzh]

**story (tale)** histoire, f. [eestwahr]

**strange** bizarre [beezahr]

**strawberry** fraise, f. [frehz]

**street** rue, f. [rew]

**string** ficelle, f. [feesehl]

**stringbeans** haricots, m.pl. [ahreekoh]

**stripe** rayure, f. [rayewr]

**strong** fort [fohr]

**suburb** banlieue, f. [bah(n)lyuh]

**subway** métro, m. [maytroh]

**subway station** station de métro, f. [stahsyoh(n) duh maytroh]

**suede** daim, m. [da(m)]

**sugar** sucre, m. [sewkr]

**suit** complet, m. [koh(m)play]

**suitcase** valise, f. [vahleez]

**sum** somme, f. [sohm]

**summer** été, m. [aytay]

**sun** soleil, m, [sohlehy]

**Sunday** dimanche [dee-mah(n)sh]

**sunglasses** lunettes de soleil, f.pl. [lewneht duh sohlehy]

**suntan lotion** huile de bronzage, f. [weel duh broh(n)zahzh]

**superior, higher** supérieur [sewpayryuhr]

**supermarket** supermarché, m. [sewpehrmahrshay]

**supplement** supplément, m. [sewplaymah(n)]

**sure** sûr [sewr]

**surf board** planche de surf, f. [plah(n)sh duh sewrf]

**sweater** chandail, m. [shah(n)dahy]

**sweet** doux, m. [doo] douce, f. [doos] sucré [sewkray]

**sweet wine** vin doux, m. [va(n) doo]

**to swim** nager [nahzhay] se baigner [suh behnyay]

**swimmer** nageur, m. [nahzhuhr]

**swimming** natation, f. [nahtahsyoh(n)]

**swimming pool** piscine, f. [peeseen]

**Swiss** suisse [swees]

**Switzerland** Suisse, f. [Swees]

**synagogue** synagogue, f. [seenahgohg]

# T

**table** table, f. [tahbl]

**tailor** tailleur, m. [tahyuhr]

**to take** prendre [prah(n)dr]

**tampon** tampon, m. [tah(m)-poh(n)]

**tangerine** mandarine, f. [mah(n)dahreen]

**tap (water faucet)** robinet, m. [rohbeenay]

**to taste** goûter [gootay]

**tavern, restaurant** bistrot, m. [beestroh]

**tax** taxe, f. [tahks]

**taxi** taxi, m. [tahksee]

**tea** thé, m. [tay]

**tea room** salon de thé, m. [sahloh(n) duh tay]

**to teach, learn** apprendre [ahprah(n)dr]

**team** équipe, f. [aykeep]

**telegram** télégramme, m. [taylaygrahm]

**telephone** téléphone, m. [taylayfohn]

**to telephone** téléphoner [taylayfohnay]

**telephone directory** annuaire, m. [ahnewehr]

**television** télévision, f. [taylayveezyoh(n)]

**telex** télex, m. [taylehks]

**to tell** raconter [rahkon(n)tay]

**ten** dix [dees]

**tennis** tennis, m. [tehnees]

**tent** tente, f. [tah(n)t]

**terrace** terrasse, f. [tehrahs]

**to thank** remercier [ruhmehr-syay]

**thank you** merci [mehrsee]

**that (thing)** ça [sah] cela [suhlah]

**that (which)** que [kuh]

**the** le/la/les [luh/lah/lay]

**theater** théâtre [tayahtr]

**their** leur/leurs [luhr/luhr]

**them** les/leur/se [lay/luhr/suh]

**then** donc [doh(n)k]

**there** là *[lah]*

**there, there is** voilà *[vwahlah]*

**there is** il y a *[eel yah]*

**therefore** donc *[doh(n)k]*

**these** ces *[say]*

**they** ils, *m.pl.* *[eel]*
elles, *f.pl.* *[ehl]*

**thief** voleur, *m.* *[vohluhr]*

**thigh** cuisse, *f.* *[kwees]*

**thin** mince *[ma(n)s]*

**thing** chose, *f.* *[shohz]*

**to think** penser *[pah(n)say]*

**third** troisième *[trwahzyehm]*

**thirst** soif *[swahf]*

**to be thirsty** avoir soif
*[ahvwahr swahf]*

**thirteen** treize *[trehz]*

**thirty** trente *[trah(n)t]*

**this** ce/cet, *m.* *[suh/seht]*
cette, *f.* *[seht]*

**this one** ceci *[suhsee]*
celui *[suhlwee]*

**those** ces *[say]*

**thousand** mille *[meel]*

**three** trois *[trwah]*

**throat** gorge, *f.* *[gohrzh]*

**through** à travers *[ah trahvehr]*

**Thursday** jeudi *[zhuhdee]*

**thyme** thym, *m.* *[ta(m)]*

**ticket** billet, *m.* *[beeyay]*

**ticket window** guichet, *m.*
*[gheeshay]*

**tie** cravate, *f.* *[krahvaht]*

**tie pin** épingle à cravate, *f.*
*[aypa(n)gl ah krahvaht]*

**time** heure, *f.* *[uhr]*
temps, *m.* *[tah(m)]*

**on time** à l'heure *[ah luhr]*

**What time is it?** Quelle
heure est-il? *[Kehl uhr ehteel?]*

**tip** pourboire, *m.* *[poorbwahr]*

**tire** pneu, *m.* *[pnuh]*

**tired** fatigué *[fahteegay]*

**tissues** mouchoirs en papiers, *m.pl.* *[mooshwahr ah(n)
pahpyay]*

**to** à *[ah]*

**to the** à la, *f.* *[ah lah]*
au, *m.* *[oh]*
aux, *m.pl. and f.pl.* *[oh]*

**toast** pain grillé, *m.* *[pa(n)
greeyay]*

**tobacco** tabac, *m.* *[tahbah]*

**tobacco shop** bureau de
tabac, *m.* *[bewroh duh
tahbah]*

**today** aujourd'hui
*[ohzhoordwee]*

**together** ensemble *[ah(n)-
sah(m)bl]*

**toilet, bathroom** cabinet
de toilette, *m.* *[kahbeenay
duh twahleht]*
toilettes, *f.pl.* *[twahleht]*
W.C., *m.* *[vay say]*

**toilet paper** papier hygiénique, *m.* *[pahpyay eezhy-
ayneek]*

**toilet water** eau de toilette,
*f.* *[oh duh twahleht]*

**token** jeton, *m.* *[zhuhtoh(n)]*

**toll** péage, *m.* *[payahzh]*

**tomato** tomate, *f.* *[tohmaht]*

**tomorrow** demain *[duhma(n)]*

**tongue** langue, *f.* *[lah(n)g]*

**too many, too much** trop
*[troh]*

**tooth** dent, f. [dah(n)]
**toothpaste** dentifrice, m. [dah(n)teefrees]
**toothpick** cure-dent, m. [kewr-dah(n)]
**to touch** toucher [tooshay]
**to touch up** retoucher [ruhtooshay]
**tour** tour, m. [toor]
**tourism** tourisme, m. [tooreezm]
**tourist** touriste, m. or f. [tooreest]
**touristic** touristique [tooreesteek]
**toward** vers [vehr]
**towel** serviette, f. [sehrvyeht]
**tower** tour, f. [toor]
**town** ville. f. [veel]
**town hall** hôtel de ville, m. [ohtehl duh veel]
**traffic** circulation, f. [seerkewlahsyoh(n)]
**traffic lights** feux de circulation, m.pl. [fuh duh seerkewlahsyoh(n)]
**trailer** caravane, f. [kahrahvahn]
**train** train, m. [tra(n)]
**bullet train** TGV, m. [tay zhay vay]
**train station** gare, f. [gahr]
**to translate** traduire [trahdweer]
**travel agency** agence de voyage, f. [ahzhah(n)s duh vwahyahzh]
**traveler's check** chèque de voyage, m. [shehk duh vwahyahzh]
**tree** arbre, m. [ahrbr]

**trip** trajet, m. [trahzhay] voyage, m. [vwahyahzh]
**trouble** difficulté, f. [deefeekewltay]
**trout** truite, f. [trweet]
**truck** camion, m. [kahmyoh(n)]
**true** vrai [vreh]
**trunk** malle, f. [mahl]
**truth** vérité, f. [vayreetay]
**to try** essayer [ehsayay]
**Tuesday** mardi [mahrdee]
**tune-up** mise au point, f. [meez oh pwa(n)]
**turkey** dinde, f. [da(n)d]
**turn** virage, m. [veerahzh] tour, m. [toor]
**to turn** tourner [toornay]
**turnip** navet, m. [nahvay]
**TV set** téléviseur, m. [taylayveezuhr]
**twelve** douze [dooz]
**twenty** vingt [va(n)]
**two** deux [duh]
**type, sort** genre, m. [zhah(n)r]
**typical** typique [teepeek]

## U

**ugly** laid [leh]
**umbrella** parapluie, m. [pahrahplwee]
**unbelievable** incroyable [a(n)krwahyahbl]
**uncle** oncle, m. [oh(n)kl]
**under** sous [soo]
**underpants** slip, m. [sleep]
**to understand** comprendre [koh(m)prah(n)dr]

243

**understood, included**
compris [koh(m)pree]

**underwear** sous-vêtements,
m.pl. [soo-vehtmah(n)]

**unhappy** malheureux
[mahluhruh]

**unique** unique [ewneek]

**united, solid** uni [ewnee]

**United States** Etats-Unis,
m.pl. [aytah-zewnee]

**university** université, f.
[ewneevehrseetay]

**unlimited** illimité
[eeleemeetay]

**unmarried** célibataire
[sayleebahtehr]

**until** jusqu'à [zhewskah]

**up, upstairs** en haut [ah(n)
oh]

**urgent** urgent [ewrzhah(n)]

**us** nous [noo]

**to use** employer [ah(m)-
plwahyay]

**useful** utile [ewteel]

**useless** inutile [eenewteel]

**usher** ouvreuse, f. [oovruhz]

**U-turn** demi-tour, m.
[duhmee-toor]

**V**

**vacation** vacances, f.pl.
[vahkah(n)s]

**valley** vallée, f. [vahlay]

**value** valeur, f. [vahluhr]

**varied** varié [vahryay]

**veal** veau, m. [voh]

**vegetable** légume, m.
[laygewm]

**velvet** velours, m. [vuhloor]

**to verify** vérifier [vayreefyay]

**vervain (infusion)** verveine,
f. [vehrvehn]

**very** très [treh]

**video recorder** magnétoscope, m. [mahnyaytohskohp]

**view** vue, f. [vew]

**villa** villa, f. [veelah]

**village** village, m. [veelahzh]

**vineyard** vignoble, m.
[veenyohbl]

**visit** visite, f. [veezeet]

**W**

**waist, size** taille, f. [tahy]

**wait** attente, f. [ahtah(n)t]

**to wait for** attendre
[ahtah(n)dr]

**waiter** garçon, m. [gahr-
soh(n)]

**waiting room** salle d'attente, f. [sahl dahtah(n)t]

**waitress** serveuse, f. [sehr-
vuhz]

**walk** promenade, f. [proh-
muhnahd]

**to walk** marcher [mahrshay]

**to take a walk** faire une
promenade [fehr ewn proh-
muhnahd]

**wall** mur, m. [mewr]

**wallet** porte-feuille, m.
[pohrtuh-fuhy]

**to want** vouloir [voolwahr]

**war** guerre, f. [gehr]

**warm** chaud [shoh]

**to wash** laver [lahvay]

**watch** montre, f. [moh(n)tr]

**to watch** regarder *[ruhgahr-day]*
**water** eau, f. *[oh]*
**water skiing** ski nautique, m. *[skee nohteek]*
**waterfall** chute d'eau, f. *[shoot doh]*
**watermelon** pastèque, f. *[pahstehk]*
**way** moyen, m. *[mwahya(n)]*
**way out** issue, f. *[eesew]* sortie, f. *[sohrtee]*
**we** nous *[noo]*
**weak** faible *[fehbl]*
**to wear** porter *[pohrtay]*
**weather** temps, m. *[tah(m)]*
**weather forecast** météo, f. *[maytayoh]*
**wedding ring** alliance, f. *[ahlyah(n)s]*
**Wednesday** mercredi *[mehrkruhdee]*
**week** semaine, f. *[suhmehn]*
**to weigh** peser *[puhzay]*
**weight** poids, m. *[pwah]*
**welcome** bienvenu *[bya(n)-vuhnew]*
**you're welcome** de rien *[duh reeya(n)]*
**well** bien *[byeh(n)]*
**well, then** alors *[ahlohr]*
**well-done (meat)** bien cuit *[bya(n) kwee]*
**west** ouest, m. *[wehst]*
**wet** mouillé *[mooyay]*
**wharf, platform** quai, m. *[keh]*
**what** quel/quelle *[kehl]* quoi *[kwah]* qu'est-ce que *[kehskuh]*

**when** quand *[kah(n)]*
**where** où *[oo]*
**which** quel/quelle *[kehl]*
**white** blanc *[blah(n)]*
**white bread** pain de mie, m. *[pa(n) duh mee]*
**white wine** vin blanc, m. *[va(n) blah(n)]*
**who** qui *[kee]*
**whole** entier *[ah(n)tyay]*
**whole wheat bread** pain complet, m. *[pa(n) koh(m)-play]*
**why** pourquoi *[poorkwah]*
**wide** large *[lahrzh]*
**widow** veuve, f. *[vuhv]*
**widower** veuf, m. *[vuhf]*
**wife** femme, f. *[fahm]*
**wild** sauvage *[sohvahzh]*
**win** gagner *[gahnyay]*
**wind** vent, m. *[vah(n)]*
**window** fenêtre, f. *[fuhnehtr]*
**windsurfing** planche à voile, f. *[plah(n)sh ah vwahl]*
**wine** vin, m. *[va(n)]*
**wine cellar** cave, f. *[kahv]*
**winter** hiver, m. *[eevehr]*
**wish** envie, f. *[ah(n)vee]*
**to wish** souhaiter *[soowehtay]*
**with** avec *[ahvehk]*
**without** sans *[sah(n)]*
**wolf** loup, m. *[loo]*
**woman, wife** femme, f. *[fahm]*
**wonderful** merveilleux *[mehrvehyuh]*
**wool** laine, f. *[lehn]*
**word** mot, m. *[moh]*
**work** travail, m. *[trahvahy]*

**to work** travailler *[trahvah-yay]*
**work site** chantier, m. *[shah(n)tyay]*
**workshop** atelier, m. *[ahtuh-lyay]*
**world** monde, m. *[moh(n)d]*
**it is worth** il vaut *[eel voh]*
**to wrap up** emballer *[ah(m)-bahlay]*
**wrist** poignet, m. *[pwahnyay]*
**to write** écrire *[aykreer]*
**written** écrit *[aykree]*
**to be wrong** avoir tort *[ahvwahr tohr]*

## X

**x-ray** radio, f. *[rahdyoh]*

## Y

**year** an, m. *[ah(n)]*
 année, f. *[ahnay]*
**yellow** jaune *[zhohn]*

**yes** oui *[wee]*
**yesterday** hier *[yehr]*
**yet** encore *[ah(n)kohr]*
**yield!** cédez le passage *[sayday luh pahsahzh]*
**yogurt** yaourt, m. *[yahoort]*
**you (singular, familiar)** tu/te/toi *[tew/tuh/twah]*
**you (plural or formal)** vous *[voo]*
**young** jeune *[zhuhn]*
**younger** cadet *[kahday]*
**your (s. or familiar)** ta/ton/tes *[tah/toh(n)/tay]*
**your (pl. or formal)** votre/vos *[votr/voh]*

## Z

**zero** zéro *[zayroh]*
**zipper** fermeture éclair, f. *[fehrmuhtewr ayklehr]*
**zoo** jardin zoologique, m. *[zhahrda(n) zoh-ohlohzheek]*

# FRENCH-ENGLISH DICTIONARY

See usage note under English-French Dictionary, page 213.

## A

**à** [ah] at, to

**abricot,** m. [ahbreekoh] apricot

**accepter** [ahksehptay] to accept

**accompagner** [ahkoh(m)-pahnyay] to accompany

**acheter** [ahshuhtay] to buy

**addition,** f. [ahdeesyoh(n)] bill

**adorer** [ahdohray] to adore, love

**adresse,** f. [ahdrehs] address

**adulte,** m. [ahdewlt] adult

**aérogramme,** m. [ah-ehrohgrahm] air-letter

**aéroport,** m. [ah-ehrohpohr] airport

**affaires,** f.pl. [ahfehr] business

**âge,** m. [ahzh] age

**agence,** f. [ahzhah(n)s] agency

**agence de location de voiture,** f. [ahzhah(n)s duh lohkahsyoh(n) duh vwahtewr] car rental agency

**agence de voyage,** f. [ahzhah(n)s duh vwahyahzh] travel agency

**agent de police,** m. [ahzhah(n) duh pohlees] policeman

**agrandissement,** m. [ahgrah(n)deesmah(n)] enlargement

**aider** [ehday] to help

**ailleurs** [ahyuhr] elsewhere

**aimer** [ehmay] to like, love

**aîné** [ehnay] eldest

**Allemagne,** f. [ahluhmah-nyuh] Germany

**allemand** [ahluhmuh(n)] German

**aller** [ahlay] to go

**aller-retour,** m. [ahlay-ruhtoor] round-trip ticket

**aller simple,** m. [ahlay sa(m)pl] one-way ticket

**alliance,** f. [ahlyah(n)s] wedding ring

**allumer** [ahlewmay] to light

**allumette,** f. [ahlewmeht] match

**alors** [ahlohr] well, then

**amandes,** f.pl. [ahmah(n)d] almonds

**amener** [ahmnay] to bring

**amer** [ahmehr] bitter

**Amérique,** f. [Ahmayreek] America

**américain** [ahmayreeka(n)] American

**ami,** m. [ahmee] friend

**amie,** f. [ahmee] friend

**amitié,** f. [ahmeetyay] friendship

**amour,** m. [ahmoor] love

**ampoule,** f. *[ah(m)pool]* bulb

**(s')amuser** *[sahmewzay]* to amuse, have fun

**an,** m. *[ah(n)]* year

**ananas,** m. *[ahnahnahs]* pineapple

**anchois,** m. *[ah(n)shwah]* anchovies

**andouille,** f. *[ah(n)dooy]* sausage

**anglais** *[ah(n)glay]* English

**Angleterre,** f. *[Ah(n)gluhtehr]* England

**anguille,** f. *[ah(n)gheey]* eel

**année,** f. *[ahnay]* year

**anniversaire,** m. *[ahneevehr-sehr]* birthday

**annuaire,** m. *[ahnwehr]* phone directory

**annuler** *[ahnewlay]* to cancel

**antiquaire,** m. *[ah(n)teekehr]* antique dealer

**antiquités,** f.pl. *[ah(n)-teekeetay]* antiques

**août** *[oot]* August

**apéritif,** m. *[ahpayreeteef]* aperitif

**appareil,** m. *[ahpahrehy]* machine

**appareil de photo,** m. *[ahpah-rehy duh fohtoh]* camera

**(s')appeler** *[sahplay]* to call, be named

**appétit,** m. *[ahpaytee]* appetite

**apporter** *[ahpohrtay]* to bring

**apprendre** *[ahprah(n)dr]* to teach, learn

**après** *[ahpreh]* after

**après-demain** *[ahpreh-duh-ma(n)]* day after tomorrow

**après-midi,** m. *[ahpreh-meedee]* afternoon

**arbre,** m. *[ahrbr]* tree

**argent,** m. *[ahrzhah(n)]* money, silver

**armoire,** f. *[ahrmwahr]* closet

**arrêt d'autobus,** m. *[ahray dohtohbews]* bus stop

**arrêter** *[ahrehtay]* to stop

**arriver** *[ahreevay]* to arrive

**art,** m. *[ahr]* art

**artichaut,** m. *[ahrteeshoh]* artichoke

**article,** m. *[ahrteekl]* article

**ascenseur,** m. *[ahsah(n)suhr]* elevator

**asperge,** f. *[ahspehrzh]* asparagus

**assez** *[ahsay]* enough

**(s')asseoir** *[sahswahr]* to sit down

**assiette,** f. *[ahsyeht]* plate

**atelier,** m. *[ahtuhlyay]* work-shop

**attacher** *[ahtahshay]* to attach, buckle

**attendre** *[ahtah(n)dr]* to wait for

**attente,** f. *[ahtah(n)t]* wait

**attention,** f. *[ahtah(n)syoh(n)]* attention

**attraper** *[ahtrahpay]* to catch

**au** *[oh]* to the, at

**au delà de** *[oh duhlah duh]* beyond

**au lait** *[oh leh]* with milk

**au revoir** *[oh rvwahr]* good-bye

**auberge,** f. *[ohbehrzh]* inn

**aubergine,** f. *[ohbehrzheen]* eggplant

**aujourd'hui** *[ohzhoordwee]* today

**aussi** *[ohsee]* also

**auto,** f. *[ohtoh]* car

**autobus,** m. *[ohtohbews]* bus

**automatique** *[ohtohmahteek]* automatic

**automne,** m. *[ohtohn]* autumn

**autoroute,** f. *[ohtohroot]* highway

**autre** *[ohtr]* other

**aux** (pl.) *[oh]* to the, at

**avant** *[ahvah(n)]* before

**en avant** *[ah(n) nahvah(n)]* forward

**avec** *[ahvehk]* with

**avion,** m. *[ahvyoh(n)]* airplane

**avocat,** m. *[ahvohkah]* avocado, lawyer

**avoir** *[ahvwahr]* to have

**avoir besoin de** *[ahvwahr buhzwa(n) duh]* to need

**avril** *[ahvreel]* April

## B

**bagages,** m.pl. *[bahgahzh]* luggage

**bague,** f. *[bahg]* ring

**baguette,** f. *[bahgeht]* French bread

**(se) baigner** *[(suh) behnyay]* to bathe, swim

**bain,** m. *[ba(n)]* bath

**balcon,** m. *[bahlkoh(n)]* balcony

**banane,** f. *[bahnahn]* banana

**banlieue,** f. *[bah(n)lyuh]* suburb

**banque,** f. *[bah(n)k]* bank

**bar,** m. *[bahr]* bar

**barbe,** f. *[bahrb]* beard

**barque,** f. *[bahrk]* boat

**barque à rames,** f. *[bahrk ah rahm]* rowboat

**bas** *[bah]* low

**bas,** m.pl. *[bah]* stockings

**basket,** m. *[bahskeht]* basketball

**bateau,** m. *[bahtoh]* boat

**bâton,** m. *[bahtoh(n)]* stick, pole

**beau,** m. *[boh]* beautiful, handsome

**beau-frère,** m. *[boh-frehr]* brother-in-law

**beau-père,** m. *[boh-pehr]* father-in-law

**beaucoup** *[bohkoo]* much, many, a lot

**beaux arts,** m.pl. *[boh zahr]* fine arts

**beaux-parents,** m.pl. *[boh-pahrah(n)]* in-laws

**beignet,** m. *[behnyay]* donut

**belge** *[behlzh]* Belgian

**Belgique,** f. *[Behlzheek]* Belgium

**belle** (f.) *[behl]* beautiful

**belle-mère,** f. *[behl-mehr]* mother-in-law

**belle-soeur,** f. *[behl-suhr]* sister-in-law

**betterave,** f. *[behtrahv]* beet

**beurre,** m. *[buhr]* butter

**bibliothèque,** f. *[bee-bleeohtehk]* library

**bien** [byeh(n)] well
**bien cuit** [byeh(n) kwee] well-done (meat)
**bien sûr** [byeh(n) sewr] of course
**bientôt** [byeh(n)toh] soon
**bienvenu** [byeh(n)vuhnew] welcome
**bière,** f. [byehr] beer
**biftek,** m. [beeftehk] steak
**bigoudis,** m.pl. [beegoodee] curlers
**bijouterie,** f. [beezhootree] jewelry shop
**bijoux,** m.pl. [beezhoo] jewels
**billet,** m. [beeyay] ticket
**biscuits,** m.pl. [beeskwee] cookies
**bisque,** f. [beesk] soup, chowder
**bistro,** m. [beestroh] tavern, restaurant
**bizarre** [beezahr] strange
**blanc** [blah(n)] white
**blanchisserie,** f. [blah(n)-sheesree] laundry
**bleu** [bluh] blue
**blond** [bloh(n)] blond
**blouse,** f. [blooz] blouse
**bocal,** m. [bohkahl] jar
**boeuf,** m. [buhf] beef
**boire** [bwahr] to drink
**boisson,** f. [bwahsoh(n)] drink
**boîte,** f. [bwaht] box
**boîte aux lettres,** f. [bwaht oh lehtr] mailbox
**boîte de nuit,** f. [bwaht duh nwee] nightclub
**bon,** m. [boh(n)] good

**bon appétit** [boh(n) nahpay-tee] hearty appetite
**bon marché** [boh(n) mahrshay] cheap
**bonjour** [boh(n)zhoor] hello
**bonne,** f. [bohn] good
**bonne chance!** [bohn shah(n)s!] good luck!
**botte,** f. [boht] boot
**bouche,** f. [boosh] mouth
**boucherie,** f. [booshree] butcher shop
**boucle,** f. [bookl] curl
**boucle d'oreille,** f. [bookl dohrehy] earring
**bougie** f. [boozhee] candle
**bouillabaisse,** f. [booy-ahbehs] fish soup
**bouilli** [booyee] boiled
**boulangerie,** f. [boolah(n)zhree] bake shop
**bourse,** f. [boors] stock exchange
**bouteille,** f. [bootehy] bottle
**boutique,** f. [booteek] shop
**bouton,** m. [bootoh(n)] button
**bracelet,** m. [brahslay] bracelet
**bras,** m. [brah] arm
**briquet,** m. [breekay] lighter
**briser** [breezay] to break
**brosse,** f. [brohs] brush
**brouillard,** m. [brooyahr] fog
**brugnon,** m. [brewnyoh(n)] nectarine
**brûler** [brewlay] to burn
**brun** [bruh(n)] brown
**Bruxelles** [Brewsehl] Brussels

**buffet-express,** m. *[bewfay-ehksprehs]* snack bar

**bureau,** m. *[bewroh]* office, desk

**bureau de change,** m. *[bewroh duh shah(n)zh]* currency exchange office

**bureau d'objets trouvés,** m. *[bewroh dohbzhay troovay]* lost and found

**bureau de poste,** m. *[bewroh duh pohst]* post office

**bureau de tabac,** m. *[bewroh duh tahbah]* tobacco shop

## C

**ça** *[sah]* that

**cabaret,** m. *[kahbahray]* cabaret

**cabine,** f. *[kahbeen]* booth

**cabinet de toilette,** m. *[kahbeenay duh twahleht]* toilet, bathroom

**cadeau,** m. *[kahdoh]* gift

**cadet** *[kahday]* younger

**café,** m. *[kahfay]* café, coffee

**café au lait,** m. *[kahfay oh leh]* coffee with milk

**café complet,** m. *[kahfay koh(m)play]* continental breakfast

**café soluble,** m. *[kahfay sohlewbl]* instant coffee

**cahier,** m. *[kahyay]* notebook

**caisse,** f. *[kehs]* cash register

**caissier,** m. *[kehsyay]* cashier

**camion,** m. *[kahmyoh(n)]* truck

**camomille,** m. *[kahmohmeel]* camomile

**campagne,** f. *[kah(m)pahɲyuh]* country (landscape)

**camper** *[kah(m)pay]* to camp

**Canada,** m. *[Kahnahdah]* Canada

**canadien** *[kahnadya(n)]* Canadian

**canard,** m. *[kahnahr]* duck

**caneton,** m. *[kahntoh(n)]* duckling

**cannelle,** f. *[kahnehl]* cinnamon

**car,** m. *[kahr]* bus

**carafe,** f. *[kahrahf]* carafe

**caravane,** f. *[kahrahvahn]* trailer

**carburateur,** m. *[kahrbewrahtuhr]* carburetor

**carnet,** m. *[kahrnay]* book of tickets

**carotte,** f. *[kahroht]* carrot

**carrefour,** m. *[kahrfoor]* intersection

**carte,** f. *[kahrt]* map, menu

**carte d'accès à bord,** f. *[kahrt dahksay ah bohr]* boarding pass

**carte de crédit,** f. *[kahrt duh kraydee]* credit card

**carte postale,** f. *[kahrt pohstahl]* postcard

**carte routière,** f. *[kahrt rootyehr]* road map

**cassé** *[kahsay]* broken

**cassoulet,** m. *[kahsoolay]* stew

**cathédrale,** f. *[kahtaydrahl]* cathedral

cave, f. [kahv] basement, wine cellar
ce, m. [suh] this
ceci [suhsee] this
cédez le passage [sayday luh pahsahzh] yield
ceinture, f. [sa(n)tewr] belt
cela [suhlah] that
céleri, m. [saylree] celery
célibataire [sayleebahtehr] single (unmarried)
cellule, f. [sehlewl] cell
celui [suhlwee] this one
cendrier, m. [sah(n)dreeay] ashtray
cent [sah(n)] hundred
centime, m. [sah(n)teem] centime (1/100 franc)
centre, m. [sah(n)tr] center
centre commercial, m. [sah(n)tr kohmehrsyahl] shopping center
centre ville, m. [sah(n)truh veel] downtown
cerise, f. [suhreez] cherry
certainement [sehrtehn-mah(n)] certainly
cervelle, f. [sehrvehl] brain
ces (pl.) [say] these, those
c'est [seh] it is, this is
cet (m.) [seht] this
cette f. [seht] this
chacun [shahkuh(n)] each one
chaînette, f. [shehneht] chain
chaise, f. [shehz] chair
chambre, f. [shah(m)br] room, bedroom
chambre d'hôte, f. [shah(m)br doht] bed and breakfast
champ, m. [shah(m)] field

champignon, m. [shah(m)-peenyoh(n)] mushroom
chance, f. [shah(n)s] luck
chandail, m. [shah(n)dahy] sweater
change, m. [shah(n)zh] currency, exchange
changer [shah(n)zhay] to change
chanson, f. [shah(n)soh(n)] song
chanter [shah(n)tay] to sing
chantier, m. [shah(n)tyay] work site
chapelle, f. [shahpehl] chapel
chaque [shahk] every, each
charcuterie, f. [shahrkewtree] delicatessen, cold cuts
chariot, m. [shahryoh] cart
chasseur, m. [shahsuhr] bellboy
chat, m. [shah] cat
château, m. [shahtoh] castle
chaud [shoh] warm, hot
chauffage, f. [shohfahzh] heat
chaussette, f. [shohseht] sock
chaussure, f. [shohsewr] shoe
chef, m. [shehf] boss
chef d'orchestre, m. [shehf dohrkehstr] orchestra leader
chemin, m. [shuhma(n)] road, way
chemin de fer, m. [shuhma(n) duh fehr] railroad
chemise, f. [shuhmeez] shirt
chèque, m. [shehk] check
chèque de voyage, m. [shehk duh vwahyahzh] traveler's check

**cher** [shehr] dear, expensive
**chercher** [shehrshay] to look for
**cheval,** m. [shuhvahl] horse
**cheveux,** m.pl. [shuhvuh] hair
**chez** [shay] at the house of
**chien,** m. [shya(n)] dog
**chiffre,** m. [sheefr] number
**choisir** [shwahzeer] to choose
**choix,** m. [shwah] choice
**chose,** f. [shohz] thing
**chou,** m. [shoo] cabbage
**chou de Bruxelles,** m. [shoo duh Brewsehl] Brussels sprouts
**chou-fleur,** m. [shoo-fluhr] cauliflower
**chute d'eau,** f. [shewt doh] waterfall
**cidre,** m. [seedr] cider
**ciel,** m. [syehl] sky
**cigare,** f. [seegahr] cigar
**cigarette,** f. [seegahreht] cigarette
**cil,** m. [seel] eyelash
**cimetière,** m. [seemtyehr] cemetery
**cinéma,** m. [seenaymah] film, movies, movie theater
**cinq** [sa(n)k] five
**cinquante** [sa(n)kah(n)t] fifty
**cintre,** m. [sa(n)tr] hanger
**circuit touristique,** m. [seerkwee tooreesteek] scenic route
**circulation,** f. [seerkewlah-syoh(n)] traffic
**ciseaux,** m.pl. [seezoh] scissors

**citron,** m. [seetroh(n)] lemon
**citron pressé,** m. [seetroh(n) prehsay] lemonade
**citron vert,** m. [seetroh(n) vehr] lime
**clair** [klehr] clear
**classique** [klahseek] classic
**clé,** f. [klay] key
**client,** m. [kleeah(n)] customer
**clignotant,** m. [kleenyoh-tah(n)] blinker
**climatisé,** m. [kleemahteezay] air-conditioned
**cochon,** m. [kohshoh(n)] pig
**coeur,** m. [kuhr] heart
**coffre-fort,** m. [kohfruh-fohr] safe
**coffret à bijoux,** m. [kohfray ah beezhoo] jewelry box
**cognac,** m. [kohnyahk] cognac
**coiffeur,** m. [kwahfuhr] hairdresser, barber
**coin,** m. [kwa(n)] corner
**col,** m. [kohl] mountain pass, collar
**colis,** m. [kohlee] package
**collègue,** m. or f. [kohlehg] colleague
**collier,** m. [kohlyay] necklace
**colline,** f. [kohleen] hill
**combien** [koh(m)bya(n)] how many, how much
**commander** [kohmah(n)day] to order
**comme** [kohm] like, as
**commencer** [kohmah(n)say] to begin
**comment** [kohmah(n)] how

**comment dit-on . . .** *[kohmah(n) dee toh(n) . . . ]* how do you say. . .

**commissariat,** m. *[koh-meesahryah]* police station

**compagnie,** f. *[koh(m)pah-nyee]* company

**compartiment,** m. *[koh(m)-pahrteemah(n)]* compartment

**complet,** m. *[koh(m)play]* suit

**composer** *[koh(m)pohzay]* to dial

**comprendre** *[koh(m)-prah(n)dr]* to understand

**compris** *[koh(m)pree]* understood, included

**compter** *[koh(m)tay]* to count

**concert,** m. *[koh(n)sehr]* concert

**concierge,** m. or f. *[koh(n)-syehrzh]* hall porter

**concombre,** m. *[koh(n)-koh(m)br]* cucumber

**conduire** *[koh(n)dweer]* to drive

**confirmer** *[koh(n)feermay]* to confirm

**confiture,** f. *[koh(n)feetewr]* jam

**connaissance,** f. *[kohneh-sah(n)s]* acquaintance

**connaître** *[kohnehtr]* to know (be familiar with)

**consigne automatique,** f. *[koh(n)seen yohtohmahteek]* baggage locker

**contenu,** m. *[koh(n)tuhnew]* contents

**continuer** *[koh(n)teeneway]* to continue

**contraire,** m. *[koh(n)trehr]* opposite

**contre** *[koh(n)tr]* against

**coq,** m. *[kohk]* rooster, cock

**coquillage,** m. *[kohkeeyahzh]* shell

**cornet de glace,** m. *[kohrnay duh glahs]* ice-cream cone

**cornichon,** m. *[kohrneeshoh(n)]* pickle

**corps,** m. *[kohr]* body

**correspondence,** f. *[kohrehspoh(n)dah(n)s]* correspondence, change of train or bus

**côte,** f. *[koht]* hill, rib, coast

**côté,** m. *[kohtay]* side

**côté de stationnement,** m. *[kohtay duh stahsyohnmah(n)]* parking side

**côtelette,** f. *[kohtleht]* cutlet

**coton,** m. *[kohtoh(n)]* cotton

**cou,** m. *[koo]* neck

**couche,** f. *[koosh]* diaper

**couchette,** f. *[koosheht]* sleeping berth

**couleur,** f. *[kooluhr]* color

**coupe,** f. *[koop]* cut, haircut

**coupe de cheveux,** f. *[koop duh shuhvuh]* haircut

**coupe-ongles,** m. *[koop-oh(n)gl]* nail cutter

**couper** *[koopay]* to cut, cut off

**courgette,** f. *[koorzheht]* squash

**courir** *[kooreer]* to run

**courrier,** m. *[kooryay]* mail

**cours,** m. *[koor]* course

**court** *[koor]* short

**cousin,** m. *[kooza(n)]* cousin
**cousine,** f. *[koozeen]* cousin
**couteau,** m. *[kootoh]* knife
**coûter** *[kootay]* to cost
**couvert** *[koovehr]* cloudy, covered
**couvert,** m. *[koovehr]* cover charge
**couverture,** f. *[koovehrtewr]* blanket
**couvrir** *[koovreer]* to cover
**crabe,** m. *[krahb]* crab
**cravate,** f. *[krahvaht]* necktie
**crayon,** m. *[krayoh(n)]* pencil
**crème,** f. *[krehm]* cream
**crème à raser,** f. *[krehm ah rahzay]* shaving cream
**créole** *[krayohl]* creole
**crêpe,** f. *[krehp]* pancake
**crêperie,** f. *[krehpree]* creperie
**crevette,** f. *[kruhveht]* shrimp
**cric,** m. *[kreek]* jack (car)
**croire** *[krwahr]* to believe
**croûte,** f. *[kroot]* crust
**crudités,** f.pl. *[krewdeetay]* raw vegetables
**cuillère,** f. *[kweeyehr]* spoon
**cuir,** m. *[kweer]* leather
**cuisine,** f. *[kweezeen]* kitchen, cooking
**cuisinier,** m. *[kweezeenyay]* cook (chef)
**cuisse,** f. *[kwees]* thigh
**cuit** *[kwee]* cooked
**bien cuit** *[byeh(n) kwee]* well-done (meat)
**curiosité,** f. *[kewryohzeetay]* attraction

**cyclisme,** m. *[seekleezm]* cycling

# D

**d'accord** *[dahkohr]* okay, agreed
**daim,** m. *[da(m)]* suede
**dangereux** *[dah(n)zhuhruh]* dangerous
**dans** *[dah(n)]* in
**danse,** f. *[dah(n)s]* dance
**danser** *[dah(n)say]* to dance
**datte,** f. *[daht]* date (fruit)
**de** *[duh]* of, from
**débutant,** m. *[daybewtah(n)]* beginner
**décaféiné** *[daykahfayeenay]* decaffeinated
**décembre** *[daysah(m)br]* December
**décider** *[dayseeday]* to decide
**déclarer** *[dayklahray]* to declare
**déçu** *[daysew]* disappointed
**dedans** *[duhdah(n)]* inside
**défense d'entrée** *[dayfah(n)s dah(n)tray]* no entry, entry prohibited
**déjeuner,** m. *[dayzhuhnay]* lunch
**demain** *[duhma(n)]* tomorrow
**demander** *[duhmah(n)day]* to ask
**démarrer** *[daymahray]* to start (a car)
**démarreur,** m. *[daymahruhr]* starter
**demi** *[duhmee]* half
**demi-bouteille,** f. *[duhmee-bootehy]* half bottle

**demi-tour,** m. *[duhmee-toor]* U-turn

**dent,** f. *[dah(n)]* tooth

**dentelle,** f. *[dah(n)tehl]* lace

**dentifrice,** m. *[dah(n)teefrees]* toothpaste

**dépannage,** m. *[daypahnahzh]* emergency road service

**se dépêcher** *[suh daypehshay]* to hurry

**dépenser** *[daypah(n)say]* to spend

**déposer** *[daypohzay]* to drop off

**depuis** *[duhpwee]* since

**Depuis quand?** *[Duhpwee kah(n)?]* Since when?

**déranger** *[dayrah(n)zhay]* to disturb

**dernier** *[dehrnyay]* last (adj.)

**derrière** *[dehryehr]* in back of, behind

**des** (pl.) *[day]* of the, from the

**descendre** *[dehsah(n)dr]* to go down, get off

**désolé** *[dayzohlay]* sorry

**dessous** *[duhsoo]* beneath

**dessus** *[duhsew]* above, over

**deux** *[duh]* two

**deuxième** *[duhzyehm]* second

**devant** *[duhvah(n)]* in front of

**devenir** *[duhvuhneer]* to become

**déviation,** f. *[dayvyahsyoh(n)]* detour

**devoir** *[duhvwahr]* to be obliged to

**diabétique** *[dyahbayteek]* diabetic

**diamant,** m. *[dyahmah(n)]* diamond

**diapositive,** f. *[dyahpoh-zeeteev]* slide (photographic)

**dictionnaire,** m. *[deek-syohnehr]* dictionary

**différent** *[deefayrah(n)]* different

**difficile** *[deefeeseel]* difficult

**difficulté,** f. *[deefeekewltay]* trouble

**dimanche** *[deemah(n)sh]* Sunday

**diminuer** *[deemeeneway]* to diminish

**dinde,** f. *[da(n)d]* turkey

**dîner** *[deenay]* to dine

**dîner,** m. *[deenay]* dinner

**dire** *[deer]* to say

**direction,** f. *[deerehksyoh(n)]* direction

**disque,** m. *[deesk]* record

**distance,** f. *[deestah(n)s]* distance

**divorcé** *[deevohrsay]* divorced

**dix** *[dees]* ten

**dix-huit** *[deez-weet]* eighteen

**dix-neuf** *[deez-nuhf]* nineteen

**dix-sept** *[deez-seht]* seventeen

**doigt,** m. *[dwah]* finger

**dois/doit** *[dwah]* must (see devoir)

**donc** *[doh(n)k]* then, therefore

**donner** *[dohnay]* to give

**dormir** *[dohrmeer]* to sleep

**dos,** m. *[doh]* back

**douane,** f. *[dwahn]* customs

**doublé** [dooblay] dubbed (film)
**douce** f. [doos] sweet, soft
**douche,** f. [doosh] shower
**douleur,** f. [dooluhr] pain
**doux** (m.) [doo] sweet, soft
**douzaine,** f. [doozehn] dozen
**douze** [dooz] twelve
**drame,** m. [drahm] drama
**drap,** m. [drah] sheet (bed)
**droit,** m. [drwah] right
**droite,** f. [drwaht] right (direction)
**du** [dew] of the, from the (m.s.)
**durer** [dewray] to last

# E

**eau,** f. [oh] water
**eau de toilette,** f. [oh duh twahleht] toilet water
**eau minérale,** f. [oh meenay-rahl] mineral water
**échanger** [ayshah(n)zhay] to exchange
**échelle,** f. [ayshehl] ladder
**éclair,** m. [ayklehr] éclair (type of pastry)
**école,** f. [aykohl] school
**écouter** [aykootay] to listen
**écrire** [aykreer] to write
**écrit** [aykree] written
**église,** f. [aygleez] church
**électricité,** f. [aylehk-treeseetay] electricity
**elle,** f. [ehl] she
**elles,** f.pl. [ehl] they
**emballer** [ah(m)bahlay] to wrap up

**embrasser** [ah(m)brahsay] to kiss
**employer** [ah(m)plwahyay] to use
**emprunter** [ah(m)pruh(n)tay] to borrow
**en** [ah(n)] in, to
**en bas** [ah(n) bah] below, downstairs
**en haut** [ah(n) oh] up, upstairs
**en plein air** [ah(n) pleh nehr] outside
**enceinte** [ah(n)sa(n)t] pregnant
**enchanté** [ah(n)shah(n)tay] delighted
**encore** [ah(n)kohr] again, still, yet
**endroit,** m. [ah(n)drwah] place
**enfant,** m. or f. [ah(n)fah(n)] child
**enregistrement,** m. [ah(n)rehzheestruhmah(n)] recording, registration
**enregistrer** [ah(n)rehzheestray] to register
**enseigne,** f. [ah(n)sehnyuh] sign
**ensemble** [ah(n)sah(m)bl] together
**ensuite** [ah(n)sweet] next, afterward
**entendre** [ah(n)tah(n)dr] to hear
**entendu** [ah(n)tah(n)dew] agreed, understood
**entier** [ah(n)tyay] whole
**entre** [ah(n)tr] between
**entrée,** f. [ah(n)tray] entrance

**envie,** f. *[ah(n)vee]* desire, wish

**envoyer** *[ah(n)vwahyay]* to send

**épaule,** f. *[aypohl]* shoulder

**épeler** *[ayplay]* to spell

**épicerie,** f. *[aypeesree]* grocery

**épinards,** m.pl. *[aypeenahr]* spinach

**épingle,** f. *[aypa(n)gl]* pin

**épingle à cravate,** f. *[aypa(n)glah krahvaht]* tie pin

**épingle de sûreté,** f. *[aypa(n)gl duh sewrtay]* safety pin

**épouse,** f. *[aypooz]* spouse

**époux,** m. *[aypoo]* spouse

**épreuve,** f. *[aypruhv]* print

**épuisé** *[aypweezay]* exhausted

**équipe,** f. *[aykeep]* team

**équipement de ski,** m. *[aykeepmah(n) duh skee]* ski equipment

**erreur,** f. *[ehruhr]* error

**escale,** f. *[ehskahl]* layover, stop

**escalier,** m. *[ehskahlyay]* staircase

**escargot,** m. *[ehskahrgoh]* snail

**Espagne,** f. *[Ehspahnyuh]* Spain

**espagnol** *[ehspahnyohl]* Spanish

**espérer** *[ehspayray]* to hope

**essayer** *[ehsayay]* to try

**essence,** f. *[ehsah(n)s]* gasoline

**est,** m. *[ehst]* east

**est-ce que** *[ehskuh]* is, do (introduces a question)

**estomac,** m. *[ehstohmah]* stomach

**et** *[eh]* and

**étage,** m. *[aytahzh]* story (of a building)

**étang,** m. *[aytah(n)]* pond

**état,** m. *[aytah]* state

**Etats-Unis,** m.pl. *[Aytah-zewnee]* United States

**été,** m. *[aytay]* summer

**êtes** *[eht]* are (see être)

**étranger** *[aytrah(n)zhay]* foreign

**étranger,** m. *[aytrah(n)zhay]* foreigner

**à l'étranger** *[ah laytrah(n)zhay]* overseas, abroad

**être** *[ehtr]* to be

**étroit** *[aytrwah]* narrow

**étui,** m. *[aytwee]* cigarette case

**excellent** *[ehksehlah(n)]* excellent

**excursion,** f. *[ehkskewrsyoh(n)]* excursion

**s'excuser** *[sehkskewzay]* to apologize

**exemple,** m. *[ehksah(m)pl]* example

## F

**en face de** *[ah(n) fahs duh]* opposite (prep.)

**facile** *[fahseel]* easy

**faible** *[fehbl]* weak

FRENCH/ENGLISH

**faim,** f. *[fa(m)]* hunger

**faire** *[fehr]* to do, make

**faire cuire** *[fehr kweer]* to cook

**faire des achats** *[fehr day zahshah]* to shop

**fait à la main** *[feh tah lah ma(n)]* handmade

**faites** *[feht]* do/make (see faire)

**faites le plein** *[feht luh pla(n)]* fill it up

**falaise,** f. *[fahlehz]* cliff

**famille,** f. *[fahmeey]* family

**fard,** m. *[fahr]* makeup

**farine,** f. *[fahreen]* flour

**fatigué** *[fahteegay]* tired

**faut** *[foh]* is necessary

**faute,** f. *[foht]* mistake

**fauteuil,** m. *[fohtuhy]* armchair

**faux** *[foh]* false

**félicitations!** *[fayleeseetah-syoh(n)!]* congratulations!

**femme,** f. *[fahm]* woman, wife

**femme de chambre,** f. *[fahm duh shah(m)br]* maid

**fenêtre,** f. *[fuhnehtr]* window

**fer,** m. *[fehr]* iron

**ferme,** f. *[fehrm]* farm

**fermer** *[fehrmay]* to close

**fermeture éclair,** f. *[fehr-muhtewr ayklehr]* zipper

**fête,** f. *[feht]* holiday

**février** *[fayvreeyay]* February

**feu,** m. *[fuh]* fire

**feu de circulation,** m. *[fuh duh seerkewlahsyoh(n)]* traffic light

**ficelle,** f. *[feesehl]* string

**fiche,** f. *[feesh]* card

**fièvre,** f. *[fyehvr]* fever

**figue,** f. *[feeg]* fig

**filet,** m. *[feelay]* filet, net

**fille,** f. *[feey]* girl, daughter

**fils,** m. *[fees]* son

**fin,** f. *[fa(n)]* end

**fin d'autoroute** *[fa(n) dohtohroot]* highway ends

**finir** *[feeneer]* to finish

**fixe** *[feeks]* fixed

**flan,** m. *[flah(n)]* custard

**fleur,** f. *[fluhr]* flower

**fleuve,** m. *[fluhv]* river

**flûte,** f. *[flewt]* flute

**foie,** m. *[fwah]* liver

**folklorique** *[fohlklohreek]* folkloric

**foncé** *[foh(n)say]* dark

**fond d'artichaut,** m. *[foh(n) dahrteeshoh]* artichoke heart

**fontaine,** f. *[foh(n)tehn]* fountain

**footing,** m. *[footeeng]* running, jogging

**forêt,** f. *[fohreh]* forest

**format,** m. *[fohrmah]* format, size

**formulaire,** m. *[fohrmewlehr]* form

**fort** *[fohr]* strong

**forteresse,** f. *[fohrtuhrehs]* fortress

**four,** m. *[foor]* oven

**fourchette,** f. *[foorsheht]* fork

**frais** *[freh]* cool, fresh

**fraise,** f. *[frehz]* strawberry*

**framboise,** f. *[frah(m)bwahz]* raspberry

**franc,** m. *[frah(n)]* franc

**français** *[frah(n)seh]* French

**France,** f. *[Frah(n)s]* France

**frapper** *[frahpay]* to knock

**freins,** m.pl. *[fraa(n)]* brakes

**frère,** m. *[frehr]* brother

**frit** *[free]* fried

**froid** *[frwah]* cold

**froid,** m. *[frwah]* cold (weather)

**fromage,** m. *[frohmahzh]* cheese

**frontière,** f. *[froh(n)tyehr]* border

**fruit,** m. *[frwee]* fruit

**fruits de mer,** m.pl. *[frwee duh mehr]* seafood

**fruits secs,** m.pl. *[frwee sehk]* dried fruit

**fumé** *[fuwmay]* smoked

**fumeurs,** m.pl. *[foomuhr]* smokers

## G

**gagner** *[gahnyay]* to earn, win

**galerie d'art,** f. *[gahlree dahr]* art gallery

**gant,** m. *[gah(n)]* glove

**garage,** m. *[gahrahzh]* garage

**garçon,** m. *[gahrsoh(n)]* boy, waiter

**garde d'enfants,** f. *[gahrd dah(n)fah(n)]* babysitter

**garder** *[gahrday]* to keep

**gare,** f. *[gahr]* train station

**(se) garer** *[(suh) gahray]* to park

**garniture,** f. *[gahrneetewr]* accompanying vegetables

**gas-oil,** m. *[gahzwahl]* diesel fuel

**gastronomique** *[gahstrohnohmeek]* gastronomical

**gâteau,** m. *[gahtoh]* cake

**gauche,** f. *[gohsh]* left

**gazeux** *[gahzuh]* carbonated

**gêner** *[zhehnay]* to bother

**genou,** m. *[zhuhnoo]* knee

**genre,** m. *[zhah(n)r]* type, sort

**gens,** m.pl. *[zhah(n)]* people

**gentil** *[zhah(n)teey]* nice

**gérant,** m. *[zhayrah(n)]* manager

**gibier,** m. *[zheebyay]* game

**gingembre,** m. *[zha(n)zhah(m)br]* ginger

**glace,** f. *[glahs]* ice, ice cream

**glacé** *[glahsay]* iced, frozen

**glaçon,** m. *[glahsoh(n)]* ice cube

**glissant** *[gleesah(n)]* slippery

**gorge,** f. *[gohrzh]* throat

**goûter** *[gootay]* to taste

**grand** *[grah(n)]* big

**grand magasin,** m. *[grah(n) mahgahza(n)]* department store

**grand-mère,** f. *[grah(n)-mehr]* grandmother

**grand-père,** m. *[grah(n)-pehr]* grandfather

**grenier,** m. *[gruhnyay]* attic

**grenouille,** f. *[gruhnooy]* frog
**grillé** *[greeyay]* grilled
**gris** *[gree]* gray
**gros** *[groh]* fat
**grossir** *[grohseer]* to gain
  weight
**grotte,** f. *[groht]* cave
**guerre,** f. *[gehr]* war
**guichet,** m. *[gheeshay]* ticket
  window
**guide,** m. or f. *[gheed]* guide
**guidé** *[gheeday]* guided

# H

**s'habiller** *[sahbeeyay]* to
  dress
**habiter** *[ahbeetay]* to live
**haricot,** m. *[ahreekoh]* bean
**haricots,** m.pl. *[ahreekoh]*
  stringbeans
**haricots verts,** m.pl. *[ahreekoh
  vehr]* green beans
**haut** *[oh]* high
**en haut** *[ah(n) oh]* up, upstairs
**haute cuisine,** f. *[oht kwee-
  zeen]* gourmet cooking
**hauteur,** f. *[ohtuhr]* height
**herbe,** f. *[ehrb]* grass, herb
**heure,** f. *[uhr]* hour, time
**à l'heure** *[ah luhr]* on time
**heureux** *[uhruh]* happy
**hier** *[eeyehr]* yesterday
**histoire,** f. *[eestwahr]* history,
  story (tale)
**hiver,** m. *[eevehr]* winter
**homard,** m. *[ohmahr]* lobster
**homme,** m. *[ohm]* man
**hôpital,** m. *[ohpeetahl]*
  hospital

**horaire,** m. *[ohrehr]* schedule
**hors d'oeuvres,** m.pl. *[ohr
  duhvr]* appetizers
**hôtel,** m. *[ohtehl]* hotel
**hôtel de ville,** m. *[ohtehl duh
  veel]* town hall, city hall
**hôtesse de l'air,** f. *[ohtehs duh
  lehr]* stewardess
**huile,** f. *[weel]* oil
**huile de bronzage,** f. *[weel
  duh broh(n)zahzh]* suntan oil
**huit** *[weet]* eight
**huître,** m. *[weetr]* oyster

# I

**ici** *[eesee]* here
**il,** m. *[eel]* he
**il y a** *[eel yah]* there is, there
  are, ago
**île,** f. *[eel]* island
**illimité** *[eeleemeetay]* unlimited
**ils,** m.pl. *[eel]* they
**impair** *[a(m)pehr]* odd
**impasse,** f. *[a(m)pahs]* dead
  end
**important** *[a(m)pohrtah(n)]*
  important
**impossible** *[a(m)pohseebl]*
  impossible
**incroyable** *[a(n)krwahyahbl]*
  unbelievable
**indicatif,** m. *[a(n)deekahteef]*
  area code
**indiquer** *[a(n)deekay]* to
  indicate
**infirmière,** f. *[a(n)feermyehr]*
  nurse

261

**infusion,** f. *[a(n)fewzyoh(n)]* infusion

**intelligent** *[a(n)tehleezhah(n)]* intelligent

**interdire** *[a(n)tehrdeer]* to prohibit

**interdit** *[a(n)tehrdee]* forbidden

**interdit aux piétons** *[a(n)tehrdee oh paytoh(n)]* no pedestrians

**intéressant** *[a(n)tayrehsah(n)]* interesting

**s'intéresser à** *[sa(n)tayrehsay ah]* to be interested in

**inutile** *[eenewteel]* useless

**invalide** *[a(n)vahleed]* handicapped

**inviter** *[a(n)veetay]* to invite

**issue,** f. *[eesew]* way out

**ivoire,** f. *[eevwahr]* ivory

**ivre** *[eevr]* drunk

## J

**jamais** *[zhahmay]* never

**jambe,** f. *[zhah(m)b]* leg

**jambon,** m. *[zhah(m)boh(n)]* ham

**janvier** *[zhah(n)vyay]* January

**jardin,** m. *[zhahrda(n)]* garden

**jardin zoologique,** m. *[zhahrda(n) zohohlohzheek]* zoo

**jaune** *[zhohn]* yellow

**je** *[zhuh]* I

**je voudrais** *[zhuh voodreh]* I'd like

**jeton,** m. *[zhuhtoh(n)]* token

**jeudi** *[zhuhdee]* Thursday

**jeune** *[zhuhn]* young

**joli** *[zhohlee]* pretty

**jouer** *[zhooay]* to play

**joueur,** m. *[zhoouhr]* player

**jour,** m. *[zhoor]* day

**journal,** m. *[zhoornal]* newspaper

**journaux,** m.pl. *[zhoornoh]* newpapers

**journée,** f. *[zhoornay]* day

**juger** *[zhewzhay]* to judge

**juillet** *[zhweeyay]* July

**juin** *[zhwa(n)]* June

**jupe,** f. *[zhewp]* skirt

**jus,** m. *[zhew]* juice

**jusqu'à** *[zhewskah]* until

## K

**kasher** *[kahshehr]* kosher

**kilomètre,** m. *[keelohmehtr]* kilometer

**kilométrage,** m. *[keelohmehtrahzh]* mileage

**kiosque,** m. *[keeohsk]* kiosk, newspaper stand

## L

**la** (f.) *[lah]* the, herself, itself

**là** *[lah]* there

**lac,** m. *[lahk]* lake

**laid** *[leh]* ugly

**laine,** f. *[lehn]* wool

**laisser** *[lehsay]* to leave, let

**lait,** m. *[leh]* milk

**laitue,** f. *[lehtew]* lettuce

**lampe de poche,** f. *[lah(m)p duh pohsh]* flashlight

**langouste,** f. *[lah(n)goost]* lobster

**langue,** f. *[lah(n)g]* tongue, language

**lapin,** m. *[lahpa(n)]* rabbit

**lard,** m. *[lahr]* bacon

**large** *[lahrzh]* wide

**laver** *[lahvay]* to wash

**laverie automatique,** f. *[lahvree ohtohmahteek]* laundromat

**le,** m. *[luh]* the, himself, itself

**leçon,** f. *[luhsoh(n)]* lesson

**léger** *[layzhay]* light

**légume,** m. *[laygewm]* vegetable

**lent** *[lah(n)]* slow

**lentille,** f. *[lah(n)teey]* lens

**lentement** *[lah(n)tuhmah(n)]* slowly

**les** (pl.) *[lay]* the

**lettre,** f. *[lehtr]* letter

**leur/leurs** *[luhr]* their, them

**se lever** *[suh luhvay]* to get up

**lévier,** m. *[layvyay]* lever

**librairie,** f. *[leebrehree]* bookstore

**libre** *[leebr]* free

**au lieu de** *[oh lyuh duh]* instead of

**ligne,** f. *[leenyuh]* line

**lime à ongles,** f. *[leem ah oh(n)gl]* nail file

**lin,** m. *[la(n)]* linen

**liqueur,** f. *[leekuhr]* liquor

**lire** *[leer]* to read

**liste,** f. *[leest]* list

**lit,** m. *[lee]* bed

**litre,** m. *[leetr]* liter

**livre,** m. *[leevr]* book

**local** *[lohkahl]* local

**loger** *[lohzhay]* to stay, lodge

**loin** *[lwa(n)]* far

**long** *[loh(n)]* long

**longtemps** *[loh(n)tah(m)]* for a long time

**louer** *[looay]* to rent, hire

**loup,** m. *[loo]* wolf

**lourd** *[loor]* heavy

**loyer,** m. *[lwahyay]* rent

**lui** *[lwee]* her, him

**lumière,** f. *[lewmyehr]* light

**lundi** *[luh(n)dee]* Monday

**lune,** f. *[lewn]* moon

**lunettes,** f.pl. *[lewneht]* eyeglasses

**lunettes de soleil,** f.pl. *[lewneht duh sohlehy]* sunglasses

**lotion,** f. *[lohsyoh(n)]* lotion

**lotion après-rasage,** f. *[lohsyoh(n) ahpreh-rahzahzh]* aftershave lotion

**luxe,** m. *[lewks]* luxury

**lycée,** m. *[leesay]* high school

## M

**ma,** f. *[mah]* my

**madame** *[mahdahm]* Mrs.

**mademoiselle** *[mahduhmwahzehl]* Miss

**magasin,** m. *[mahgahza(n)]* store

**magasin hors-taxe,** m. *[mahgahza(n) ohr-tahks]* duty-free shop

**magazine,** m. *[mahgahzeen]* magazine

**magnétophone à cassette,** m. *[mahnyaytohfohn ah kahseht]* cassette recorder

**magnétoscope,** m. *[mahnyaytohskohp]* video recorder

**mai** *[meh]* May

**maigrir** *[mehgreer]* to lose weight

**maillot de bain,** m. *[mayoh duh ba(n)]* bathing suit

**main** *[ma(n)]* hand

**maintenant** *[ma(n)tuhnah(n)]* now

**mais** *[meh]* but

**maïs,** m. *[mah-ees]* corn

**maison,** f. *[mehzoh(n)]* house

**maître d'hôtel,** m. *[mehtr dohtehl]* maitre d', host

**maître nageur,** m. *[mehtr nahzhur]* life guard

**mal** *[mahl]* badly

**malade** *[mahlahd]* ill, sick

**maladie,** f. *[mahlahdee]* illness, sickness

**malgré** *[mahlgray]* in spite of

**malheureux** *[mahluhruh]* unhappy

**malle,** f. *[mahl]* trunk

**mandarine,** f. *[mah(n)dahreen]* tangerine

**manger** *[mah(n)zhay]* to eat

**manque,** m. *[mah(n)k]* lack

**manquer** *[mah(n)kay]* to lack

**manteau,** m. *[mah(n)toh]* overcoat

**manucure,** f. *[mahnewkewr]* manicurist

**marchand,** m. *[mahrshah(n)]* merchant

**marché,** m. *[mahrshay]* market

**marché aux puces,** m. *[mahrshay oh pews]* flea market

**marcher** *[mahrshay]* to walk

**mardi** *[mahrdee]* Tuesday

**marée basse,** f. *[mahray bahs]* low tide

**marée haute,** f. *[mahray oht]* high tide

**mari,** m. *[mahree]* husband

**marié** *[mahryay]* married

**marjolaine,** f. *[mahrzhohlehn]* marjoram

**mars** *[mahrs]* March

**matin,** m. *[mahta(n)]* morning

**mauvais** *[mohveh]* bad

**mayonnaise,** f. *[mahyohnehz]* mayonnaise

**me** *[muh]* me, to me

**mécanicien,** m. *[maykahneesya(n)]* mechanic

**médicin,** m. *[maydsa(n)]* doctor

**médecine,** f. *[maydseen]* medicine

**médiéval** *[maydyayvahl]* medieval

**meilleur** *[mehyuhr]* better

**melon,** m. *[muhloh(n)]* melon

**même** *[mehm]* same

**menthe,** f. *[mah(n)t]* mint

**menton,** m. *[mah(n)toh(n)]* chin

**menu,** m. *[muhnew]* menu

**menu à prix fixe,** m. *[muhnew ah pree feeks]* fixed-price menu

**menu gastronomique,** m. *[muhnew gahstrohnohmeek]* gourmet menu

**mer,** f. *[mehr]* sea
**merci** *[mehrsee]* thank you
**mercredi** *[mehrkruhdee]*
  Wednesday
**mère,** f. *[mehr]* mother
**merveilleux** *[mehrvehyuh]*
  wonderful, marvelous
**mes** (pl.) *[may]* my
**messe,** f. *[mehs]* mass
**météo,** f. *[maytayoh]* weather
  forecast
**métro,** m. *[maytroh]* subway
**mettre** *[mehtr]* to put, put on
**meublé** *[muhblay]* furnished
**meubles,** m.pl. *[muhbl]*
  furniture
**midi** *[meedee]* noon
**mieux** *[myuh]* better
**milieu,** m. *[meelyuh]* middle,
  environment
  **au milieu de** *[oh meelyuh
    duh]* in the middle of
**mille** *[meel]* thousand
**mille-feuille,** m. *[meel-fuhy]*
  napoleon (type of pastry)
**mince** *[ma(n)s]* thin
**minérale** *[meenayrahl]*
  mineral
**minuit** *[meenwee]* midnight
**minute,** f. *[meenewt]* minute
**miroir,** m. *[meerwahr]* mirror
**mise en pli,** f. *[meez ah(n)
    plee]* permanent
**mise au point,** f. *[meez oh
    pwa(n)]* tune up
**moi** *[mwah]* me
**moins** *[mwa(n)]* less
  **au moins** *[oh mwa(n)]* at least
**mois,** m. *[mwah]* month
**moment,** m. *[mohmah(n)]*
  moment

**mon** *[moh(n)]* my
**monastère,** m. *[mohnahstehr]*
  monastery
**monde,** m. *[moh(n)d]* world
**monnaie,** f. *[mohnay]* money,
  change
**monsieur** *[muhsyuh]* Mister,
  sir
**montagne,** f. *[moh(n)tahnyuh]*
  mountain
**monter** *[moh(n)tay]* to go up
**montre,** f. *[moh(n)tr]* watch
**montrer** *[moh(n)tray]* to show
**morue,** f. *[mohrew]* cod
**mosquée,** f. *[mohskay]*
  mosque
**mot,** m. *[moh]* word
**mouchoir,** m. *[mooshwahr]*
  handkerchief
**mouchoirs en papiers,** m.pl.
  *[mooshwahr ah(n)pahpyay]*
  tissues
**mouillé** *[mooyay]* wet
**moules,** f.pl. *[mool]* mussels
**mousse,** f. *[moos]* mousse
**moustache,** f. *[moostahsh]*
  moustache
**moutarde,** f. *[mootahrd]*
  mustard
**mouton,** m. *[mootoh(n)]* lamb
**moyen,** m. *[mwahya(n)]* way
**moyens,** m.pl. *[mwahya(n)]*
  means
**mur,** m. *[mewr]* wall
**musée,** m. *[mewzay]* museum
**musique,** f. *[mewzeek]* music

# N

**nager** *[nahzhay]* to swim

**navet,** m. *[nahvay]* turnip

**né** *[nay]* born

**nécessaire** *[naysehsehr]* necessary

**neige,** f. *[nehzh]* snow

**neiger** *[nehzhay]* to snow

**nettoyer** *[nehtwahyay]* to clean

**nettoyer à sec** *[nehtwahyay ah sehk]* to dry clean

**neuf** *[nuhf]* nine

**nez,** m. *[nay]* nose

**niveau,** m. *[neevoh]* level

**noir** *[nwahr]* black

**noix,** f. *[nwah]* nut

**nom,** m. *[noh(m)]* name

**non** *[noh(n)]* no

**nord,** m. *[nohr]* north

**nos** (pl.) *[noh]* our

**note,** f. *[noht]* bill

**notre** *[nohtr]* our

**nouilles,** f.pl. *[nooy]* noodles

**nourriture,** f. *[nooreetewr]* food

**nous** *[noo]* we, us

**nouveau** *[noovoh]* new

**nouvelle cuisine,** f. *[noovehl kweezeen]* new cuisine

**novembre** *[nohvah(m)br]* November

**nuit,** f. *[nwee]* night

**numéro,** m. *[newmayroh]* number

**numéroté** *[newmayrohtay]* numbered

# O

**objectif,** m. *[ohbzhehkteef]* lens

**objet,** m. *[ohbzhay]* object

**obtenir** *[ohbtuhneer]* to obtain

**obturateur,** m. *[ohbtewrahtuhr]* shutter

**occasion,** f. *[ohkahzyoh(n)]* [opportunity]

**occupé** *[ohkewpay]* busy

**océan,** m. *[ohsayah(n)]* ocean

**octobre** *[ohktohbr]* October

**oeil,** m. *[uhy]* eye

**oeuf,** m. *[uhf]* egg

**offrir** *[ohfreer]* to offer

**oie,** f. *[wah]* goose

**oignon,** m. *[ohnyoh(n)]* onion

**omelette,** f. *[ohmleht]* omelette

**on** *[oh(n)]* one, we

**oncle,** m. *[oh(n)kl]* uncle

**ongle,** m. *[oh(n)gl]* nail

**onze** *[oh(n)z]* eleven

**or,** m. *[ohr]* gold

**orange,** f. *[ohrah(n)zh]* orange

**orangeade,** f. *[ohrah(n)zhahd]* orangeade

**orchestre,** m. *[ohrkehstr]* orchestra

**ordinaire** *[ohrdeenehr]* ordinary

**ordonnance,** f. *[ohrdohnah(n)s]* prescription

**oreille,** f. *[ohrehy]* ear

**oreiller,** m. *[ohrayay]* pillow

**origan,** m. *[ohreegah(n)]* oregano

**os,** m. *[ohs]* bone

**ou** *[oo]* or

**où** *[oo]* where

**oublier** *[oobleeyay]* to forget

**ouest,** m. *[wehst]* west
**oui** *[wee]* yes
**ouvert** *[oovehr]* open
**ouvreuse,** f. *[oovruhz]* usher
**ouvrir** *[oovreer]* to open

# P

**pain,** m. *[pa(n)]* bread
**pain complet,** m. *[pa(n) koh(m)play]* whole wheat bread
**pain de mie,** m. *[pa(n) duh mee]* white bread
**pain grillé,** m. *[pa(n) greeyay]* toast
**paire,** f. *[pehr]* pair
**palais de justice,** m. *[pahleh duh zhewstees]* courthouse
**pamplemousse,** m. *[pah(m)-pluhmoos]* grapefruit
**panier,** m. *[pahnyay]* basket
**panne.** f. *[pahn]* accident, car breakdown
**panne d'essence,** f. *[pahn dehsah(n)s]* gasoline emergency
**panorama,** m. *[pahnoh-rahmah]* panorama
**pantalon,** m. *[pah(n)tahloh(n)]* pants
**pantoufles,** f.pl. *[pah(n)-toofl]* slippers
**papeterie,** f. *[pahpehtree]* stationery store
**papier,** m. *[pahpyay]* paper
**papier à lettres,** m. *[pahpyay ah lehtr]* stationery
**papier hygiénique,** m. *[pahpyay eezhyayneek]* toilet paper

**paquet,** m. *[pahkay]* pack, packet
**par** *[pahr]* by
**parapluie,** m. *[pahrahplwee]* umbrella
**parc,** m. *[pahrk]* park
**parce que** *[pahrs kuh]* because
**parcomètre,** m. *[pahrkoh-mehtr]* parking meter
**pardon,** m. *[pahrdoh(n)]* excuse, apology
**pardonner** *[pahrdohnay]* to excuse
**parfait** *[pahrfch]* perfect
**parfois** *[pahrfwah]* sometimes
**parfum,** m. *[pahrfuh(m)]* perfume, flavor
**parking,** m. *[pahrkeeng]* parking lot
**parler** *[pahrlay]* to speak
**parmi** *[pahrmee]* among
**partager** *[pahrtahzhay]* to share
**partie,** f. *[pahrtee]* part
**partir** *[pahrteer]* to leave
**partout** *[pahrtoo]* everywhere
**pas** *[pah]* not (negates verb)
**pas du tout** *[pah dew too]* not at all
**passage,** m. *[pahsahzh]* passage
**passage à niveau,** m. *[pahsahzh ah neevoh]* railroad crossing
**passage clouté,** m. *[pahsahzh klootay]* pedestrian crosswalk
**passeport,** m. *[pahspohr]* passport

**passer** *[pahsay]* to pass, spend (time)

**pastèque,** f. *[pahstehk]* watermelon

**pâtes,** f.pl. *[paht]* pasta

**patinoire,** f. *[pahteenwahr]* skating rink

**pâtisserie,** f. *[pahteesree]* pastry shop

**pauvre** *[pohvr]* poor

**payer** *[payay]* to pay

**pays,** m. *[payee]* country (nation)

**paysage,** m. *[payeezahzh]* landscape

**en P.C.V.** *[ah(n) pay say vay]* collect (phone call)

**péage,** m. *[payayzh]* toll

**peau,** f. *[poh]* skin

**pêche,** f. *[pehsh]* peach

**peigne,** m. *[pehnyuh]* comb

**peintre,** m. *[pa(n)tr]* painter

**peinture,** f. *[pa(n)tewr]* painting

**pellicule,** f. *[pehleekewl]* film cartridge

**pendant** *[pah(n)dah(n)]* during

**pendule,** f. *[pah(n)dewl]* clock

**penser** *[pah(n)say]* to think

**pension complète,** f. *[pah(n)syoh(n) koh(m)pleht]* room with all meals

**perdre** *[pehrdr]* to lose

**perdu** *[pehrdew]* lost

**père,** m. *[pehr]* father

**période,** f. *[payryohd]* period

**permettre** *[pehrmehtr]* to permit

**permis,** m. *[pehrmee]* license

**persil,** m. *[pehrsee]* parsley

**personne,** f. *[pehrsohn]* person

**personnel** *[pehrsohnehl]* personal

**personnes âgées,** f.pl. *[pehrsohn zahzhay]* senior citizens

**persuader** *[pehrswahday]* to persuade

**peser** *[puhzay]* to weigh

**petit** *[puhtee]* small

**petit déjeuner,** m. *[puhtee dayzhuhnay]* breakfast

**petit fils,** m. *[puhtee fees]* grandson

**petite fille,** f. *[puhteet feey]* granddaughter

**petit pain,** m. *[puhtee pa(n)]* roll

**petits pois,** m.pl. *[puhtee pwah]* peas

**peu** *[puh]* little, few

**peu de** *[puh duh]* few

**peur,** f. *[puhr]* fear

**avoir peur de** *[ahvwahr puhr duh]* to be afraid of

**peut-être** *[puh-tehtruh]* perhaps

**peux** *[puh]* am able to (see pouvoir)

**phares,** f.pl. *[fahr]* headlights

**pharmacie,** f. *[fahrmahsee]* pharmacy

**photo,** f. *[fohtoh]* picture, photograph

**photographier** *[fohtohgrahfyay]* to photograph

**phrase,** f. *[frahz]* sentence

**pièce,** f. *[pyehs]* play (literature)

**pied,** m. *[pyay]* foot

**à pied** *[ah pyay]* on foot

**pierre,** f. *[pyehr]* stone

**pierre précieuse,** f. *[pyehr praysyuhz]* precious stone

**piéton,** m. *[pyaytoh(n)]* pedestrian

**pile,** f. *[peel]* battery

**pillule,** f. *[peelewl]* pill

**piment,** m. *[peemah(n)]* spice

**piscine,** f. *[peeseen]* swimming pool

**place,** f. *[plahs]* town square, seat

**plafond,** m. *[plahfoh(n)]* ceiling

**plage,** f. *[plahzh]* beach

**plainte,** f. *[pla(n)t]* complaint

**plaisanterie,** f. *[plehzah(n)tree]* joke

**plaisir,** m. *[plehzeer]* pleasure

**plan,** m. *[plah(n)]* map, plan

**planche à voile,** f. *[plah(n)sh ah vwahl]* windsurfing

**planche de surf,** f. *[plah(n)sh duh sewrf]* surf board

**plancher,** m. *[plah(n)shay]* floor

**planétarium,** m. *[plahnaytahryuhm]* planetarium

**plat** *[plah]* flat

**plat,** m. *[plah]* dish

**plein air** *[pleh nehr]* outdoors

**pleurer** *[pluhray]* to cry

**(il) pleut** *[(eel) pluh]* (it's) raining

**plongée sous-marine,** f. *[ploh(n)zhay soo-mahreen]* deep-sea diving

**pluie,** f. *[plwee]* rain

**plus** *[plew]* more

**plusieurs** *[plewzyuhr]* several

**plutôt** *[plewtoh]* rather

**pneu,** m. *[pnuh]* tire

**poche,** f. *[pohsh]* pocket

**poids,** m. *[pwah]* weight

**poignet,** m. *[pwahnyay]* wrist

**pointure,** f. *[pwa(n)tewr]* shoe size

**poire,** f. *[pwahr]* pear

**poireau,** m. *[pwahroh]* leek

**pois,** m. *[pwah]* peas

**poisson,** m. *[pwahsoh(n)]* fish

**poitrine,** f. *[pwahtreen]* chest

**poivre,** m. *[pwahvr]* pepper

**pomme,** f. *[pohm]* apple

**pomme de terre,** f. *[pohm duh tehr]* potato

**pont,** m. *[poh(n)]* bridge

**porc,** m. *[pohr]* pork

**port,** m. *[pohr]* harbor

**porte,** f. *[pohrt]* door

**porte-feuille,** m. *[pohrtuhfuhy]* wallet

**porter** *[pohrtay]* to carry

**porteur,** m. *[pohrtuhr]* porter

**portion,** f. *[pohrsyoh(n)]* portion

**posséder** *[pohsayday]* to possess

**poste de radio,** m. *[pohst duh rahdyoh]* radio

**poster** *[pohstay]* to mail

**poterie,** f. *[pohtree]* pottery

**poule,** f. *[pool]* hen

**poulet,** m. *[poolay]* chicken

**pour** *[poor]* for

**pourboire,** m. *[poorbwahr]*
tip

**pourquoi** *[poorkwah]* why

**pourrions** *[pooryoh(n)]* could
(see *pouvoir*)

**pousser** *[poosay]* to push

**pouvez** *[poovay]* can (see
*pouvoir*)

**pouvoir** *[poovwahr]* to be
able to

**pratique** *[prahteek]* practical

**(avec) préavis** *[(ahvehk)
prayahvee]* person-to-
person

**préférer** *[prayfayray]* to
prefer

**premier** *[pruhmyay]* first

**prendre** *[prah(n)dr]* to take

**préparer** *[praypahray]* to
prepare

**près (de)** *[preh (duh)]* near

**présenter** *[prayzah(n)tay]* to
present, introduce

**presque** *[prehsk]* almost

**pression,** f. *[prehsyoh(n)]*
pressure

**prêt** *[preh]* ready

**prêter** *[prehtay]* to lend

**prêtre,** m. *[prehtr]* priest

**printemps,** m. *[pra(n)tah(m)]*
spring

**priorité,** f. *[preeohreetay]*
priority

**privé** *[preevay]* private

**prix,** m. *[pree]* price

**prochain** *[prohsha(n)]* next

**proche** *[prohsh]* near

**profession,** f. *[prohfehsyoh(n)]*
profession

**promenade,** f. *[proh-
muhnahd]* walk

**faire une promenade** *[fehr
ewn prohmuhnahd]* to take a
walk

**promettre** *[prohmehtr]* to
promise

**prononcer** *[prohnoh(n)say]* to
pronounce

**propre** *[prohpr]* clean, own

**propriétaire,** m. *[prohpreeay-
tehr]* owner

**propriété privée,** f. *[proh-
preeaytay preevay]* private
property

**protéger** *[prohtayzhay]* to
protect

**prune,** f. *[prewn]* plum

**pruneau,** m. *[prewnoh]* prune

**public** *[pewbleek]* public

**puis-je** *[pweezh]* can I

**pyjama,** m. *[peezhahmah]*
pajamas

## Q

**quai,** m. *[keh]* wharf, platform

**qualité,** f. *[kahleetay]* quality

**quand** *[kah(n)]* when

**quarante** *[kahrah(n)t]* forty

**quart,** m. *[kahr]* quarter

**quartier,** m. *[kahrtyay]*
neighborhood

**quatorze** *[kahtohrz]* fourteen

**quatre** *[kahtr]* four

**quatre-vingts** *[kahtruh-va(n)]*
eighty

**quatre-vingt-dix** *[kahtruh-
va(n)-dees]* ninety

**que** *[kuh]* that

**quel** m. *[kehl]* what, which

**quelle** f. *[kehl]* what, which
**Quelle heure est-il?** *[Kehl uhr eh teel?]* What time is it?
**quelque(s)** *[kehlkuh]* some
**quelque chose** *[kehlkuh shohz]* something
**quelque part** *[kehlkuh pahr]* somewhere
**quelqu'un** *[kehlkuh(n)]* someone
**qu'est-ce que** *[kehskuh]* what
**Qu'est-ce qu'il y a?** *[Kehs keel yah?]* What's the matter?
**question,** f. *[kehstyoh(n)]* question
**queue,** f. *[kuh]* line (of people)
**qui** *[kee]* who
**quiche,** f. *[keesh]* quiche
**quincaillerie,** f. *[ka(n)kahy-ree]* hardware store
**quinze** *[ka(n)z]* fifteen
**quittance,** f. *[keetah(n)s]* receipt
**quoi** *[kwah]* what
**quotidien** *[kohteedyeh(n)]* daily

# R

**rabais,** m. *[rahbay]* reduction
**rabbin,** m. *[rahba(n)]* rabbi
**raconter** *[rahkoh(n)tay]* to tell
**radiateur,** m. *[rahdyahtuhr]* radiator
**radio,** f. *[rahdyoh]* radio, x-ray
**rafraîchissant** *[rahfreh-sheesah(n)]* refreshing

**raisin,** m. *[rehza(n)]* grape
**raisins sec,** m.pl. *[rehza(n) sehk]* raisins
**raison,** f. *[rehzoh(n)]* reason
**raisonnable** *[rehzohnahbl]* reasonable
**ralentir** *[rahlah(n)teer]* to slow down
**rapide** *[rahpeed]* rapid, fast
**rappeler** *[rahplay]* to call back
**se rappeler** *[suh rahplay]* to remember
**raser** *[rahzay]* to shave
**rasoir,** m. *[rahzwahr]* razor
**rayon,** m. *[rayoh(n)]* shelf, section
**rayure,** f. *[rayewr]* stripe
**récent** *[raysah(n)]* recent
**recevoir** *[ruhsuhvwahr]* to receive
**recommander** *[ruhkohmah(n)-day]* to recommend
**refuser** *[ruhfewzay]* to refuse
**regarder** *[ruhgahrday]* to look at
**régime,** m. *[rayzheem]* diet
**règle,** f. *[rehgl]* rule
**regretter** *[ruhgrehtay]* to regret
**remarquer** *[ruhmahrkay]* to notice
**rembourser** *[rah(m)boorsay]* to reimburse
**remercier** *[ruhmehrsyay]* to thank
**rencontrer** *[rah(n)koh(n)tray]* to meet
**rendez-vous,** m. *[rah(n)day-voo]* appointment

**rendre** *[rah(n)dr]* to return

**renseignements,** m.pl. *[rah(n)-sehnyuhmah(n)]* information

**renseigner** *[rah(n)sehnyay]* to inform

**rentrer** *[rah(n)tray]* to return

**réparer** *[raypahray]* to repair

**repas,** m. *[ruhpah]* meal

**repas léger,** m. *[ruhpah lay-zhay]* light meal

**repasser à la vapeur** *[ruhpah-say ah lah vahpuhr]* to iron

**répéter** *[raypaytay]* to repeat

**répondre** *[raypoh(n)dr]* to answer

**réponse,** f. *[raypoh(n)s]* answer

**repos,** m. *[ruhpoh]* rest

**se reposer** *[ruhpohzay]* to rest

**représentation,** f. *[ruhpray-zah(n)tahsyoh(n)]* performance

**représenter** *[ruhprayzah(n)-tay]* to represent

**réservation,** f. *[rayzehrvah-syoh(n)]* reservation

**réservé aux autobus** *[rayzehr-vay oh zohtohbews]* · reserved for buses

**réserver** *[rayzehrvay]* to reserve

**responsable** *[rehspoh(n)-sahbl]* responsible

**ressembler** *[ruhsah(m)blay]* to resemble

**restaurant,** m. *[rehstohrah(n)]* restaurant

**rester** *[rehstay]* to stay, remain

**résultat,** m. *[rayzewltah]* result

**retard,** m. *[ruhtahr]* delay

**retoucher** *[ruhtooshay]* to touch up

**(de) retour** *[(duh) ruhtoor]* returned

**retraite,** f. *[ruhtreht]* retirement

**rétréci** *[raytraysee]* shrunk

**réunion,** f. *[rayewnyoh(n)]* meeting

**réveil,** m. *[rayvehy]* alarm clock

**revenir** *[ruhvuhneer]* to return, come back

**rez-de-chaussée,** m. *[ray-duh-shohsay]* ground floor

**rhume,** m. *[rewm]* cold (virus)

**rien** *[ryeh(n)]* nothing

**de rien** *[duh ryeh(n)]* you're welcome

**rire** *[reer]* to laugh

**risque,** m. *[reesk]* risk

**rivière,** f. *[reevyehr]* river

**riz,** m. *[ree]* rice

**robe,** f. *[rohb]* dress

**robe de chambre,** f. *[rohb duh shah(m)br]* bathrobe

**robinet,** m. *[rohbeenay]* faucet, tap

**roman,** m. *[rohmah(n)]* novel

**romarin,** m. *[rohmahra(n)]* rosemary

**rosbif,** m. *[rohsbeef]* roast beef

**rose** *[rohz]* pink

**rôti,** m. *[rohtee]* roast

**rouge** *[roozh]* red

**rouge à lèvre,** m. *[roozh ah lehvr]* lipstick

**rouler** [roolay] to roll, drive
**route,** f. [root] road
**ruines,** f.pl. [rween] ruins

## S

**sa** (f.) [sah] his/her
**sable,** m. [sahbl] sand
**sac,** m. [sahk] handbag, bag, pocketbook
**saignant** [sehnyah(n)] rare (meat)
**sais** [seh] know (see savoir)
**saison,** f. [sehzoh(n)] season
**sale** [sahl] dirty
**salé** [sahlay] salted
**salle,** f. [sahl] room
**salle à manger,** f. [sahl ah mah(n)zhay] dining room
**salle d'attente,** f. [sahl dahtah(n)t] waiting room
**salle de bain,** f. [sahl duh ba(n)] bathroom
**salle pour non-fumeurs,** f. [sahl poor noh(n) foomuhr] non-smoking section
**salon,** m. [sahloh(n)] living room
**salon de beauté,** m. [sahloh(n) duh bohtay] hairdresser's, beauty shop
**salon de thé,** m. [sahloh(n) duh tay] tea room
**samedi** [sahmdee] Saturday
**sandales,** f.pl. [sah(n)dahl] sandals
**sang,** m. [sah(n)] blood
**sans** [sah(n)] without
**santé,** f. [sah(n)tay] health
**saucisse,** f. [sohsees] sausage

**saucisson,** m. [sohseesoh(n)] sausage
**sauvage** [sohvahzh] wild
**savez** [sahvay] know (see savoir)
**savoir** [sahvwahr] to know (facts)
**savon,** m. [sahvoh(n)] soap
**sculpture,** f. [skewltewr] sculpture
**se** [suh] reflexive pronoun for third person
**sec** [sehk] dry
**sèche-cheveux,** m. [sehsh-shuhvuh] hair dryer
**secours,** m. [suhkoor] help
**seigle,** m. [sehgl] rye
**seize** [sehz] sixteen
**séjour,** m. [sayzhoor] stay
**sel,** m. [sehl] salt
**selon** [suhloh(n)] according to
**semaine,** f. [suhmehn] week
**sembler** [sah(m)blay] to seem
**sens,** m. [sah(n)s] direction, meaning
**sens unique** [sah(n)s ewneek] one way
**se sentir** [suh sah(n)teer] to feel
**sept** [seht] seven
**septembre** [sehptah(m)br] September
**sera** [suhrah] will be
**sérieux** [sayryuh] serious
**serrez à droite** [sehray ah drwaht] keep right
**serveuse,** f. [sehrvuhz] waitress
**service à l'étage,** m. [sehrvees ah laytahzh] room service

**serviette,** f. *[sehrvyeht]* towel, napkin, briefcase

**serviettes hygiéniques,** f.pl. *[sehrvyeht eezhyayneek]* feminine napkins

**servir** *[sehrveer]* to serve

**ses** (pl.) *[say]* his, her, their

**seul** *[suhl]* alone

**seulement** *[suhlmah(n)]* only

**shampooing,** m. *[shah(m)pwa(n)]* shampoo

**si** *[see]* if

**s'il vous plaît** *[seel voo pleh]* please

**signer** *[seenyay]* to sign

**signification,** f. *[seenyeefee-kahsyoh(n)]* meaning

**site,** m. *[seet]* site

**six** *[sees]* six

**ski,** m. *[skee]* skiing

**ski de fond,** m. *[skee duh foh(n)]* cross-country skiing

**ski nautique,** m. *[skee noh-teek]* water skiing

**slip,** m. *[sleep]* underpants

**snack-bar,** m. *[snahk-bahr]* snack bar

**soeur,** f. *[suhr]* sister

**soie,** f. *[swah]* silk

**soif,** f. *[swahf]* thirst

**avoir soif** *[ahvwahr swahf]* to be thirsty

**avec soin** *[ahvehk swa(n)]* carefully

**soir,** m. *[swahr]* evening

**soirée,** f. *[swahray]* evening party

**soixante** *[swahsah(n)t]* sixty

**soixante-dix** *[swahsah(n)t-dees]* seventy

**sol,** m. *[sohl]* ground

**soleil,** m. *[sohlehy]* sun

**somme,** f. *[sohm]* sum

**sommet,** m. *[sohmay]* peak

**son** (m. or f.) *[soh(n)]* his, her

**sortie,** f. *[sohrtee]* exit

**soucoupe,** f. *[sookoop]* saucer

**soufflé,** m. *[sooflay]* soufflé

**souhaiter** *[soowehtay]* to wish

**sourire,** m. *[sooreer]* smile

**sous** *[soo]* under

**sous-vêtements,** m.pl. *[soo-vehtmah(n)]* underwear

**souvent** *[soovah(n)]* often

**spaghetti,** m.pl. *[spahgheh-tee]* spaghetti

**spécialité,** f. *[spaysyahleetay]* specialty

**spectacle,** m. *[spehktahkl]* show

**stade,** m. *[stahd]* stadium

**station,** f. *[stahsyoh(n)]* station

**station de métro,** f. *[stah-syoh(n) duh maytroh]* subway station

**station-service,** f. *[stahsyoh(n)-sehrvees]* service station

**stationnement,** m. *[stahsyohn-mah(n)]* parking

**stationnement interdit** *[stahsyohnmah(n) a(n)tehrdee]* no parking

**statue,** f. *[stahtew]* statue

**steak,** m. *[stehk]* steak

**stylo,** m. *[steeloh]* pen

**sucre,** m. *[sewkr]* sugar

**sucré** *[sewkray]* sweet

**sud,** m. *[sewd]* south

**suis** [swee] am (see être)
**Suisse,** f. [Swees] Switzerland
**suisse** [swees] Swiss
**suivre** [sweevr] to follow
**super** [sewpehr] great
**supérieur** [sewpayryuhr] superior, higher
**supermarché,** m. [sewpehr-mahrshay] supermarket
**supplément,** m. [sewplay-mah(n)] supplement, extra
**sur** [sewr] on
**sûr** [sewr] sure
**synagogue,** f. [seenahgohg] synagogue

# T

**ta,** f. [tah] your
**tabac,** m. [tahbah] tobacco
**table,** f. [tahbl] table
**tableau,** m. [tahbloh] painting
**taille,** f. [tahy] waist, size
**tailleur,** m. [tahyuhr] tailor
**talon,** m. [tahloh(n)] heel
**tampon,** m. [tah(m)poh(n)] tampon
**tant** [tah(n)] so many, so much
**tant mieux** [tah(n)myuh] so much the better
**tant pis** [tah(n) pee] so much the worse
**tante,** f. [tah(n)t] aunt
**tapis,** m. [tahpee] rug
**tard** [tahr] late
**tarif,** m. [tahreef] price, rate
**tarte,** f. [tahrt] pie
**tasse,** f. [tahs] cup
**taxe,** f. [tahks] tax

**taxi,** m. [tahksee] taxi
**te** [tuh] you (reflexive)
**teinturerie,** f. [ta(n)tewruhree] dry cleaners
**télégramme,** m. [taylay-grahm] telegram
**téléphone,** m. [taylayfohn] telephone
**téléphoner** [taylayfohnay] to telephone
**téléphoniste,** m. or f. [taylay-fohneest] operator
**téléski,** m. [taylayskee] ski lift
**téléviseur,** m. [taylayveezuhr] TV set
**télévision,** f. [taylayvee-zyoh(n)] television
**télex,** m. [taylehks] telex
**tempête,** f. [tah(m)peht] storm
**temps,** m. [tah(m)] time, weather
**tennis,** m. [tehnees] tennis
**tente,** f. [tah(n)t] tent
**tenue,** f. [tuhnew] outfit, way of dressing
**terminer** [tehrmeenay] to end
**terrain de golf,** m. [tehra(n) duh gohlf] golf course
**terrain de jeu,** m. [tehra(n) duh zhuh] playground
**terrasse,** f. [tehrahs] terrace
**terre,** f. [tehr] land
**tes** (pl.) [tay] your
**tête,** f. [teht] head
**TGV,** m. [tay zhay vay] bullet train
**thé,** m. [tay] tea
**théâtre,** m. [tayahtr] theater
**thym,** m. [ta(m)] thyme

**tiens!** *[tyeh(n)!]* goodness!

**timbre,** m. *[ta(m)br]* stamp (postage)

**tire-bouchon,** m. *[teer-booshoh(n)]* corkscrew

**toi** *[twah]* you, to you

**toile de coton,** f. *[twahl duh kohtoh(n)]* calico

**toilettes,** f.pl. *[twahleht]* toilet

**toit,** m. *[twah]* roof

**tomate,** f. *[tohmaht]* tomato

**tombe,** f. *[toh(m)b]* grave

**tomber** *[toh(m)bay]* to fall

**ton** (m. or f.) *[toh(n)]* your

**avoir tort** *[ahvwahr tohr]* to be wrong

**tôt** *[toh]* early

**toucher** *[tooshay]* to touch

**tour,** f. *[toor]* tower

**tour,** m. *[toor]* turn, tour

**tourisme,** m. *[tooreezm]* tourism

**touriste,** m. or f. *[tooreest]* tourist

**touristique** *[tooreesteek]* touristic

**tourne-disque,** m. *[toornuh-deesk]* record player

**tourner** *[toornay]* to turn

**tournevis,** m. *[toornuhvees]* screwdriver

**tousser** *[toosay]* to cough

**tout** *[too]* all, everything

**tout de suite** *[tood sweet]* right away

**tout le monde** *[too luh moh(n)d]* everybody

**toutes directions** *[toot dee-rehksyoh(n)]* all directions

**toux,** f. *[too]* cough

**traduire** *[trahdweer]* to translate

**train,** m. *[tra(n)]* train

**trajet,** m. *[trahzhay]* trip

**tranche,** f. *[trah(n)sh]* slice

**tranquil** *[trah(n)keel]* calm

**travail,** m. *[trahvahy]* job, work

**travailler** *[trahvahyay]* to work

**à travers** *[ah trahvehr]* through

**traverser** *[trahvehrsay]* to cross

**treize** *[trehz]* thirteen

**trente** *[trah(n)t]* thirty

**très** *[treh]* very

**triste** *[treest]* sad

**trois** *[trwah]* three

**troisième** *[trwahzyehm]* third

**trop** *[troh]* too many, too much

**trottoir,** m. *[trohtwahr]* sidewalk

**trou,** m. *[troo]* hole

**trouver** *[troovay]* to find

**truite,** f. *[trweet]* trout

**typique** *[teepeek]* typical

## U

**un** (m.) *[uh(n)]* one, a

**une** (f.) *[ewn]* one, a

**uni** *[ewnee]* united, solid

**unique** *[ewneek]* unique

**université,** f. *[ewneevehr-seetay]* university

**urgence,** f. *[ewrzhah(n)s]* emergency

**urgent** *[ewrzhah(n)]* urgent

**usine,** f. *[ewzeen]* factory, plant

**utile** *[ewteel]* useful

## V

**vacances,** f.pl. *[vahkah(n)s]* vacation

**vais** *[veh]* am going (see *aller*)

**valeur,** f. *[vahluhr]* value

**valise,** f. *[vahleez]* suitcase

**vallée,** f. *[vahlay]* valley

**varié** *[vahryay]* varied

**vaut** *[voh]* is worth

**veau,** m. *[voh]* veal

**velours,** m. *[vuhloor]* velvet

**velours côtelé,** m. *[vuhloor kohtuhlay]* corduroy

**vendeur,** m. *[vah(n)duhr]* salesman

**vendeuse,** f. *[vah(n)duhz]* saleswoman

**vendre** *[vah(n)dr]* to sell

**vendredi** *[vah(n)druhdee]* Friday

**venir** *[vuhneer]* to come

**vent,** m. *[vah(n)]* wind

**vente,** f. *[vah(n)t]* sale

**verglas,** m. *[vehrglah]* frost

**vérifier** *[vayreefyay]* to verify

**vérité,** f. *[vayreetay]* truth

**vernis à ongles,** m. *[vehrnee ah oh(n)gl]* nail polish

**verre,** m. *[vehr]* glass

**verre de contact,** m. *[vehr duh koh(n)tahkt]* contact lens

**vers** *[vehr]* toward

**vert** *[vehr]* green

**verveine,** f. *[vehrvehn]* vervain (infusion)

**veston,** m. *[vehstoh(n)]* jacket

**vêtements,** m.pl. *[vehtmah(n)]* clothes

**veuf,** m. *[vuhf]* widower

**veuve,** f. *[vuhv]* widow

**veux** *[vuh]* want (see *vouloir*)

**viande,** f. *[vyah(n)d]* meat

**vide** *[veed]* empty

**vie,** f. *[vee]* life

**vieille** (f.) *[vyehy]* old

**vieux** (m.) *[vyuh]* old

**vignoble,** m. *[veenyohbl]* vineyard

**villa,** f. *[veelah]* villa

**village,** m. *[veelahzh]* village

**ville,** f. *[veel]* town, city

**vin,** m. *[va(n)]* wine

**vin blanc,** m. *[va(n) blah(n)]* white wine

**vin brut,** m. *[va(n) brewt]* dry wine

**vin doux,** m. *[va(n) doo]* sweet wine

**vin du pays,** m. *[va(n) dew payee]* local wine

**vin léger,** m. *[va(n) layzhay]* light wine

**vin mousseaux,** m. *[va(n) moosuh]* sparkling wine

**vin rosé,** m. *[va(n) rohzay]* rosé wine

**vin rouge,** m. *[va(n) roozh]* red wine

**vingt** *[va(n)]* twenty

**violet** *[vyohlay]* purple

**virage,** m. *[veerahzh]* turn

**visage,** m. *[veezahzh]* face

**visite,** f. *[veezeet]* visit

277

**vite** *[veet]* quickly
**vitesse,** f. *[veetehs]* speed
**vitrine,** f. *[veetreen]* store window
**voici** *[vwahsee]* here is
**voie sans issue,** f. *[vwah sah(n) zeesew]* dead end
**voilà** *[vwahlah]* there, there is
**voir** *[vwahr]* to see
**voisin,** m. *[vwahza(n)]* neighbor
**voiture,** f. *[vwahtewr]* car
**vol,** m. *[vohl]* flight
**vol direct,** m. *[vohl deerehkt]* direct flight
**volaille,** f. *[vohlahy]* fowl
**voler** *[vohlay]* to fly, steal
**voleur,** m. *[vohluhr]* thief
**vos** (pl.) *[voh]* your
**votre** *[vohtr]* your
**voudrais** *[voodreh]* would like (see *vouloir*)
**vouloir** *[voolwahr]* to want

**vouloir dire** *[voolwahr deer]* to mean
**vous** *[voo]* you, yourself
**voyage,** m. *[vwahyahzh]* trip
**vrai** *[vreh]* true
**vraiment** *[vrehmah(n)]* really
**vue,** f. *[vew]* view

# W

**wagon-lit,** m. *[vahgoh(n)-lee]* sleeping car
**W.C.,** m. *[vay say]* toilet

# Y

**y** *[ee]* there
**y a-t-il** *[yah teel]* are there
**yaourt,** m. *[yahoort]* yogurt

# Z

**zéro** *[zayroh]* zero
**zone bleue,** f. *[zohn bluh]* blue zone (parking area)